A History of Islamic Schooling in North America

This insightful text challenges popular belief that faith-based Islamic schools isolate Muslim learners, impose dogmatic religious views, and disregard academic excellence. This book attempts to paint a starkly different picture. Grounded in the premise that not all Islamic schools are the same, the historical narratives illustrate varied visions and approaches to Islamic schooling that showcase a richness of educational thought and aspiration.

A History of Islamic Schooling in North America traces the growth and evolution of elementary and secondary private Islamic schools in Canada and the United States. Intersecting narratives between schools established by indigenous African American Muslims as early as the 1930s with those established by immigrant Muslim communities in the 1970s demonstrate how and why Islamic education is in a constant, on-going process of evolution, renewal, and adaptation. Drawing on the voices, perspectives, and narratives of pioneers and visionaries who established the earliest Islamic schools, chapters articulate why Islamic schools were established, what distinguishes them from one another, and why they continue to be important.

This book will be of great interest to graduate and postgraduate students, researchers, academics, teaching professionals in the fields of Islamic education, religious studies, multicultural education curriculum studies, and faith-based teacher education.

Nadeem A. Memon is Senior Lecturer in the Centre for Islamic Thought and Education, University of South Australia, Australia.

Routledge Research in Religion and Education

Series Editor
Michael D. Waggoner,
University of Northern Iowa, USA

Public Theology, Religious Diversity, and Interreligious Learning
Edited by Manfred L. Pirner, Johannes Lähnemann, Werner Haussmann, and Susanne Schwarz

Religious Education as a Dialogue with Difference
Fostering democratic citizenship through the study of religions in schools
Kevin O'Grady

Investigating Political Tolerance at Conservative Protestant Colleges and Universities
George Yancey, Laurel Shaler and Jerald H. Walz

Faith, Diversity, and Education
An Ethnography of a Conservative Christian School
Alison H. Blosser

The First Amendment and State Bans on Teachers' Religious Garb
Analyzing the Historic Origins of Contemporary Legal Challenges in the United States
Nathan C. Walker

Improving the Pedagogy of Islamic Religious Education in Secondary Schools
The Role of Critical Religious Education and Variation Theor
Ayse Demirel Ucan

A History of Islamic Schooling in North America
Mapping Growth and Evolution
Nadeem Ahmed Memon

For more information about this series, please visit: www.routledge.com/Routledge-Research-in-Religion-and-Education/book-series/

A History of Islamic Schooling in North America
Mapping Growth and Evolution

Nadeem Ahmed Memon

NEW YORK AND LONDON

First published 2020
by Routledge
52 Vanderbilt Avenue, New York, NY 10017

and by Routledge
2 Park Square, Milton Park, Abingdon, Oxon, OX14 4RN

Routledge is an imprint of the Taylor & Francis Group, an informa business

© 2020 Taylor & Francis

The right of Nadeem Ahmed Memon to be identified as authors of this work has been asserted by him in accordance with sections 77 and 78 of the Copyright, Designs and Patents Act 1988.

All rights reserved. No part of this book may be reprinted or reproduced or utilised in any form or by any electronic, mechanical, or other means, now known or hereafter invented, including photocopying and recording, or in any information storage or retrieval system, without permission in writing from the publishers.

Trademark notice: Product or corporate names may be trademarks or registered trademarks, and are used only for identification and explanation without intent to infringe.

Library of Congress Cataloging-in-Publication Data
A catalog record for this book has been requested

ISBN: 978-1-138-33688-9 (hbk)
ISBN: 978-0-429-44279-7 (ebk)

Typeset in Sabon
by Apex CoVantage, LLC

For Luqman and Afiya

Contents

Book Series Foreword viii
Acronyms xi
Glossary of Arabic Terms xii

1 Introduction: Context of Islamic Schooling
   in North America   1

2 Protest: Resistance and Renewal: Schooling
   in the Nation of Islam   35

3 Preservation: Preserving Islamic Identity:
   Indigenous and Immigrant Muslim Educators Meet   66

4 Pedagogy: Models of Islamic Schooling Emerge   112

5 Praxis: Reviving the Tradition of Learning and
   Teaching in Islam   161

6 Conclusion: Potential and Possibilities of Islamic
   Schooling in North America   201

   Index   213

Book Series Foreword

The opening years of the 21st century brought increased attention to religion as an important dimension of culture and politics. Early in this period, the dramatic multi-pronged attacks of September 11, 2001 came as a jolting reminder of the potential for violent action that can have a basis in religious motivations. Over the same period, we came to see an increase in religiously motivated activity in politics. In the US, we see this in the evolution from the silent majority to the moral majority movement that emerged as a force in the late 1970s as the beginning of the new religious right. On further reflection, however, we can see the involvement of religion extending much further back as a fundamental part of our social organization rather than a new or emerging phenomenon. We need only recall the religious wars of early modern Europe through to the contentious development of US church and state relations as evidence of the longstanding role religion has played as a source of competing values and beliefs. We also recognize religion as a positive source of motivation for social action, seen in the 19th century abolitionist movement, the social gospel and its humanitarian contributions, and the Civil Rights movement, to name a few. That said, there has been a significant upturn in research and scholarship across many disciplines relative to the study of religion in the last 20 years. This is particularly the case in the area of the interplay of education and religion.

While religious education—study *toward formation* in a particular faith tradition—has been with us for millennia, religious education—study *about* religion as an academic subject apart from theology—is more recent. Whereas theology departments proceeded from religious assumptions aiming to promulgate a faith tradition, the religious studies field emerged as a discipline that sought to bring a more objective social scientific approach to the study of religion. The origins of this approach date back to the European research centers that influenced US scholars beginning in the 18th century. The formalization of this trend, however, is a fairly recent phenomenon, as illustrated by the 1949 formation of the Society for the Scientific Study of Religion, with its own scholarly journal, and the creation of religious studies departments across the U.S.

in the wake of the U.S. Supreme Court decision in 1963 that allowed teaching *about* religion (rather than *for*) in public education institutions. It was also that same year that the American Academy of Religion was born out of a group of scholars that had since 1909 been meeting under the various names related to biblical study.

It is out of this relatively recent increase in scholarly attention to religion and education that this book series arises. Routledge Publishers have long been an important presence in the respective fields of religion and of education. It seemed like a natural step to introduce a book series focused particularly on Research in Religion and Education. My appreciation extends to Max Novick for guiding this series into being and now to Elsbeth Wright for continuing Routledge's oversight.

In this 16th book in the series, Dr. Nadeem A. Memon takes us through the development of Islamic schools in North America. Dr. Memon and his colleague, Dr. Mujadad Zaman, edited an earlier book in this series, *Philosophies of Islamic Education: Historical Perspectives and Emerging Discourses*. In this latest volume, solely authored by Dr. Memon, he pursues two overarching objectives: 1) "trace the historical growth of Islamic schools in North America" and 2) "explore the ideological and philosophical values that have shaped the vision of these schools." In so doing, Memon elucidates "the ways Islamic education is defined differently based upon generational, contextual, and ideological perspectives." In his account, he focuses on two distinct communities among Sunni Muslims: indigenous, which includes African American Muslims associated with the community of Imam Warith Deen Mohammed, and immigrants, which include those Sunni Muslims who settled in North America in the 1960s and 1970s. He suggests that the evolution of Islamic schools can be best understood as proceeding in four overlapping phases: Protest (1930–1975), focusing on the roots of Islamic schools in North America; Preservation (1965–1990), a period where indigenous and immigrant Muslims worked to secure educational opportunities as a bulwark against the undue influence of Western secular values; Pedagogy (1985–2001), where established schools, now more secure, could begin to refine their pedagogy and curriculum to distinguish themselves from each other; and Praxis (9/11 to present), where the aim is to translate these theoretical distinctives into practice.

Dr. Memon delineates some important nuances at the outset that one should take into a reading of this book. He addresses Islamic schools rather than Muslim schools, distinguishing Islamic schools "as institutions that strive to define school ethos, curriculum, and pedagogy through traditional sources of Islamic knowledge: the Qur'an and the Prophetic tradition," whereas Muslim schools are "institutions where a learning environment conducive to Muslim dress, diet, and observance are made possible, but where no actual restructuring of the educational philosophy or curriculum of the school is considered." To place this in a broader context, he uses a typology of Islamic education developed by Douglass and Shaikh (2004) consisting of four strands:

> education *of* Muslims, where emphasis is placed on religious instruction; education *for* Muslims, commonly known as Islamic schools, where Muslim children attend these schools for both secular academic and religious instruction; education *about* Islam where textbooks and other sources serve as the medium for educating students in secular public schools about Islam; and, lastly education *in the* Islamic spirit, where knowledge is sought, without distinguishing between religious and secular knowledge in order to cultivate humanity.
> (Author's paraphrasing of Douglass and Shaikh, 17)

Dr. Memon's history pertains to the schools pursuing education *for* Muslim children to nurture a sense of faith-consciousness through basic beliefs, practices, and an Islamic worldview.

A particularly significant contribution made in this volume by Dr. Memon relates to recognizing the internal diversity within Islam—a topic of increasing interest and importance across all religious traditions. With Islam, Memon asserts, there is "difference with sameness," reinforcing "the simple truth that [Islamic schools] are not all the same, nor are they static."

A final important set of ideas one must take into this reading involves Memon's frames of analysis. First, he uses anti-colonial discourse and post-colonial theory to "inform the context and conflicts within which Islamic schools have emerged." Second, he uses a critical faith-based epistemology to illuminate his study participants' values and motivations, "re-positioning faith-centered ways of knowing from the margins to the center." This second point is similar to an argument made by Dr. Ayse Demeriel Ucan in a prior volume in this series, *Improving the Pedagogy of Islamic Religious Education in Secondary Schools*.

Dr. Memon's history of Islamic schools in North America is an important addition to the literature of the educational history of this continent, and his capturing of the oral histories brought into the story here provides invaluable resources that enrich our understanding.

Michael D. Waggoner
Series Editor
Research in Religion and Education

Acronyms

AMM	American Muslim Mission
CISNA	Council of Islamic Schools in North America
CMS	Clara Muhammad schools
IIIT	International Institute of Islamic Thought
ISNA	Islamic Society of North America
MAS	Muslim American Society
MSA	Muslim Students Association
NOI	Nation of Islam
SCMS	Sister Clara Muhammad schools
WCIW	World Community of Al-Islam

Glossary of Arabic Terms

'Aqida/'Aqa'id	foundational beliefs/tenets of faith
Asabiyya	group solidarity, cultural community building
'Ilm	knowledge
Akhlaq	character/behavior
Allah	God
Ayah	sign, verse of the Qur'an
Fiqh	Islamic law
Fitrah	natural inclination, natural state
Hadith	a saying, teaching of the Prophet Muhammad
Ibadah	worship
Imam	religious leader of a congregation
Islam	the religion of Muslims
Jahiliyyah	ignorance
Khalifah	vicegerent
Madrasah (pl. madaris)	traditional school, place of learning
Mizan	balance, scale
Muhammad (Prophet)	the final prophet of Islam
Mujaddid	renewer of faith
Nafs	inner self
Qadr	power, strength
Qur'an	final revelation of Islam
Salafiyyah	an ideology/perspective of contemporary Islam that emphasizes returning to core Islamic beliefs as they were practiced by the *salaf* (earliest generations of Muslims)
S.A.W	refers to an Arabic phrase of "salallahu alayhi wa salam" which translates to "peace and blessings be upon the Prophet" Muhammad—a customary saying among Muslims
Seerah	the life of the Prophet Muhammad
Sheikh/Shaykh	scholar of the Islamic sciences, not necessarily a leader of a congregation

Sunnah	the way of the Prophet Muhammad
Tafsir	interpretation of the Qur'an
Taqwa	belief, certainty of God
Tarbiyah	nurturing wholeness
Tawhid	the belief in One God and in the finality of the Prophet Muhamad
Ummah	global Muslim community

1 Introduction
Context of Islamic Schooling in North America

Positioning Myself

A decade ago, when I was a graduate student at the University of Toronto, I vividly recall sitting in seminars on philosophy of education while reading Freire in particular and feeling something resonate deeply about the intersection between my Islamic faith-identity and critical educational theory. While sitting in the seminar, I began to question, what are Muslim perspectives on education? Is there a philosophy of education rooted in the Islamic tradition? And what makes education "Islamic"?

I grew up in Toronto, Canada as a second-generation Muslim whose parents immigrated from Pakistan to the United States and later Canada in the 1970s for graduate studies. I grew up attending public schools but always being conscious of my Muslim identity. I also grew up in a context that is home to the largest concentration of Islamic Schools in North America (Memon 2012, 73). Although I never attended a formal, full-time Islamic school or taught in one, during my graduate studies, I gained a keen interest in exploring them.

The implicit stigma of Islamic schools within Muslim communities in North America is real. Despite Islamic schools growing rapidly over the past few decades, still only an estimated 3–5% of the North American Muslim population send their children to Islamic schools (Keyworth 2009, 28). The vast majority of Muslim parents believe Islamic schools will isolate their children, emphasize religious studies at the expense of core academic achievement, and provide their children with a substandard education (Elbih 2012; Hussain and Read 2015; Brooks 2019). The larger public stigma of faith-based schools, but in particular of Islamic schools and specifically post-9/11, is damning and increasingly vociferous. Common perceptions are that Islamic schools are dogmatic, insular, and contribute to the breakdown of core national commitments of social cohesion (Parker-Jenkins et al. 2005; Wertheimer 2015; Pring 2018; Hannam 2019).

Pre-9/11 and prior to me delving into graduate studies in education, I attended an education conference at the University of Toronto organized by a group of burgeoning Muslim activists and thought leaders. The conference was entitled "Beyond Schooling: Building Communities that Matter" and held in April 2001. The conference was also dubbed the "Zarnuji Conference" because it relied on a classical educational treatise penned by Imam Zarnuji (Burhan al-Islam al-Zarnuji) in the 12th century. It was a transformative moment for me as an aspiring educator to be exposed to Muslim educational thought. To know that Muslim scholars had written about teaching and learning and that these reflections were derived through interpretations of the Islamic tradition moved me. It was particularly jolting because I grew up thinking that learning about Islam was solely about imparting rudiments of faith. I had not considered that a grounded theory of education, better termed pedagogy, could be derived from a faith tradition.

The combination of being intimately aware of the stigma associated with Islamic schools, being introduced to an archive of Muslim educational thought, and delving into everything from Freire to Foucault during graduate studies encouraged me to look at Islamic schools differently. My intrigue grew about who established Islamic schools and what they envisioned, about whether Islamic schools considered themselves as having a distinct pedagogy, and about what distinguished them from other Islamic schools, other faith-based schools, and from public schools in general.

Setting aside the internal and external stigma of Islamic schooling, I embarked on a study to meet the visionaries and pioneers of the earliest Islamic schools in North America. I wanted to hear their perspectives on what they intended to do, to understand their impetus, and to appreciate their struggle. Essential to this study was the intent to unpack the complexities of Islamic schooling. I recognized from the outset that Islamic schools are not the same, and so the distinguishing aspects of their perspectives and approaches became a salient part of this work.

In response to the widely held stigmas, I made a decision early on that this book will not set out to make a case for Islamic schools or to prove that Islamic schools foster civic engagement, deserve public funding, reinforce gender equity, or any of the larger contemporary debates about faith-based schooling. Rather this book focuses on tracing a journey—an untold story—of sacrifice, dissent, and aspiration by North American Muslim pioneers who grappled with defining the vision of the Islamic schools we have today. The stories shared provide insights about how and why shaping these schools remains a work in progress. This book reveals the messiness of educators not knowing what they are doing while telling parents they have it all figured out. It illustrates how societal factors and tumultuous historical events can shape and reshape the work of schools. And it closes with more questions than answers about what Islamic schooling is and can be. But in all of this, this history of Islamic schooling in North America reveals that there is difference within sameness. This book reinforces the simple truth that they are not all the same nor are they static. Islamic schools are evolving, renewing, reconnecting, questioning, adapting, and challenging themselves.

I should mention three important caveats at the outset. Firstly, that this book is "a history" and not "the history" of Islamic schooling in North America. This book is crafted on the shoulders, stories, and sentiments of pioneering voices in the field but far from an exhaustive list of those whose voices could have been included—some passed away before I could meet them, others I was unable to get to, and most I likely do not even know. Undoubtedly there are voices left out—not silenced intentionally—but missed, not heard, and as a result not acknowledged. This is but one meagre attempt to tell a story of an important part of North American Muslim history that I hope others will develop and expand on in the years to come. Secondly, this study is an oral history, which means that I relied largely on the voices of those whom I met to retell their stories. There may be unintended inaccuracies such as misspelled names, inaccurate dates, places, and historical details. The richness in the narrative derives from the deep sentiments, raw emotions at times, and inner reflections that my participants shared. Lastly, I should position myself. I am a Muslim Canadian of Pakistani heritage writing about a history that is significantly American with a large focus on the experience of indigenous African American Muslims. I wrote this book conscious of the power and privilege that my identity affords me among North American Muslim communities. Being Sunni, male, middle-class, born in Canada, of South Asian heritage—together have likely informed the way that I interpreted the voices of my participants and have written this work. At the same time, I hope that my familiarity with the discourses that have taught me to acknowledge power and privilege have also informed some semblance of equitable representation of the voices and perspectives of my participants. Where I have fallen short, know that it was unintended.

Mapping the Terrain

The historical growth of Islamic schools in North America has been led by two distinct and largely separate communities among Sunni Muslims: the indigenous and the immigrant. Although within these two communities many sub-distinctions can be made, when I speak of "indigenous" in this study, my research will focus primarily on the African American Muslim community of Imam Warith Deen Mohammed (1933–2008) whose roots can be traced back to the Nation of Islam. Similarly, when I speak of the "immigrant" Muslim community, I refer specifically to the generation of Sunni Muslims who immigrated both to Canada and the United States in the 1960s and 1970s.

The use of the term "indigenous" to refer to African American Muslims seems odd in a North American context when the term is most often used and rightfully attributed to Aboriginal Native Canadians and Americans. However, within Muslim communities in North America (in the United States in particular), "indigenous" distinguishes the historical presence of Muslims *in* America (Jackson 2005). The use of the term indigenous versus immigrant easily demarcates who came first. The distinction is particularly important for this study, given the way that both communities that comprise my participants have articulated their experience with one another. For a community historically oppressed and then marginalized once again in their encounter with immigrant Islam in America, the use of the term indigenous gives African American Muslims a sense of authority over what it means to be "American" if not what it means to be "Muslim." This friction will become clearer in the study, but as an initial note, I have chosen the labels of "indigenous" and "immigrant" to help characterize the relationship between the two communities.

These two communities are the first to have aspired toward establishing Islamic elementary and secondary schools as full-time alternatives to the North American public education system. Their histories, contexts, and objectives are distinct and rightfully deserve two separate narratives, as has been done in the handful of literature that exists (Merry 2007; Cristillo 2009; Jasser 2011; Khan and Siddiqui 2017; Pring 2018). However, I wish to tell a different story. This book traces how the two broader North American Muslim communities, indigenous and immigrant, aspired, struggled, collaborated, and, in some instances, parted ways on their journeys toward separate faith-based schools.

This work is an oral history that relies in large part on the voices and memories of those who worked tirelessly to establish the earliest Islamic schools. The voices, perspectives, and narratives of these participants seek to articulate why Islamic schools were established and why they continue to be important. The voices represent what I contend are visions of Islamic education by the visionaries themselves. In other words, by speaking with those who established the schools and listening to how they articulated their intent, I seek to convey some semblance of vision of the history of Islamic Schools in North America that has so far been untold.

In organizing both the historical and philosophical objectives of this work, I have developed four overlapping historical phases through which I feel the visions of Islamic schooling in North America have evolved. The first phase spans from 1930 to 1975. I have entitled this period "Protest," in order to represent the roots of Islamic schools established under the Nation of Islam as a response to the absence of equitable educational opportunities for African American children in the pre-, and, arguably, post-Civil Rights era. The second phase is entitled "Preservation" and spans from 1965 to 1990. This phase represents the initial reaction of early Muslim immigrants as well as indigenous Muslims to protect and preserve their children from perceived immorality in American culture, and by virtue, schools. By the third historical phase, early Islamic schools in both communities were better established and could begin thinking about defining themselves in relation to their school philosophy and curriculum. I have called this third phase "Pedagogy," and it spans from 1985 to 2001. The last phase is largely informed by the tumultuous events of 9/11 and continues to this day. This last phase serves as the catalyst for Islamic schools to perform what they had theoretically set out to do. I call the last phase "Praxis." Together, the four phases of protest, preservation, pedagogy, and praxis frame the historical growth of Islamic schooling through the evolution of its vision.

Semantics: Islamic Schools Versus Muslim Schools

The terms "Islamic school" and "Muslim school" are often used interchangeably in contemporary literature. Following Parker-Jenkins et al. (2005), I define Islamic schools as institutions that strive to define school ethos, curriculum, and pedagogy through the traditional sources of Islamic knowledge: the Qur'an and the Prophetic tradition. Muslim schools, on the other hand, are institutions where a learning environment conducive to Muslim dress, diet, and observance is made possible, but where no actual restructuring of the educational philosophy or curriculum of the school is considered (45).

To further elaborate on the distinction, I rely on Douglass and Shaikh's (2004) typology of Islamic education in America. Their typology also consists of four strands: education *of* Muslims, where emphasis is placed on religious instruction; education *for* Muslims, commonly known as Islamic schools, where Muslim children attend these schools for both secular academic and religious instruction; education *about* Islam, where textbooks and other sources serve as the medium for educating students in secular public schools about Islam; and lastly, education *in the* Islamic spirit, where knowledge is sought without distinguishing between religious and secular knowledge in order to cultivate humanity (2). With Douglas and Shaikh's typology in mind, all of the schools upon which my study focuses fall under the category of education *for* Muslims, or "Islamic schools." The schools that my participants have established or administer are not traditional *madaris* (sing. *madrasah*) or seminaries where Muslim children are educated to become Muslim scholars and theologians. Rather, Islamic schools provide an education *for* Muslim children to nurture a sense of faith-consciousness through basic beliefs, practices, and an Islamic worldview. To an extent, these are schools which strive to eventually nurture an education *in the* Islamic spirit, as Douglass and Shaikh's typology defines and is further discussed in Chapter 4, entitled Pedagogy.

Keyworth (2009) provides the most systematic data tracking of Islamic schools in the United States to date that I have come across. Given that there is no overarching registration board or accrediting body that Islamic schools are tied to, accurately accounting for schools is difficult. Her study found that there were 235 full-time Islamic schools as of 2009 and approximately 32,000 students attending out of the 850,000 school aged students in the country (approximately 3.8%). At the time of her study, she found that 85% of the schools were less than ten years old, which suggests that the majority of American Islamic schools were established between the late 1990s and early to mid 2000s. On average, an Islamic school has approximately 300 students, close to 50% of the academic staff certified teachers, and 75% of the schools independently or autonomously governed (i.e. not affiliated to a mosque) (Keyworth 2009, 28–33). To my knowledge, a statistical study of the sort has not been conducted in Canada, however, anecdotally, similar demographic details can be expected. In my own efforts to determine the number of Islamic schools in Canada through Ministry of Education websites in 2012, I found 60 Islamic schools across the country, with approximately 50% of those located in Toronto, Ontario, alone. In a 2019 search of the Ontario Ministry of Education's website, I found a total of 87 Islamic schools in the province of Ontario, with 64 Islamic schools located in the Greater Toronto Area.

Relevance of This Study

The relevance of the study is threefold. Firstly, the history of Islamic schools as a movement in North America is a story largely untold. Recognizing the handful of published studies specifically on Islamic schools, the emphasis is, for the most part, upon how Muslim students negotiate their Islamic identity in schools, the views of Muslim parents, teachers, or leaders, and whether Islamic schools are able foster or hinder social cohesion (Elbih 2012; Jasser 2011; Brooks 2019; Zine 2008; Cristillo 2009; Merry 2007; Decuir 2016). This work aspires to contribute broader context to the important contributions already published by narrating a history of Islamic schools that explores the collaborations and complexities within and between communities.

Secondly, to date we do not have a concise, descriptive study that seeks to understand the "Islamic" in Islamic schools from the perspective of those who initiated them. Studies on specific schools provide much needed depth and perspective. However, a macro view of the contesting visions, theories, practices, and curricular formats that have been developed over the past 75 years remains a story untold. The intent of this book is not to judge or assess the validity or effectiveness of the vision as it manifests itself in practice but to understand the motives and approaches which underlie varying visions of Islamic schooling. Through attempting to understand the events, people, and perspectives that shaped the evolving approaches of Islamic schools, I hope to contribute to a deeper appreciation of the multiplicity of views on education within North American Muslim communities. It is hoped that this will extend the singular explanation that Islamic schools arose solely out of fear of the unknown or a response to the overt secularity of public schooling.

Lastly, on account of the limited research in this area and growing skepticism due to media sensationalism following 9/11, the need to understand Islamic schooling has increased. I will employ the case in England as a tangential example: the White Paper which formalized the government's intention to expand faith-based schools was published in and around the same time as 9/11. Combined with the Bradford Riots which preceded 9/11, growing public opinion at the time and ever since has become more insistent that segregating communities by ethnic and religious affiliations will increase hostility and misunderstanding between peoples in the larger societal framework. In fear that faith-based schools (particularly minority faith-based schools) will be divisive and exclusionary, public polls have shown decreasing support for the establishment of faith-based schools (Parker-Jenkins 2014; Parker-Jenkins et al. 2005; Breen 2018) Exploring the objectives, nuances, and complexities that distinguish one Islamic school from another would challenge simplistic interpretations and perceptions of their potential or lack thereof. In the past decade, the issues within religion and schooling have intensified. As with the case of England, so too have the United States and Canada experienced a heightened concern over what is taught in private religious schools and whether faith-based schools ought to be supported, financed, or even allowed to exist.

Phases of Islamic School Growth

In describing his "historical method," Marshall Hodgson, author of the ageless *Venture of Islam*, argues that a historian must be forthright in identifying the goal of their inquiry. He says even if the questions that shape a historical study are of the normative "date-bound" type, "one can still distinguish historical viewpoints further in terms of what sort of date-bound questions are regarded as primary, the answer to which is the goal of the inquiry." (Hodgson 1977, 23). To understand historical inquiry, he creates a dichotomy between two types of historians: "typicalizers" and "exceptionalizers." Typicalizers, he says, are concerned with inquiries that unpack the "total cultural environment" of a particular historical circumstance in an attempt to understand the ways in which interacting events contribute to cultural change. These historians employ an "exceptional" lens only so far as it can help understand the interacting events. The exceptionalizer, on the other hand, conducts historical inquiry employing the same tools as the typicalizer with the intent not only to understand a total cultural environment, but to recognize why that circumstance is exceptional. From the latter perspective, the beliefs, motivations, and visions of individuals who make history become central. Hodgson insists that "it is such personal vision that is the most human part of human history. . . . For when habitual, routine thinking will no longer work, it is the man or woman with imagination who will produce the new alternatives" (Hodgson 1977, 26). The role of the exceptionalizer is then to concern themselves with the concerns, commitments, and ways that individuals know and interact with the world that shapes their intentions and actions.

The growth of Islamic schools can be understood through the typical events, people, and places that have shaped their existence today, which is part of what I have tried to achieve. But from Hodgson's category of "exceptionalizer," I think part of my purpose in choosing to use oral history has also been my subconscious attempt at deeply engaging with the "beliefs, motivations, and visions" of my participants. More importantly, my analysis seeks to explore how these "visions" of Islamic schooling are understood by my participants historically in relation to their life purpose. And as the schools progress and improve, what are they moving toward? With these questions in mind, looking back and looking forward historically in time, I use Murata and Chittick (1994) to help frame my philosophy of history; they write, "Surely one of the deepest gulfs separating the modern Western perspective from the traditional Islamic worldview is the understanding of history" (321). In this, study I have outlined four phases of Islamic school growth in North America. However, these phases must not be understood as evolving or progressing toward new directions per se. The phases are not meant to imply that each new phase renders the previous inadequate. To make sense of the historical vision of Islamic schooling in North America, I will employ a distinctly Islamic perspective on history, what can be referred to as "sacred history."

My intention of mapping four distinct phases in the growth of Islamic schools is not to predict a fifth, intrinsic of a Marxist take on historical method (Popper 1959, 277). Nor do the phases understand the growth through a materialist conception of history as devised by Engels. Such an approach would explain the evolving vision of Islamic schools largely by the class divisions and access to wealth that have divided the indigenous from the immigrant (Russell 1959, 287). Essential to the Islamic perspective on history is "the very centrality and totality of the human state which makes any 'linear' and 'horizontal' evolution of man impossible" (Nasr 2007, 69). I rely on an Islamic worldview of history that is spiritually based and emphasizes history as the unraveling of the wisdom embedded in the Qur'an. "Everything that happened in the past was a sign of God. Hence, the *significance* of the past was already established before people learned anything about its details" (Murata and Chittick 1994, 324). From such a perspective, the events of the past, the future, and agency that human beings have in shaping those events are all intertwined in a grander notion of Islamic ontology.

The conception of a "sacred history" must be understood through the role and responsibility of human beings from an Islamic perspective. The concept of *khalifat Allah fi'l-ard* (the vicegerent of God on earth) is a recurring theme that comes out throughout this study by my participants as the rationale for their effort in envisioning and establishing Islamic schools. The concept of *khalifat Allah* is central to an Islamic ontology. Reflection on the term's centrality will elucidate the individual motivations of my participants and, from a methodological perspective, can also inform the way one reads history. From an Islamic perspective, the ultimate reality is to know God and to understand the Divine Will. The role of a human being from an Islamic worldview is the "impossible ascent" toward this reality (Eaton 1987, 375). In comparison and in relation to agency, from a Western, secular perspective, freedom and agency are considered to be the freedom to do something, but from an Islamic worldview, "freedom is the freedom to *be*, to experience pure existence itself" (Nasr 1981, 16). If the spiritual purpose is to experience the countenance of God, the very purpose of the human state transcends the physical world as we know it. Human beings are not evolving physically, then, but returning spiritually. The position of being *khalifa* places particular responsibilities on human beings that are unlike those on any other creation of God. The physical work, or fulfillment of these responsibilities (i.e. establishing justice, seeking understanding), are embedded in a metaphysical reality. The evolution of human beings in any linear or horizontal trajectory does not exist. The existence and effort of human beings are exerted then toward the fulfillment of their responsibility as *khalifa*, which shapes the way the world is read (Eaton 1987, 375). This conception provides an alternative view of history that transcends the limitations of time and space in the physical sense and recognizes what lies beyond creation.

Sacred history is what I think the great Muslim historian, Ibn Khaldun, called the inner meaning of history, which "involves speculation and an attempt to get at the truth, subtle explanation of the causes and origins of existing things, and deep knowledge of the why of events. [History,] therefore, is firmly rooted in philosophy" (Khaldun 1958, 6). I see the history of Islamic schools from the lens of sacred history, one that recognizes the human responsibility of *khalifa* and the growth of individuals, communities, and in this case schools as a movement in search of fulfilling this covenant that God has placed on them. The growth of Islamic schools through the phases of protest, preservation, pedagogy, and praxis is not an outline for the evolution of Islamic schools toward new methods and models of schooling per se, but a move back toward pedagogical practices that are more closely aligned with the immutable principles of Islam (Oludamini 2018). Although the movement is progressively forward, it is at the same time inherently defined by a return.

Common words used to conceptualize the forward motion of historical trajectories are "development," "progress," "renewal," and "renaissance" (Lings 1968, 1). Inherent in the concepts of development and progress is a move away from principles. But the further away a community shifts from past principles, the closer it moves toward degeneration. Counter to Hegel's view of history that suggests progress is based on the decisions of individuals (Russell 1959, 291), the Islamic worldview understands progress as an attempt to renew and relive principles of the past within the structures of the present. "Progress," then, is a movement of return, "a restoration of something of the primordial vigour of Islam" (Lings 1968, 1). As Islamic schools "progress" from protest to praxis, the movement forward is intrinsically about returning closer toward finding the most effective ways to nurture a student's natural inclinations. Progress "implies a direction, a goal, and standards whereby it can be judged" (Murata and Chittick 1994, 330). The question for Islamic schooling, then, is on what basis do we measure the progress of schools historically? And if, the measure of success for Islamic schooling is on the basis of its ability to fulfill the covenant discussed earlier, then our conception of success drastically changes. Hence, each phase of Islamic school growth represents an attempt to improve pedagogical aims and practices toward the same goal. In what follows, I briefly outline the four phases of growth.

Protest (1930–1975)

I employ the term protest reflective of the necessary confrontation of racism and discrimination that was central to most African American Islamic movements. More accurately, the term spiritual protest (Auston 2017) ought to be used because of the intersection between a search for justice and equality grounded with an intimate connection to a faith-tradition. Chapter 2, entitled Protest, focuses on the American experience of racial segregation. Systemic racism in the United States served as the catalyst for numerous African American responses, including the Nation of Islam (NOI). Although the NOI is a community outside the teachings and practices of orthodox Islam, the African American experience of establishing separate schools under the NOI serves as the roots of the earliest Islamic schools on the continent. In the chapter, I trace the historical growth of the NOI's separate elementary and secondary schools, called the University of Islam. I contextualize the growth of the consortium of University of Islam schools through the rhetoric of protest that defined the leadership of Elijah Muhammad, co-founder of the NOI. The narrative of the University of Islam schools spans from the emergence of the NOI in the 1930s to the death of Elijah Muhammad in 1975. I close this section by transitioning with the transformation of the NOI under the leadership of Imam Warith Deen Mohammed, Elijah's prodigal son. Under Imam Warith Deen, his father's community is aligned with the teachings of orthodox Islam, and inevitably many of the existing University of Islam schools make a formal transition to becoming Islamic schools.

Preservation (1965–1990)

Preservation continues where Protest left off. Among the changes made in the years following his father's death, Imam Warith Deen Mohammed renames and re-envisions the University of Islam schools after his mother, Sister Clara Muhammad. Part of the aim of this section is to trace how the Clara Muhammad schools align with the orthodox teachings of Islam and the impact that such changes had on the community of Imam Warith Deen while acknowledging the necessity of the early schools under the NOI. The chapter then spirals back in time to introduce the wave of Muslim immigration to both the United States and Canada in the mid-1960s. Through networks and the establishment of community organizations to preserve an Islamic identity in a new land, I explore how and why the need for educational outlets arose among immigrant Muslims. By the early 1980s, when both the indigenous and immigrant communities established a number of schools, I shift my attention toward the collaboration between communities around improving the quality of Islamic education.

Pedagogy (1985–2001)

Pedagogy is less confined by time than the previous two parts. Although the data is informed by particular historical events, the ideologies and perspectives that I attempt to explain here cannot fall neatly within a fixed time frame. The focus of this part is to elucidate the theoretical underpinnings that have shaped the objectives of Islamic schools in North America. The term pedagogy will be used not to refer to the conventional conception of pedagogy as teaching or the art of instruction but rather pedagogy as a human science, a philosophy of education that espouses values, intentions, and aspirations of learning and teaching (Smith et al. 2010). Through contemporary Muslim theorists, ideologies, and perspectives, I attempt to make sense of the unique ways in which an Islamic education has been defined and how curriculum models have been informed. I argue that during the mid-1980s to mid-1990s, numerous individuals, many of whom were my participants in this study, sought to develop models of education that would serve the growth of Islamic schools. These models, however, are distinct from one another and mirror particular perspectives within the Islamic tradition.

Praxis (2001 to the Present)

Praxis brings the reader to the present era shaped by the tragic events of 9/11. The increasing scrutiny, hesitation, and misinformation of seemingly everything Muslim or "Islamic" post-9/11 has evolved the mission of Islamic schools once again. In the words of one of my participants, Islamic schools need to "stop teaching *about* Islam and start teaching *how* to be Muslim." Numerous similar sentiments pushed me to call Chapter 5 "Praxis" since Islamic schools have been catapulted into an era where students must actualize the generosity, civility, and humanity that have thus far largely only been taught theoretically in Islamic schools. Related to a push toward praxis, in this part I also explore the role that second-generation Muslims of immigrant families and indigenous Muslim converts who did not come through the NOI play in complicating my dichotomy. I explain how the visions of "protest," "preservation," and "pedagogy" have been criticized by the two groups mentioned earlier as having fallen short of an "Islamic" education. In response, a growing number of Muslims now seek to find alternative educational models, including home schools, community schools, and reforms within public schools.

History of Muslims in North America

Among the two different groups of Muslims in America—the indigenous and the immigrant—there are additional subcategories and complexities. Indigenous Muslims, for example, include African American Muslims who came through the slave trade and Anglo Muslim converts (Haddad and Lummis 1987). And some scholars have traced the presence of African American Muslims to pre-Columbus America (Weiner 1920).

The history of immigrant Muslims in America has similar, yet relatively more recent complexity. Haddad and Lummis (1987) outline five separate waves of Muslim immigration to America. The first major wave was in the 1900s (1875–1912), with the arrival largely of dock workers from Palestine, Lebanon, Syria, and Jordan. The second wave of immigration was from 1918–1922, where many relatives of the already established immigrants were coming over after the First World War. The third wave occurred between 1930–1938, where American immigration laws allowed for more relatives to come. The fourth wave was 1948–1960, where the arrival of a larger number of Muslims from the Subcontinent, the Far East, and Russia migrated. The fifth stage is from 1967 to the present, where America is being chosen for economic and political reasons.

In addition to the Muslim migration from the Middle East, Nyang (2002) insists in his chapter on continental African Muslim immigrants to the United States that we not forget the arrival of African Muslims since the late 19th century. In telling the tale of the growth of Islam among African Americans and Canadians, Nyang's work serves as a perspective often overshadowed. These Africans, however, also contributed to the growth of Muslim America since its earliest stages. Many of the early Africans migrated by choice largely from West Africa to America through their collaboration with Christian missionaries who had hoped for their conversion upon arrival. They, like the Arabs, came for educational opportunities, but not necessarily permanent residence. Once financially established, however, marital relationships often confirmed their decision to stay permanently. Later waves of African immigrants came as political refugees from East Africa (Nyang 2002, 250).

In Canada, the first Muslims similarly came from Syria and Lebanon as traders to sell goods in the Canadian northwest. Lake La Biche in Alberta is considered the first Canadian Muslim community (McDonough and Hoodfar 2005; Abu-Laban 1980). In his history of Arabs in Canada, Abu Laban describes the religious diversity amongst the early Arab immigrants as primarily Christian. It was not until later phases of immigration that large numbers of Arab Muslims arrived. Karim (2002) traces the first Muslim presence in Canada to 1871, when the national census recorded 13 Muslim residents (263). Hamdani's (1984) study of archival documents suggests that an immigrant Muslim couple lived in Ontario as early as 1854 (8). Earliest records of the Muslim presence remain contested. Although small numbers of Muslims continued to immigrate prior to and after the First World War, the largest wave of Muslim immigration came in the post-war period and especially in the 1970s, when Prime Minister Pierre Trudeau established the celebrated multicultural policy on October 8, 1971.

In both the American and Canadian experience, the most substantial wave of Muslim immigrants came in the 1960s and 70s. Until then, the Muslim presence in North America was dispersed across the continent in small communities often practicing their faith individually. With the recent waves of immigration, greater diversity with respect to ethnicity and ideology has reshaped the North American Muslim experience.

Diversities and Complexities Within North American Muslims

Between the indigenous and immigrant communities, there also exists much diversity on the basis of Islamic sect, socioeconomic class, and perceived authority over the Islamic tradition that together inform ideological differences. McCloud (2003) describes the American Muslim community as a mosaic and a tattered quilt at the same time. She argues that religious interpretation among Muslims in America is so diverse that the "cacophony of voices raised is dynamic, if sometimes deafening. The variety of discourses is as wide as the many ethnicities in the Muslim community" (159).

The contemporary thrust of immigrants either came out of refuge from political turmoil in the South Asia and Middle East or immigrated seeking new opportunities in the rapidly developing industrial complex of North America. The majority of Muslims to have immigrated in the post-World War II period belonged to the Sunni Muslim communities, even though Shi'is from South Asia, Iran, and the Near East, along with Ismailis from East Africa and Ahmadis largely from India, also came in substantial numbers (McDonough and Hoodfar 2005, 136–137). It was not until the Civil Rights movement of the 1960s that large numbers of Muslim as well as other non-European immigrants of color settled in the United States.

The Civil Rights movement created great opportunities for minority immigration. The African American struggle for equal rights served as a platform from which other racial, ethnic, and religious minorities could benefit. As a result, changes to the American immigration law in 1964 opened recruitment of skilled professionals in the areas of medicine, pharmacy, and engineering and provided student visas and funding for skill development training for minorities. By this latter wave of immigration,

> Muslims on the whole were better educated, more economically advantaged, and generally competent in English. Often recruited to study and work in this country, they came as professionals in the fields of medicine, engineering, and other sciences prepared to join the American middle and upper classes of the professionally successful.
> (McDonough and Hoodfar 2005, 136–137)

Professionally trained and educated, yet the economic status of North American Muslims informs differing views on socio-political participation in civic affairs of the country. Khan (2003) dichotomizes this phenomenon as the two images of America held by Muslims. We have "America the democracy versus America the colonial power" (178). America the democracy describes those Muslims who cherish the freedom granted through individual and community rights based on race, ethnicity, and religion to hold on to indigenous identities. Those who view America as a colonial power emphasize the role of American foreign policy in aiding, abetting, instigating, and carrying out military offences in Muslim countries overseas. Finding a home somewhere between the two ideologies, some Muslim intellectuals who found themselves serving the leadership of the American Muslim community held one common overriding goal: to revive Islamic civilization (ibid., 181).

The Islamization of Knowledge project in the 1960s and 1970s is likely the best example of this sort of revivalist ideology shaping the North American landscape. The work of Ismail Faruqi and other Muslim intellectuals, such as Seyyed Hossein Nasr and Naquib al-Attas, was institutionalized through the establishment of the Association of Muslim Social

Scientists (AMSS) and the International Institute of Islamic Thought (IIIT), both based in the United States. Other similar think tanks, such as the Islamic Foundation in the United Kingdom, were also established around the same time. But all this institutional activity began through campus student networks in the 1970s. Muslim Student Associations (MSA) served as the meeting ground for blossoming Muslim intellectuals to network and initiate community projects. Study circles and prayer rooms were established for Muslims to meet while fulfilling religious observances. With the Muslim leadership graduating from university, religious activism was gradually taken to a broader arena in establishing organizations such as those mentioned earlier as well as mosques and Islamic schools. At this historical stage of the Muslim community, much of the emphasis was on fighting the pressure of assimilation, and as a result, community based energy was largely placed on building Islamic centers and schools in the 1970s and 1980s.

Toward Muslim Organizational Structures

To appreciate the intricacies behind early Muslim organizational structures, I employ Mattson's (2003) three Islamic paradigms to explain the different political outlooks that exist within the Muslim communities of North America. Mattson argues that Muslims who are willingly connected to a religious discourse will fit into one of her paradigms: resistance, embrace, and selective engagement. The paradigm of resistance is espoused by those who passionately critique American society as *jahili*, backward, hedonistic, lawless, and immoral. The stance of such Muslims is to isolate themselves from areas of American society where they might be influenced by such culture in order for them to ground themselves in an Islamic way of life so as to change American society from its roots. In her paradigm of embrace, Muslim immigrants who have escaped repressive regimes value the freedom of expression and individuality of North America. They embrace American commitments of not imposing religious values on anyone while at the same time respecting the religious rights of those who choose to practice a religious faith. The final paradigm that Mattson presents is that of selective engagement, where Muslims feel strongly about fulfilling the religious command of changing wrongs and contributing to societal growth. These Muslims choose active participation in the public sphere through social, political, economic, and environmental activism around issues that affect all citizens. Within such a framework, the vision and purpose of many Muslim organizations can be explored.

The histories of two major Muslim organizations in America are necessary for laying the groundwork for the establishment of Islamic schools. The Islamic Society of North America (ISNA), based in Plainfield, Indiana, and Warith Deen Muhammad's American Muslim Mission (AMM), based out of Chicago, Illinois, are organizations that emphasize a very pragmatic approach to community involvement. ISNA and AMM differ from more politically fervent groups such as Hizb at Tahrir and Ikhwan al Muslimun as well as the revivalist/pietistic based groups of Jamaat-e-Islami, Tabligh Jamaat, and the Islamic Circle of North America (ICNA) in advocating "the idea that American Muslims are simultaneously part of the worldwide community of Muslim believers and of the pluralistic society" (Nimer 2002, 171). Members of these organizations believe that political and civic involvement can benefit the community at large and show appreciation for an opportunity to fulfill the Qur'anic command of enjoining good and forbidding evil. Using Mattson's framework, both ISNA and the community of Imam Warith Deen would fall under the category of selective engagement, which will be briefly outlined in what follows and discussed in further detail in subsequent chapters.

From the Muslim Student's Association (MSA) to the Islamic Society of North America (ISNA): Aspirations of Immigrant Muslims

The roots of ISNA can be traced back to earlier attempts in the 1950s of community building initiatives, such as the Federation of Islamic Associations (FIA) and the Muslim Student's Association (MSA), which represented the diversity and internationalism of Islam. Organizations such as the FIA were largely social networks divided on ethnic lines. The MSA, however, united the Arabs, Iranians, South Asians, Malaysians, Turks, and others under a single mission of serving Islam. Ahmed (1991) argues that the catalyst for such unity was not only that university campuses served as a fertile meeting place for academic activists but also the political context of the time. The year of the official consolidation of the MSA, 1963, was the same year that Ayatollah Khomeini was expelled from Iran, Maulana Maududi was sent to jail in Pakistan, the *Ikwaan al Muslimun* were jailed in Egypt (and Sayyid Qutb was executed shortly thereafter), the Masjumi Party and its leader in Indonesia were thrown into jail, and the Algerian revolution was in its final stages of victory (14). The students who envisioned the MSA model and were active on university campuses across North America represented these life stories and political tensions. Creating awareness and providing financial assistance toward the tensions of the Islamic world were of primary importance to young Muslim immigrants in North America.

By the mid-1960s, an elaborate network of local chapters was established at every major university campus nationwide, and zonal structures were put in place. Memberships increased and donations from overseas followed to assist the work of the MSA. In 1975, more consolidation and coordination was needed, and as a result of the growth, land was purchased to serve as the headquarters in Plainfield, Indiana. Departments, subsidiary organizations, and professional organizations by field were created to keep graduated members active in the MSA mission. By 1977, task forces were set up to again restructure the exponential growth of the organization. By 1981, it was decided that the MSA should focus their work on university campuses, while a separate organization, the Muslim Community Organization (MCA), would oversee larger community initiatives. Both the MSA and MCA, however, would remain bound under the same umbrella organization of the Islamic Society of North America (ISNA). ISNA was envisioned to serve as the glue under which student led initiatives (MSA), community led initiatives (MCA), professional organizations such as the Association of Muslim Social Scientists (AMSS), and service organizations such as the North American Islamic Trust (NAIT) would all work collectively. Today, under the auspices of ISNA (which represents the MCA) and the MSA, these organizations have shaped the mainstream discourse of Muslims in North America. Their annual convention held in Chicago brings together over 50,000 Muslims to be inspired by important and influential Muslim scholars, leaders, and activists. Professional development seminars, issue-specific working groups, youth activities, and an international bazaar are also held at this convention. The intent of the convention, along with zonal conferences and symposia, are to educate and stimulate Muslims both young and old toward personal betterment and community activism.

The Nation of Islam and the American Muslim Mission: From Elijah Muhammad to His Son Warith Deen

The American Muslim Mission (AMM) is the result of Warith Deen Mohammed's transformed vision of the Nation of Islam (NOI). The AMM was preceded by the Nation of Islam, which incorporated the tradition of the Moorish Science Temple of Noble Drew Ali (d. 1929) and the International Negro Improvement Movement of Marcus Garvey (d. 1940) (Ahmed 1991, 18). Noble Drew Ali, who claimed to be a prophet, adapted Islam to create his own creed and entice African Americans who had lost their faith over time through the slave trade. From 1886–1929, Drew Ali was the predecessor of Fard Muhammad and later Elijah Muhammad. In the spirit of Noble Drew Ali, the Nation of Islam was created in 1932 by the anointing of Elijah Muhammad as the Messenger of God. Advocating unique forms of Black Nationalism, this movement assisted in forming the ideology of the NOI based on the charismatic leadership of Elijah Muhammad. Claiming to be the messenger of God, Elijah Muhammad established the most effective Black indigenous community in North America. With a hierarchical, centralized leadership, the NOI put into place their own organized militia (the Fruit of Islam, FOI), community owned businesses, temples, and schools, named the University of Islam schools (Curtis 2006; Walker 2005).

Warith Deen Mohammed, Elijah's eldest son, succeeded his father after his father's death in 1975 and steered the Nation of Islam back toward orthodox Sunni Islam. He transformed the NOI by declaring that his father was not a prophet and replaced the Nation's ideology with orthodox, mainstream Islamic practices. In 1980, further changes to the organization were made when Warith Deen changed the name of his movement to the American Muslim Mission, its weekly paper into the *Muslim Journal*, and the schools were renamed and re-envisioned as the Sister Clara Muhammad schools after his mother. Under the leadership of Warith Deen Mohammed, the vision of the Nation of Islam became more inclusive, less oppositional, and overall closer to adopting the mainstream principles of Islam through the Qur'an and Prophetic tradition. Imam Warith Deen's ideology for Black Nationalism was definitely opposed to his father's position of preaching hate. On February 5, 1992, he addressed the Pentagon on the fundamentals of the Islamic faith. The following day, he became the first Muslim in the history of the United States to deliver the invocation in the Senate. On January 20, 1993, he was invited by President Clinton to represent Muslims at the Inaugural Interfaith Prayer Service. The community of Imam Warith Deen is hailed as the largest Muslim organization or mass movement in the United States. Unlike ISNA, which serves the Muslim population of North America but does not necessarily represent them, the community of Imam Warith Deen is unique in being led by a single leader and voice.

The history and ideology of both of these organizations will be further developed in the subsequent parts. This initial synopsis is intended to lay the foundation for the two umbrella communities that will shape the voices and perspectives of Islamic schooling in North America.

An Oral History of Islamic Schooling

Oral history allows for the multiple layers of time, events, and people that overlap within North American Muslim communities to connect. The dynamics of intersections and peculiarities will help characterize the growth of Islamic schools as an unfolding story rather than a fixed entity in time and space. By retracing history through unheard voices, history can be deepened, and alternative narratives can arise. In the case of my research, tracing the growth of Islamic schools in North America through the voices and lives of those who established them provided new insights and greater depth in understanding the contextual origin and objectives of Islamic schooling. In the words of Paul Thompson (1998), "it can give back to the people who made and experienced history, through their own words, a central place" (22). Documenting these voices is vital to the continual growth, reflection, and regeneration of Islamic schooling. Pioneers and advocates, such as Imam Warith Deen Mohammed, for example, inspired a nation for the past 40 years in re-envisioning the Nation of

Islam and the Clara Muhammad schools (the largest consortium of Islamic schools in America), and yet there is little written about what he aimed to achieve through these schools. Nor is there a documented history of the struggles he endured to transform these schools from the Nation of Islam or the challenges of integrating them with the vision of the global Muslim community in America. His voice and the voices of those who stood by his side are central to the historical growth and vision of Islamic schooling.

The history of Islamic schools in North America is also relatively recent, and as a result of its newness and sporadic growth, the resources to tell such a history are also limited. Few schools or Islamic educational organizations have kept archives of their school's history and growth. Many schools likely did not even consider keeping one, and others have not considered the importance of an archive enough to maintain it. Most schools also were established with limited funds and the over-reliance on a few individuals who have not had the time to consider anything beyond the day to day functioning of the school. Focusing on archival research would have limited the breadth of history I would have been able to cover. I was informed by Sheikh Abdalla Idris, founder of the first Islamic School in Canada, that the ISNA Headquarters in Plainfield, Indiana, for example, does have an archive of old ISNA newsletters and videos. However, the archives, from what I have been told, are far from cataloged or organized in any sequential order, which had the potential of making a researcher's life miserable. The more important point is that if I were to depend on ISNA's archives, I would have only been given a history of ISNA's role in Islamic schools and not the various communities and individuals who have done work outside of ISNA.

Setting aside archives, then, I realized that tracing the history of Islamic schools through the voices of those who first established them, who pioneered the work, and who envisioned the importance of their work would be the richest way of retelling the history of Islamic schools. I also feel that oral history has allowed me to transcend individual schools and organizations. It has allowed me to provide a breadth of lived experiences that inform the complexities of the growth of these schools over the span of close to 80 years, highlighting contexts, people, and visions that have collaborated and collided along the way. Speaking with, often meeting, and in some cases even living with my participants for short periods of time have given me insights and narratives that documents cannot. I was also given insight through the passion of personal influences and ideologies that have shaped individual motivations that could not be gained through texts.

An Insider's Perspective

As a researcher from within the community of Muslims in North America, being born and raised in Canada and active in organizing and attending national events, my ability to conduct effective oral history heightened. What Tuchman (1984) refers to as being able to distinguish the significant from the insignificant in oral history, being an "insider" not in the sense of being a participant in the growth of Islamic schools but in the sense of knowing community leaders and initiatives intimately, gave me access to people who are otherwise quite difficult to meet. The day before I got my first interview with Shaykh Hamza, for example, I attended a public lecture of his entitled "Misreading History" held at Columbia University. Dr. Richard Bulliet, Professor of History at Columbia, preceded Shaykh Hamza on the program and remarked to a standing room only audience that "opening for Shaykh Hamza is like opening for the Rolling Stones." It was not the first time that I have heard academics from across the United States refer to Shaykh Hamza's near rock star status. For me to procure an hour of his time twice, as well as a number of phone conversations, was no simple task. Had I not been close to people who were close to him, I likely would not have secured the interviews. Similarly, but less successfully, my access to the community allowed me to get in touch with people close to Imam Warith Deen Mohammed, but I was unable to secure a formal interview with him. Having spoken to his eldest daughter numerous times, visited his office in Chicago at the *Muslim Journal*, met his youngest daughter and son, all of whom were quite supportive of my research, I began to eventually realize how difficult it is to secure interviews with prominent community leaders. After a year of failed attempts, faxed letters, personal phone calls to his advisors, security, family, visits to his hometown, and cross country drives to meet him at public conferences, I needed to move forward. It was only months after a first draft of this book that I received communication that Imam Warith Deen Mohammed passed away on September 9, 2008. My own educated conclusion after speaking to many people close to him is that given his age, his limited energy and memory, coupled with the numerous requests for his time, it would likely have been more of an honor to simply meet with him than to actually gain from what he would be able to remember. What I did gain from my failed attempts of meeting Imam Warith Deen, however, were interviews with people who have worked closely with him on educational initiatives who I did not know of at the outset of this oral history journey.

By interviewing people who did not necessarily agree with each other or work with one another, I was able to delve into the complex perspectives that shaped particular voices. Especially within the immigrant established Islamic schools, I interviewed people who directly challenged the views of other participants. And more importantly, they challenged the limitations of my own framework. People like Shabbir Mansuri, who established and directed the Council of Islamic Education (CIE), for instance, challenged the very need for Islamic schools. Others, like Afeefa Syeed, questioned whether I was being over-simplistic by labeling particular schools from a particular era as "immigrant established schools," which is the conventional language used amongst many of the educators with whom I spoke. She frankly told me that the school she established is often labeled as an immigrant school, but she herself is a second generation Muslim in America, and the parents that her school caters to are the same—people who do not relate to the immigrant but rather indigenous experience of Muslims in America. My participants, therefore, not only represented the complexity of the Sunni Muslim experience in North America but also pushed my own thinking around the dynamic nature of this project of schooling.

I attempt to retell the history of Islamic schools through a series of chronological events. Major events in this narrative are important to contextualize because, as Gaddis (2002) says, they serve as "punctuated equilibrium." Punctuated equilibrium helps me explain that the evolution of Islamic schooling in North America did not happen at a steady rate, one school after the other, but periods of growth were stimulated or "punctuated" with "abrupt and destabilizing changes" (98). In the case of the growth of Islamic schools, the death of Elijah Muhammad, for example, was abrupt. Similarly, the terrorist attacks of 9/11 were gravely destabilizing. Gaddis (2002) argues that these destabilizing moments give rise to new species and ways of doing things. In the case of Islamic schools, after the death of Elijah Muhammad in 1975 and the reformation of the Nation of Islam, Imam Warith Deen transformed the existing schools under his father's leadership to be *Islamic*. Similarly, post-9/11, Islamic schools both in Canada and the United States redefined the vision of an Islamic education. I highlight major historical moments emphasized by my participants to inform the shifts and evolution of the aims and objectives of Islamic schools that I have found.

Limitations of Oral History

There are a number of limitations of oral history, some of which have been addressed by the distinctiveness of my study. Among the limitations are that individual recollections can be vague, imprecise, or limited. An unreliability of memory often leads to either unintentional or sometimes even deliberate falsification of lived experiences. In the case of the latter, the participant may have a personal end for which they embellish their own role or diminish someone else's (Seldon and Pappworth 1983). I feel that I have been able to avoid some of the stated shortcomings because of the nature of my study. My purpose for employing oral history is not with the intent of retracing a detailed chronology of events but to highlight overarching themes that were shaped by major events, personalities, and perspectives. I also feel that my participants themselves were all guided by an ethical code and driven by a higher purpose that disallowed them to see my work as anything other than a sacred act. Channeled by their *taqwa*, God consciousness, my participants were all very aware, if not afraid, of the unethical potential of misrepresenting and misappropriating the truth. I found that such awareness came naturally to them. Humility was a deep part of their being. I found, for instance, that many of them would first ask me whether I had spoken to others and questioned whether they were the right person for me to be interviewing, even though I had often been recommended by numerous other people of my participants' unparalleled contributions in the field of Islamic schooling. Others would often shy away from answering questions that they did not feel they had authority over. I remember interviewing Dr. Qadir Abdus Sabur, founder and director of the Muslim Teacher's College, as one of my first participants. When I asked him about Imam Warith Deen's vision of education, he told me frankly that I should ask the Imam about that directly. When I interviewed him for the second time, I reshaped the same question hoping for an answer, and he again forthrightly told me that if I am going to ask about the views of someone else or about someone else, I should ask them directly of that person. This sentiment comes from an Islamic consciousness of speaking of someone else who is not present, even if speaking well of someone. Dr. Abdus Sabur's *taqwa* in this instance illustrates the strong sense of moral uprightness that my participants embodied.

Similarly, my participants would often avoid issues that might be deemed slanderous or hurtful to others in the community. They all lived through difficult times when community politics created rifts between individuals, families, and even within communities based on race, culture, and ideology. And indeed, I do acknowledge these tensions within my work because denial of their existence would be untruthful to the history of Islamic schooling in North America. But I have consciously focused on larger issues versus the minute details that created rifts between individuals and communities. I recognized early in my research that it was not my project to delve into the particulars of unfortunate frictions which individuals have grown to reconcile. Nor did my participants insist on reliving such moments of friction. In oral history, participants often use interviews to impose their own perspective on controversial historical moments, yet in the case of my research, I found the opposite. Dr. Zakiyyah Muhammad, for example, an African American Muslim woman who administered an immigrant established Islamic school for many years in California, did not retrace the time she took the school community to court on the basis of racism against her. Nor did Br. Rafiq Iddin, who is currently reviving the Philadelphia CMS, tell me about the internal corruption and mismanagement of funds that led to the closure of the school. Both certainly did not deny the events, but were wary of giving me a biased, one-sided opinion and recommended I research the events myself since they were well documented in the news for me to make my own judgment. Dr. Abdul Alim Shabazz, director of education who was ousted from the community of Imam Warith Deen Mohammed shortly after the death of the Honorable Elijah Muhammad, told me to do the same thing if I wanted to know more about that particular event. These are people that are living their faith in practice. They approached my work with a sincerity and commitment to tell the truth without hiding historical tensions but at the same time were very conscious of the potential of giving biased opinions on issues that they themselves recognize to be complex. I felt at times myself that a number of participants, especially in the scenarios mentioned, could have used my work as an opportunity to redress wrongs leveled against them, but they proved to be more gracious than to demean themselves with petty individual tensions in a much grander project. They recognized that my project was not about individual schools or communities but about the overall trajectory of an evolving vision of education. These were people who did not use excessive discretion in embellishing their roles and efforts. In fact, most times I was often left to probe into the tremendous personal sacrifices that each of them made.

Focus of the Study

In organizing this work among two distinct Muslim communities in North America, the indigenous and immigrant, my work focuses on two types of schools which I feel have enhanced the depth of this study. However, as a result, I have had to make numerous over-simplifications that I wish to explain. Firstly, when I speak of indigenous Muslim schools, I am referring to African American Muslim schools established by the Nation of Islam and later the community of Imam Warith Deen. However, many African Americans do not trace their conversion to Islam through the NOI, nor are all existing African American Muslim schools a part of either the University of Islam or the Clara Muhammad schools systems (Danin 2002). On the same point, then, another conscious decision I made in my research was to focus on Sunni Islamic schools. My explanation of the growth of University of Islam schools in the chapter entitled "Protest" is solely to give credence to the roots of the Clara Muhammad schools. However, that does not mean that when Imam Warith Deen transformed the schools into Sunni Islamic schools all of them transitioned. Many schools today continue to exist as University of Islam schools under the leadership of Louis Farrakhan.

Similarly, when I speak of immigrant established schools, not all Islamic schools were established by immigrants. Many were established by second-generation Muslims whose parents were immigrants (which I address in the chapter entitled "Praxis"), and others were established by African American and Anglo American converts. When I speak of home schooling in "Praxis," I explore how it became a growing trend specifically after the advocacy of home schools of prolific Muslim orators like Shaykh Hamza Yusuf. However, the complexity of home schooling makes accuracy difficult because of its private, often unregistered nature. I do know that there have been Muslim home schooling networks in Canada and the United States well before Shaykh Hamza's advocacy. There have also been home schoolers within the Nation of Islam and the community of Imam Warith Deen Mohammed. All of these have been beyond the scope of my study but provide interesting narratives for future research.

Thirdly, with a focus on full-time Islamic schools, I do not deeply explore the work around supplementary (weekend and after school) Islamic schooling, the work being done in public schools around teacher sensitivity training or equitable representations of Muslims in public school textbooks, or even traditional *madaris* (pl. *madrasa*) that also have a rich history of schooling in North America.

Lastly, I chose to focus my work on the Sunni Muslim community partly because that is the community that represents my own identity but also because it represents the majority of Islamic schools in North America by far. Most other Muslim sectarian communities do not aspire to establish full-time school alternatives for their children, with the exception of a few Shi'a schools and a more recent Ismail'i education program that I am aware of designed for preparing supplementary (weekend) school teachers.

Frames of Analysis

I rely on two overarching frames of analysis that informed the types of questions I asked and themes I wrote about in this book. On the one hand, anti-colonial discourse and post-colonial theory together inform the context and conflicts within which Islamic schools have emerged. On the other, a critical faith-based epistemology assists in understanding the ways in which my participants make sense of their life purpose and work in establishing Islamic schools.

Anti-Colonial Discourse and Post-Colonial Theory

In the context of the Civil Rights movement, the assassination of Malcolm X, and the split of the Nation of Islam in the 1960s and 70s, issues of race, class, privilege, power, cultural identity, and faith were interwoven quite tightly in affecting the life and struggle of indigenous Black Muslims. The establishing of schools was directed by a particular agenda that linked Black Nationalism with Islam.

The growth of the Sister Clara Muhammad schools must be understood within an anti-racist and an anti-colonial perspective. Such perspectives re-position and re-inform reality in relation to the local experiences of African Americans. Critiquing contemporary Western knowledge and socio-political structures as dominated by European-American cultures and epistemologies, an anti-colonial framework seeks to employ indigenous knowledge as a source of power and resistance. Such a frame "interrogates the power configurations embedded in ideas, cultures, and histories of knowledge production, validation, and use" (Dei and Asgharzadesh 2001, 300). In relation to schools and schooling, the anti-colonial framework recognizes the roles that institutions play in producing and reproducing social inequities and knowledge hierarchies. Such inequities can be addressed, from the perspective of this framework, through questioning, challenging, and "subsequently subvert[ing] the oppressive structures of power and privilege" (ibid.). Dei and Asgharzadesh (2001) argue that a colonized and/or marginalized nation or community is revived through a process of "indigenization." Such indigenous ways of knowing emerge when knowledge is articulated from one's own cultural terms, history, geography, language, and spirituality. Legitimizing indigenous knowledge provides the lens by which privileged knowledge can then be challenged, ruptured, and leveled (Dei 1996; Dei et al. 2004; Asante 2003).

Karumanchery (2005) argues that among the strategies sought by disenfranchised peoples is to reestablish community. He describes how racism and other forms of oppression rupture the equilibrium of social relationships among discriminated peoples. The trauma of racism is combated with the reconstruction of circles of healing through the solidarity of community and shared heritage. "The solidarity and sense of safety that arises in these 'places,' are simply not available to the oppressed when they are in mainstream environments. In fact, this would account for the often noted 'need for them to stick together'" (185). Islamic schools are sites of opposition to dominant secular forms of knowledge that are privileged in public schools. Islamic schools challenge the notion not only of valid knowledges but, more importantly, of the priority that certain forms of knowledge are given over others. For example, Islamic schools would privilege (ideally) moral, spiritual, and religious forms of knowledge that nurture spiritual consciousness and religious observance as a primary goal of the educative process.

The experience for immigrant Muslims with colonialism is distinct from that of the indigenous African American Muslim experience. Although immigrants also sought to reestablish community as Karumanchery suggests, many immigrant Muslims in the 1960s and 1970s were influenced by formal, higher education in colonial schools. For the immigrant Muslim, colonialism and the effects of post-colonialism were felt largely in their home country and in many ways were far less oppressive or direct in relation to the subjugation of outright systemic racism experienced by African Americans. To fully understand the immigrant experience, I rely more heavily on the concepts of hybridity, mimicry, and diaspora that inform the plight of identity formation for Muslim immigrants in North America.

For many early immigrant Muslims, public schools represented a form of socialization of their children that would help attain, in the words of Fanon, the whiteness to which he aspires (Gordon et al. 1996). These immigrants in particular often endured what Benedict Anderson calls the "mental miscegenation" of post-colonial educational policy that nurtured "a class of persons, Indian in blood and colour, but English in taste, in opinion, in morals and in intellect'" (Loomba 1989, 173).

Most commonly, through Western secular institutions or Catholic schools in former British colonies, educated immigrant elites came to North America with an imprinted sense of educational quality. But there were exceptions. Loomba argues,

> [The] colonialist presence was felt differently by various subjects of the Empire—some never even saw Europeans in all their lives, and for them the authority still wore a native face. For others, the foreign presence was daily visible but space was still divided into 'their' sphere and 'ours.' For others still, colonialism had penetrated still deeper into their everyday existence. Thus, the resonances of both 'hybridity' and mimicry are enormously variable.
> (Loomba 1989, 179)

Two points of relevance can be drawn from such variance. Firstly, the intended process of hybridization did not fully succeed because "[i]n practice . . . anti-colonial movements and individuals often drew upon Western ideas and vocabularies to challenge colonial rule. Indeed, they often hybridized what they borrowed by juxtaposing it with indigenous ideas, reading it through their own interpretative lens, and even using it to assert cultural alterity or insist on an unbridgeable difference between the colonizer and the colonized. This for me speaks to the process of Islamization that Muslim intellectuals in the 1960s and 1970s so fervently articulated for gaining support for organizations, religious centers, and schools to preserve Islamic identity.

Secondly, I feel that it is this variance in the colonial experience that Loomba describes that explains why the immigrant and African American Muslims have had such difficulty in collaborating for an Islamic presence in North America. Uniting with fellow immigrant Muslims from various parts of the world has been relatively less complicated. Each era or evolution or stage of Islamic schooling represents, to a degree, a form of resistance. The level and form of resistance, however, have been shaped by the colonial and post-colonial experience of each Muslim community differently. The experience of African American Muslims who came to Sunni Islam through the Nation of Islam would recall, for example, the social, political, and economic subjugation through both formal and informal slavery and its impact on the access to civil liberties and rights in America. Immigrant Muslims would rely on very different colonial experiences depending on their country of origin, class, and access to varying levels of education. The level of trust, involvement, and resistance for the indigenous Muslim and the immigrant in North America can vary based on their past experiences with the unraveling of the post-colonial period. Immigrant Muslim engagement with America can vary between forced assimilation, internalized self-rejection, political co-optation, social conformism, cultural mimicry, or creative transcendence (Shohat 1994, 110).

Critical Faith-Centered Epistemology

Critical, spiritually-centered theoretical frameworks re-position spiritual, faith-centered ways of knowing from the margins to the center. Whether Dantley's framework on critical, African American spirituality or Zine's critical faith-centered epistemology, such frameworks serve as forms of resistance and liberation for those who seek to "reflect on hermeneutic kinds of inquiries that ultimately question the efficacy of the status quo" (Dantley 2002, 334). These frameworks create a space for critical academic discussions that recognize that faith, spirituality, and indigenous ways of knowing have been the subject of oppression and marginalization while also in many circumstances the cause of reproducing oppressions (Zine 2004, 167). Applying a critical lens when centering faith-based discussions is particularly relevant to this study to fully understand the rationale for the establishment of early Islamic schools as sites of resistance while not overlooking the ways in which the schools have also been sites of discrimination.

Zine (2004) argues that it is through a faith-centered understanding that some people understand, challenge, counter, and resist the world around them. In the case of Islamic education, the educational aspirations of many Muslims are similarly intrinsically directed by an Islam-based epistemology. Whether an individual is united to the Divine through personal self-reflexive practices that are self-determined or within the boundaries that are shaped through particular religious doctrines, Zine insists that "Islamic frameworks are also rarely used as analytical tools for the study of Muslim societies. . . . they are traditionally regarded as elements of 'false consciousness' or dogmas to be elided by 'rational' scholarly thought" (183). In an era where logical positivism has been embraced by the dominant academic culture, alternative, intuitive, and spiritual ways of knowing are denied the possibility to contribute (Dantley 2002, 335). A critical faith-centered framework, therefore, aspires to establish faith-based and spiritual ways of knowing as valid sites for academic knowledge (Zine 2004, 183).

In relation to this study, Zine's faith-centered framework is most effective because it provides a guideline by which to understand the issues, challenges, perspectives, and unique identities of Islamic schools. Her principles especially ground Islamic schools within their unique multiple identities of negotiation: Muslim by choice/lineage, Western by context, immigrant/diasporic by virtue of the global community, and ethnic/racial by lineage. Such interplay is dynamic and multifaceted in combining both their national and civic identities while upholding the primacy of their faith identities.

The framework is based on seven principles that can be applied as analytic tools. In what follows, I will briefly outline each while explaining its relevance to this study. The first principle is holism. Ontology has traditionally been the first point of entry in understanding an Islamic worldview emphasizing the interconnections between the physical, intellectual, and spiritual components of being. In *Wholeness and Holiness in Education: An Islamic Perspective*, al Zeera (2001) explains that an Islamic ontology is the realization of the unity of nature, the universe, and the metaphysical realms. Holism unites knowledge of the world around a person with the Divine wisdom that is inherent in all things, including one's existence, which informs life and death and recognition of the inevitable direction of every living creature. The result of such recognition is an awareness of a person's time and responsibility both in this world and the hereafter. The overarching principle that unites each of these elements is *tawhid*, which is commonly translated as God's oneness or "unity." *Tawhid* is defined by the divine, spiritual, religious, eternal, constant, absolute, and ideal awareness of God while at the same time recognizing the human, material, rational, temporary, mutable, and relative nature of existence (67).

Essential to a *tawhidic* perspective is the unity of knowledge where an education unites the physical with the spiritual, and in the words of Nasr (1987), where seeking knowledge is "always a journey from the outward to the abode of the inward" (xviii). When knowledge and its pursuit are united purposefully, all mundane actions have the potential to be a form of *ibadah*, worship (Zine 2008, 53). Understanding such motivation is particularly important in this study as the rationale for most of my participants is articulated. Most will speak of their work in Islamic schools as an act of *ibadah* or as a benefit to their own spiritual growth.

Zine's second principle emphasizes the need for historically and culturally situated analyses of faith-centered individuals in relation to their personal growth. Formal practices of *ibadah*, such as prayer, fasting, charity, and remembrance/invocation of God's names and attributes, "establish a rhythm to daily life" for many Muslims (ibid., 54). These religious practices affect the ways in which faith-centered Muslims interact, work, eat, dress, and wake/sleep, for instance. Muslims who pray *fajr*, the morning prayer, for example, are up the early hours of the day. Similarly, those who restrict themselves to eating *halal* will be selective, at times scrupulous, in what they eat. These are simple, everyday examples, but to fully understand the ways in which faith-centered Muslims function in a diasporic context, there has to be recognition and understanding of how religious practices shape their daily lives (Zine 2008). In relation to Islamic schooling, or any form of religious schooling for that matter, much of the purpose of establishing faith-based schools is to nurture this "rhythm" of daily *ibadah* in the lives of young children.

Among the essential contributions of this study on the historical growth of Islamic schools is its attempt to grapple with how unique perspectives and ideologies interpret the Islamic tradition to shape the aims of Islamic education. Zine's third principle centers such a discussion which analyzes how "[r]eligious and spiritual world views and/or contestations of those world views continue to shape human social, cultural, and political development" (ibid., 54–55). There are multiple ways in which the religious orientations and beliefs of Muslim communities can be understood. Firstly, communities can be distinguished by sectarian difference: Sunni, Shi'a, Ismaili, Ahmadi, and so on. Within a particular sect, of which I have chosen to focus on the Sunni community, communities have also been traditionally understood within schools of thought (amongst Sunnis there are four schools: Hanafi, Shafi', Maliki, and Hanbali). Each school of thought equally represents a codified and accepted method of interpreting and practicing the Islamic tradition. However, in particular parts of the Muslim world, some schools of thought are more dominant than others. The predominance of particular schools in distinct geographic locations often embeds the practices of the school as part of the ethnic culture. Lastly, within a sect such as Sunni Islam, adherents can be understood through faith-centered ideologies and perspectives. Among such perspectives are spiritually based orientations, such as Sufism, which has existed for centuries, while others are more ideological and shaped by more contemporary socio-political circumstances, such as the *Salafiyyah*, *Deobandi*, and *Wahhabi* movements. These distinctions are especially important to this study because they complicate the perceived uniformity of religious organizations and institutions in North America, such as mosques and Islamic schools. But these distinctions also become useful when analyzing the ways in which schools determine curricular emphases.

I combine my discussion of Zine's fourth and seventh principles, which build on one another to demand the recognition of indigenous ways of knowing in academia. The fourth principle states that indigenous ways of knowing are oppositional to the Eurocentric and Western ways of knowing that have become hegemonic. Acceptance of indigenous ways of knowing, Zine insists, cannot, however, be superficial or an "uncritical moral relativism" that is understood through dominant ways of knowing. In order for acceptance of indigenous ways of knowing as valid sites for analysis, Zine's final principle, which is the recognition that not all knowledge is socially constructed, is essential. She argues that "the validation of religious and spiritual knowledge is important as a means to apprehend non-secular ways in which people make sense of the world and their place in it" (ibid., 65). From this stance, divine revelation, prophets, messengers, and angels must be accepted as valid ways of knowing the world. In particular, reference to the Qur'an and *Sunnah* (Prophetic tradition) are two essential sources for understanding Muslim perspectives and interpretations. The final two principles of Zine's critical faith-centered epistemology that I have yet to discuss are related to the ways that religions have been oppressed, become complicit in that oppression, and have resisted oppression. The fifth principle insists that in addition to race, class, gender, and ethnicity, religion has also been an aspect of one's identity that has been marginalized and discriminated against. A case in point is 9/11, which is a central theme in the final part of this study that recognizes the ways in which anti-Islamic sentiments have reshaped the vision of Islamic schools with a new sense of direction. In response to those who seek to debunk the relevance of Islamophobia as cultural and not faith-based discrimination, this principle allows for issues related to religious practice to come to the fore. Similarly, much of this study examines the ways in which the intersections of race, class, and religion within the post-colonial experience also inform the challenges to co-existence for African American and immigrant Muslims in the United States. Cultural and racial perceptions held by immigrant Muslims must be understood within the discourse of religious authenticity, however, when interrogating the American Muslim experience largely shaped by the racial ideology of the Nation of Islam. With Zine's framework, the ways in which religious ideologies are complicated between being complicit in oppression and yet resistant to injustice becomes possible.

Speaking of liberatory praxis, liberation theology, and not silencing the political element of spirituality, Zine argues that a "spiritual education" creates a holistic understanding of inward purification and outward civic engagement. This principle highlights the concept of community and societal responsibility that is embedded in the Islamic tradition to emphasize the necessity of living in accordance to Divine law in a manner that upholds justice for all (al-Zeera 2001, 67). In keeping with the Islamic intellectual tradition *'amal* (action) is inseparable from knowledge. A well-known Prophetic tradition states, "it is charity (*sadaqah*) to learn (*'-l-m*), to act accordingly, and to teach" and confirms the necessary precedence of knowledge over action while recognizing the inseparability of the two (Rozenthal 1970, 242). On the relationship between knowledge and action, it is said that "Knowledge is the beginning of action, and action is the end of knowledge; a beginning without an end is futile, and an end without a beginning is absurd" (ibid., 243). The essential interreliance between knowledge and action becomes evident in the final part of this study in particular, as Islamic schools move from protest to praxis. Zine's framework allows for the analysis to recognize that the movement to establish Islamic schools that began out of protest against oppression became more aware over time not only of internal contradictions but also the need to put knowledge into action. The principles of a critical faith-centered epistemology not only center the relevance of faith-based ways of knowing in a study that is inherently about faith-centered individuals, but they also provide the multiple angles with which to examine the development of Islamic schools.

References

Abu Laban, Baha. *An Olive Branch on the Family Tree: The Arabs in Canada*. Toronto: McClelland and Stewart, 1980.
Ahmed, Gubti Mahdi. "Muslim Organizations in the United States." In *The Muslims of America*, edited by Yvonne Y. Haddad. New York: Oxford University Press, 1991, p. 18.
Al-Zarnuji, Burhan Al-Islam. *Instruction of the Student: The Method of Learning*, 2nd ed. Translated by G.E. von Grunebaum and Theodora M. Abel. Burr Ridge, IL: Starlatch, 2001.
Al Zeera, Zahra. *Wholeness and Holiness in Education: An Islamic Perspective*. Herndon, VA: The International Institute of Islamic Thought, 2001.
Asante, Molefi K. *Afrocentricity: The Theory of Social Change*. Chicago: African American Images, 2003.
Auston, Donna. "Prayer, Protest, and Police Brutality: Black Muslim Spiritual Resistance in the Ferguson Era." *Transforming Anthropology* 25, no. 1 (2017): 11–22.
Breen, D. *Muslim Schools, Communities and Critical Race Theory Faith Schooling in an Islamophobic Britain?* London: Palgrave Macmillan, 2018.
Brooks, M. *Education and Muslim Identity During a Time of Tension: Inside an American Islamic School*, 1st ed. London and New York: Routledge, 2019.
Cristillo, Louis. "The Case for the Muslim School as a Civil Society Actor." In *Educating the Muslims of America*, edited by Yvonne Y. Haddad, Farid Senzai, and Jane I. Smith. New York: Oxford University Press, 2009.
Curtis IV, Edward. *Black Muslim Religion in the Nation of Islam, 1960–1975*. Chapel Hill: University of North Carolina Press, 2006.
Dannin, Robert. *Black Pilgrimage to Islam*. New York: Oxford University Press, 2002.
Dantely, M. "Uprooting and Replacing Positivism, the Melting Pot, Multiculturalism, and Other Impotent Notions in Educational Leadership Through an African American Perspective." *Education and Urban Society* 34, no. 3 (May 2002): 334–352.
Decuir, A. "Roles & Responsibilities of the Women Leading American Islamic Schools." *International Journal of Educational Leadership Preparation* 11, no. 1 (2016): 18.
Dei, George. *Anti-Racism Education: Theory and Practice*. Halifax, NS: Fernwood Pub., 1996.
Dei, George and Asgharzadesh, Alireza. "The Power of Social Theory: The Anti-Colonial Discursive Framework." *Journal of Educational Thought* 35, no. 3 (2001).
Dei, George, Karumanchery, Leeno, and Karumanchery-Luik, Nisha. *Playing the Race Card*. New York: Lang, 2004.

Douglass, Susan L. and Shaikh, Munir A. "Defining Islamic Education: Differentiation and Applications." *Current Issues in Comparative Education* 7, no. 1 (2004).

Eaton, Charles Le Gai. "Man." In *Islamic Spirituality: Foundations*, edited by Seyyed Hossein Nasr. New York: Crossroad Publishing Company, 1987.

Elbih, Randa. "Debates in the Literature on Islamic Schools." *Educational Studies: Journal of the American Educational Studies Association* 48, no. 2 (2012): 156–173.

Gaddis, John. *The Landscape of History: How Historians Map the Past*. New York: Oxford University Press, 2002.

Gordon, Deneane Sharpley-Whiting and White, Renee, eds. *Fanon: A Critical Reader*. Cambridge, MA: Blackwell Publishers, 1996.

Haddad, Yvonne and Lummis, Adair. *Islamic Values in the United States: A Comparative Study*. New York: Oxford University Press, 1987.

Hamdani, Daood Hassan. "Muslim in the Canadian Mosaic." *Journal Institute of Muslim Minority Affairs* 5, no. 1 (1984): 7–16.

Hannam, P. *Religious Education and the Public Sphere*. Abingdon: Routledge, 2019.

Hodgson, M. *The Venture of Islam: Conscience and History in a World Civilization*. Chicago: University of Chicago Press, 1977.

Hussain, S. and Read, J.G. "Islamic Schools in the United States and England: Implications for Integration and Social Cohesion." *Social Compass* 62, no. 4 (2015): 556–569.

Jackson, Sherman. *Islam and the Blackamerican: Looking Toward the Third Resurrection*. New York: Oxford University Press, 2005.

Jasser, M. "Islamic Schools and American Civic Culture." *Academic Questions* 24, no. 1 (2011): 24–31.

Karim, Karim H. "Crescent Dawn in the Great White North: Muslim Participation in the Canadian Public Sphere." In *Muslims in the West: From Sojourners to Citizens*, edited by Yvonne Yazbeck Haddad. New York: Oxford University Press, 2002.

Karumanchery, Leeno, ed. *Engaging Equity: New Perspectives on Anti-Racist Education*. Calgary: Detselig Enterprises Ltd., 2005.

Keyworth, K. "Islamic Schools of America: Data-Based Profiles." In *Educating the Muslims of America*. New York: Oxford University Press, 2009.

Khaldun, Ibn. *The Muqaddimah: An Introduction to History*, Vol. 1. Translated by Franz Rosenthal. Princeton, NJ: Princeton University Press, 1958.

Khan, M.A. "Constructing the American Muslim Community." In *Religion and Immigration: Christian, Jewish, and Muslim Experiences in the United States*, edited by Yvonne Y. Haddad, Jane I. Smith, and John L. Esposito. New York: Altamira Press, 2003.

Khan, Sabith and Siddiqui, Shariq. *Islamic Education in the United States and the Evolution of Muslim Non-Profit Institutions: New Horizons in Nonprofit Research*. Cheltenham, UK and Northampton, MA: Edward Elgar Publishing, 2017.

Lings, Martin. "The Spiritual Function of Civilization." *Studies in Comparative Religion* 2, no. 4 (Autumn 1968).

Loomba, Anita. *Colonialism/Postcolonialism*. New York: Routledge, 1989.

Mattson, Ingrid. "How Muslims Use Islamic Paradigms to Define America." In *Religion and Immigration: Christian, Jewish, and Muslim Experiences in the*

United States, edited by Yvonne Y. Haddad, Jane I. Smith, and John L. Esposito. New York: Altamira Press, 2003.

McCloud, Aminah Beverly. "Islam in America: The Mosaic." In *Religion and Immigration: Christian, Jewish, and Muslim Experiences in the United States*, edited by Yvonne Y. Haddad, Jane I. Smith, and John L. Esposito. New York: Altamira Press, 2003.

McDonough, Sheila and Hoodfar, Homa. "Muslims in Canada: From Ethnic Groups to Religious Community." In *Religion and Ethnicity in Canada*, edited by Paul Bramadat and David Seljak. Toronto: Pearson Canada, 2005.

Memon, N. "Between Immigrating and Integrating: The Challenge of Defining an Islamic Pedagogy in Canadian Islamic Schools." In *Discipline, Devotion, and Dissent: Jewish, Catholic, and Islamic Schooling in Canada*. Waterloo, Canada: Wilfrid Laurier University Press, 2012, pp. 73–97.

Merry, Michael. *Culture, Identity and Islamic Schooling: A Philosophical Approach*. New York: Palgrave Macmillan, 2007.

Murata, Sachiko and Chittick, William. *The Vision of Islam*. St. Paul, MN: Paragon Press, 1994.

Nasr, Seyyed Hossein. *Islamic Life and Thought*. Albany, NY: State University of New York Press, 1981, p. 16.

Nasr, Seyyed Hossein. "Islamic Spirituality: Foundations." In *World Spirituality: An Encyclopedic History of the Religions Quest*. New York: Crossroad, 1987.

Nasr, Seyyed Hossein. *The Essential Seyyed Hossein Nasr*, edited by William Chittick. Bloomington, IN: World Wisdom, 2007.

Nimer, Mohamed. "Muslims in American Public Life." In *Muslims in the West: From Sojourners to Citizens*, edited by Yvonne Yazbeck Haddad. New York: Oxford University Press, 2002, p. 71.

Nyang, Sulayman. "Continental African Muslim Immigrants in the United States: A Historical and Sociological Perspective." In *Muslims in the West: From Sojourners to Citizens*, edited by Yvonne Yazbeck Haddad. New York: Oxford University Press, 2002.

Ogunnaike, Oludamini. "Of Cannons and Canons: The Promise and Perils of Postcolonial Education." San Francisco, *Renovatio*, 2018. https://renovatio.zaytuna.edu/article/of-cannons-and-canons

Parker-Jenkins, M., Hartas, D., Irving, B.A. *In Good Faith: Schools, Religion, and Public Funding*. Aldershot, England: Ashgate, 2005.

Parker-Jenkins, M. "Identity, Belief and Cultural Sustainability: A Case-Study of the Experiences of Jewish and Muslim Schools in the UK." In *International Handbook of Learning, Teaching and Leading in Faith-Based Schools*. Dordrecht, The Netherlands: Springer, 2014, pp. 157–176.

Popper, Karl. "Prediction and Prophecy in the Social Sciences." In *Theories of History*, edited by Patrick Gardiner. New York: The Free Press, 1959.

Pring, R. *The Future of Publicly Funded Faith Schools: A Critical Perspective*, 1st ed. London: Routledge, 2018.

Rosenthal, Franz. *Knowledge Triumphant; The Concept of Knowledge in Medieval Islam*. Leiden: Brill, 1970.

Russell, Bertrand. "Dialectical Materialism." In *Theories of History*, edited by Patrick Gardiner. New York: The Free Press, 1959.

Seldon, Anthony and Pappworth, Joanna. *By Word of Mouth: Elite Oral History*. London and New York: Methuen, 1983.

Shohat, Ella. *Unthinking Eurocentrism: Multiculturalism and the Media*. New York: Routledge, 1994.
Smith, Tracey, Edwards-Groves, Christine, and Brennan Kemmis, Roslin. "Pedagogy, Education and Praxis." *Pedagogy, Culture & Society*, 18, no. 1 (2010): 1–8. doi: 10.1080/14681360903556749.
Thompson, Paul. "The Voice of the Past." In *The Oral History Reader*, edited by Robert Perks and Alistair Thompson. London: Routledge, 1998.
Tuchman, Barbara. "Distinguishing the Significant from the Insignificant." In *Oral History: An Interdisciplinary Anthology*, edited by David Dunaway and Willa Baum. Nashville, TN: American Association for State and Local History, 1984.
Walker, Dennis. *Islam and the Search for African-American Nationhood: Elijah Muhammad, Louis Farrakhan and the Nation of Islam*. Atlanta: Clarity Press, 2005.
Weiner, Leo. *Africa and the Discovery of America*. Philadelphia: Philadelphia Innes, 1920.
Wertheimer, L. *Faith Ed.: Teaching About Religion in an Age of Intolerance*. Boston: Beacon Press, 2015.
Zine, Jasmin. "Creating Faith-Centered Space for Anti-Racist Feminism: Reflections from a Muslim Scholar Activist." *Journal of Feminist Studies in Religion* 20, no. 2 (Fall 2004).
Zine, Jasmin. *Canadian Islamic Schools: Unraveling the Politics of Faith, Gender, Knowledge, and Identity*. Toronto: University of Toronto Press, 2008.

2 Protest
Resistance and Renewal: Schooling in the Nation of Islam

This chapter traces the growth and vision of Elijah Muhammad's separate school system, the University of Islam (UofI) schools. Through the voices of a handful of educators who taught, administered, and in many ways established the UofI schools, I explore Elijah Muhammad's rationale, curriculum, and evolution of educational aims. From the same voices, I then trace how many of the UofI schools eventually became the Clara Muhammad schools (CMS) they are today. This shift from the Nation of Islam's (NOI) Black Nationalist teachings to orthodox Islamic beliefs under Elijah's son, Warith Deen Mohammed, required a systematic re-envisioning of the schools as well. What the death of Elijah Muhammad meant to believers in 1975, how Warith Deen Mohammed delicately re-educated an entire community, and how in particular the schools were transformed will be investigated in the second half of this chapter.

Contextualizing Protest

The history of Islamic schools in North America ought to begin with the NOI. Historical research often begins with a particular event and then traces backward to causing events. The further back we go, the more events we uncover. In order to determine just how far back to go, however, one can apply the principle of "diminishing relevance" (Gaddis 2002, 98). For me, and for the focus on North American Islamic schooling, that event is the establishment of the first school in the NOI. African American Muslims under the NOI established separate schools more out of necessity than choice. UofI history is embedded in the larger narrative of slavery and systemic racial segregation in America. For Elijah Muhammad and the NOI, establishing their own schools was a form of protest against the absence of legitimate educational opportunities that existed for African Americans. Schools were microcosmic representations of core tenets of the NOI that were intended to separate, isolate, and re-educate African American children with a sense of self. Such re-education required extreme measures of both resistance and reverse-discrimination. Rafiq Iddin described complete separation in battleground terminology:

> When we were under the Honorable Elijah Muhammad we were at war with America—we were in a military pose—they [the entire White race] were the enemy—we didn't watch their movies, we didn't watch their TV—we were building our own community and we stayed focused on those goals. They were the bad guys; we were the good guys—we needed to separate ourselves morally, socially, culturally from them otherwise we were going to go down with them.

The NOI schools were born in a context that necessitated, from their perspective, rejecting and, to a large extent, reversing sentiments of inferiority (Pitre 2008; Dannin 2002; Diouf 1998; Rashed 1977; Essien-Udom 1966). Between the Common School Movement and Civil Rights era, there remained a great divide between the theory of an equal education for all and the practice of public educational institutions. Outright racism and discrimination on the basis of race and class codified a superiority/inferiority complex through both a hidden and formal curriculum. Students in White educational institutions, for example, were taught a similar social, political, and racial hierarchy, only in reverse. "[S]chools taught white children they were exclusive . . . [and that] they could be anything they wanted to be in a meritocratic society" (Wilson and Segall 2001, 2). Until Black communities began "to do for self," a fundamental belief of Elijah Muhammad, they and their children would be taught the facade of White supremacy (Pitre 2008). Living in an era wherein Jim Crow laws[1] stunted learning for Blacks, taking active control of their own educational fate was not considered an option for those who truly wanted to be liberated.

Such vehement discrimination and outright subjugation in schooling was devastating for generations of Blacks. Compounded with the Great Depression in the 1930s, discrimination and economic insecurity made the plight of African Americans catastrophic. High rates of unemployment and even higher rates of hiring discrimination made some African Americans desperate for a savior. The teachings of Elijah Muhammad and his Black Nationalist predecessors[2] empowered some with the rhetoric of protest and change. He felt that the only way to resist subjugation was through turning over the discourse of inferiority in favor of African Americans. Elijah Muhammad, like his integrationist contemporaries,[3] demanded equal rights, opportunities, and freedoms for Blacks in America. But his method of dissent was distinct. The root for him was a re-education of African Americans, and this process had to be free of interference. Elijah Muhammad believed that for his teachings to be successful, his system of education could not be accommodated or integrated into a public system, nor could it be constructed parallel to what the state provided; it had to be devoid of all teachings, nuances, and sentiments of White superiority and therefore had to be separate.

Voices of Resistance

With the exception of a handful of articles and theses on the historical growth of either the UofI schools or the CMS, few scholars have deeply explored the purpose of these schools, and even fewer have considered them in relation to each other or to the larger trajectory of Islamic schools in general. To address this void, I begin the narrative of this oral history on Islamic schools through the voices of those who taught, developed, and administered at the UofI schools under the leadership of Elijah Muhammad. More importantly, however, I selected participants who also transitioned through the UofI and into CMS—many of whom also collaborated with or even taught at immigrant established schools, such as Bilal Ajieb, Zakiyyah Muhammad, and Qadir Abdus Sabur. Speaking with individuals who could address the multiple transformations of Islamic schools since the late 1960s until today gave me access to the highly complex and interconnected struggle to establish and administer Islamic schools in North America.

Among the educators that inform the findings of this chapter are largely individuals who converted to the NOI in the 1960s, transitioned to mainstream Sunni Islam under the leadership of Warith Deen Mohammed, and taught in both the UofI and the CMS systems. Abdul Alim Shabazz is among the participants of this study who came into the NOI much earlier and did not transition with the rest. His role under the NOI as the Director of Education for many years and his stature as the first African American professor of mathematics (from his recollection) enriched the narrative deeply. For most of my participants, their roles within the schools vary from teachers, principals, consultants, curriculum developers, and administrators. Many of them have held all, if not most, of the aforementioned positions over the span of their educational careers. The voices of Safiyyah Shahid, principal of the Clara Muhammad "flagship" school in Atlanta, Georgia, for example, and Rafiq Iddin, involved with the Philadelphia CMS, are indispensable. Needless to say, all of these participants are African American, but noteworthy enough is that many of them, including Zakiyyah Muhammad, Qadir Abdus Sabur, Hakim Rashid, and Daaiyah Saleem are all professors of education and have authored the existing scholarship on this history.

Although finding participants for this part of my study relied on conventional conference networking and snowballing from one contact to another in addition to investigative internet research, my journey to meet Imam Warith Deen Mohammed is a story worth telling. It began by sending faxes, emails, and phone calls to his office at the Mosque Cares in Chicago. With no initial response but encouragement from his secretaries,

I then planned a road trip with my wife to visit his office in Chicago. At his office, I was fortunate enough to meet two of his children, as well as his kind staff, who supported my research, provided plenty of archival material, and promised to pass on my message to him personally. After returning to Toronto and still not hearing from him, I came close to giving up on seeking face to face contact until I heard about the Muslim Alliance of North America (MANA) conference in Philadelphia held in October 2007, where he was to be given an honorary award for a lifetime of service. With investigative research spirit, we took yet another road trip in search of an interview. Surrounded by well-coordinated security, the Imam made a brief four-minute appearance and then left through a back door. It was at this time that I learned of his ailing health and his inability to give interviews anymore. Not having met the man who defines the American Muslim trajectory, my default option took me on one last road trip to the Schomburg Center for Research in Black Culture in New York on Malcolm X Boulevard to access archival interviews of his. In all of these experiences, I may not have met the late Imam Warith Deen Mohammed, but I certainly gained a deep sense of reverence for his sacrifices through the voices of those whom I met along the way. Imam Warith Deen Mohammed returned to his Creator on September 9, 2008.

How the Story Will Unfold

The history of Islamic schools in North America is most commonly traced back to the 1970s, when the first major wave of immigrant Muslims arrived. Few immigrant Muslim scholars recognize the NOI and its schools as part of the narrative. Those who refuse to acknowledge the contributions of African American Muslims through the UofI are most commonly segments of the immigrant Muslim population who maintain that the teachings of Elijah Muhammad were outside of mainstream Islam. Albeit few would contend otherwise, including those who transitioned from the Nation of Islam to the community of Imam Warith Deen Mohammed, I still consider the history of the UofI essential to the narrative of Islamic schools for the following reasons.

Firstly, from the voices of my participants and the state of the current schools, it became increasingly apparent to me that during the transition from Elijah Muhammad to Warith Deen Mohammed, the sentiment of struggle and sacrifice diminished. Elijah's vision of nation building demanded an unparalleled level of sacrifice of his educators that Warith Deen was arguably unable to maintain. By making Islamic schooling optional and by collaborating more closely with immigrant Muslim communities, the necessity of separate schools that emphasized racial and ethnic self-identity through a Black Nationalist (and Afrocentric for a short period in the 1960s) curriculum weakened. The call for revolution, change, protest, and struggle had shifted, and many believers, including teachers in the schools, were lost in transition. As a result, the number of CMS has been consistently decreasing.

Secondly, I found a general sentiment of appreciation among Muslims in the community of Imam Warith Deen who lived through the transition from the NOI to the American Muslim Mission (AMM) for the teachings of the Hon. Elijah Muhammad. As theologically "misguided" as his own son has called him, all of the African American Muslims that I met told me that Elijah Muhammad's philosophy of education was a necessary precursor for the Clara Muhammad schools. Elijah Muhammad's teachings of racial superiority were essential to undo the ingrained racism and inferiority that had been imposed on African Americans. These teachings, however, were not limited to an ideology of racism. The essence of Elijah Muhammad's message was inherently a religious one—what Sherman Jackson (2005) calls "Black Religion."[4] Jackson (2005) argues that Black Religion is a distinctly American response similar to the Black Church, Afrocentrism, and the Civil Rights movement. Black Religion does not refer to the pre-slave trade religions of Africans but to religious beliefs that have emerged directly as a response to an American reality.[5]

The distinct features of Black Religion rely on two essential factors: "(1) an indigenously rooted vehicle via which they could successfully appropriate Islam; and (2) charismatic figures that could harness and make effective use of that vehicle" (Jackson 2005, 28). By "appropriation of Islam," Jackson refers to the "act of enlisting the aid of a set of non-indigenous ideas in one's own existential or ideological struggle" (Jackson 2005, 28). Jackson's emphasis on the appropriation of Islam is important because, as he argues, the intent of appropriation is to alter, redefine, and interpret ideas in a way that serves the psychological needs of a community without the intent to recognize the historical conceptualization of the faith tradition. That said, the intent of Elijah Muhammad of appropriating Islam was not to align Black Americans closer to mainstream Islam but to give them a deeper sense of themselves (Jackson 2005, 28). The teachings of the NOI appropriated Islam to empower Black Americans while systematically distinguishing themselves from Muslims worldwide.[6] The conception of Black Religion must, however, be understood not only through its ability to empower but also to empower at the cost of being complicit in reverse discrimination. Essential to a critical faith-based epistemology is to recognize the ways in which religious ideologies are used to reproduce oppressions (Zine 2004, 167). Implicit in the analysis of this chapter is, therefore, Warith Deen Mohammed's recognition of such complicity.

The third major finding from my interviews in this part of the narrative relates to the transition that Imam Warith Deen Mohammed made from the teachings of his father to those of orthodox Islam. By the time of transition in 1975, immigrant Muslims had made their mark on the North American landscape. The task of the young Imam Warith Deen at this time was immense. Convincing a substantial community of African American Muslims that his father had misguided beliefs about Islam was a delicate venture. At the same time, establishing credibility within the newly settled immigrant Muslim communities was arguably a greater task—one that to an extent is still on-going. I found that this two-fold task of Imam Warith Deen has had profound effects on the landscape of Islamic schools in North America in relation to race, class, and legitimacy.

Before delving into the growth of the University of Islam schools, I would like to venture into a brief historical sketch of what segregated schools in America meant to African Americans. After establishing context, I trace the emphasis of "re-education" that defined the teachings of the NOI. By exploring the teachings of Elijah Muhammad, his vision of education, and the role that the UofI schools performed, I describe how Elijah Muhammad rationalized the urgency of separate schools on the basis of abject racial subjugation. As the NOI transitioned to a second resurrection[7] at the death of Elijah Muhammad, his successor and son, Warith Deen Mohammed, took on the major task of realigning the core beliefs and practices set by his father. To close, I explore how Warith Deen Mohammed transitioned the UofI schools into the present-day Clara Muhammad schools.

Setting the Stage: Racial Segregation of American Schools

In 1954, *Brown v. Board of Education Topeka* overruled *Plessy v. Ferguson 1896*, ending state-sponsored racial segregation in public schools.[8] Prior to *Brown v. Board of Ed*, there existed a highly segmented schooling system that made racial divisions and discrimination normative both in policy and practice. Schools for Black children were poorly funded with far less than half per pupil expenditure in relation to schools reserved for Whites. High school education was officially denied by authorities in many concentrated Black districts (Patterson 2001, xvii).

Jim Crow laws in the South enforced complete and systematic racial inferiority. Blacks were not permitted equal access to everyday social spaces, including restaurants, theatres, buses, and even phone booths. But the segregation of schools instilled in young minds a sense of inferiority that was most damning. Children who were taught lessons of racial inferiority naturally questioned their own ability and potential. It made some Black proponents of integration question whether the integration of schools in particular might do more harm than good. Concerns arose that if Black students were put in the same classrooms as White students, it may just exacerbate their sense of inferiority and inequality. Prominent Civil Rights activist W.E.B. Du Bois supported the controversial stance that separate schools were needed. Citing the example of integrated public schools in parts of the northern United States, Du Bois argued that even if schools were integrated, Black students would remain tolerated, not educated (Du Bois 1935). Separated schools, he said, "are needed just so far as they are necessary for the proper education of the Negro race" (Du Bois 1935, 330). The proper education of any people includes sympathetic touch between teacher and pupil as well as knowledge on the part of the teacher, not simply of the individual taught, but of his surroundings and background and the history of his class and group. Among integrationist advocates and NAACP circles, Du Bois remained a minority voice on the issue of schooling which was consistent with the advocacy of Elijah Muhammad.

In major north-eastern American cities such as New York, Detroit, and Chicago, where the NOI planted its roots early in the 1930s, public schools outwardly seemed better than those unambiguously segregated in the South. Yet the influx of African Americans from the South in the early 20th century brought out similar sentiments of discrimination. As a result of this wave of migration northward, some states that had prohibited segregation made amendments to reverse state and school board policies. In fear of racial mixing between White children and Blacks from the South who were far less educated or presumably less accustomed to social etiquette, many public schools looked for ways to maintain segregation. In some cases, intelligence tests were implemented and mandated to ensure segregation but also to justify claims of inherent black inferiority (Douglas 2005, 123–66).

Similarly, schools in Philadelphia and smaller parts of Pennsylvania established separate schools for Blacks and Whites and ensured that regardless of place of residence, children would be transported to schools of their own race. Other schools housed children by race in separate buildings, with separate teachers, classrooms, and even American flags (Douglas 2005, 123–66). Circumstances and educational opportunities could then be differentiated. Classrooms and schools for Black students often were overcrowded, had limited resources such as textbooks, and teachers would often be either less qualified or committed. Many of my participants recalled their own educational experiences as being hindered by the working conditions and as a result the inconsistency of teacher commitment.

Qadir Abdus Sabur began his education in 1949 at a time when most schools in America were still segregated. He recalls the sacrifices his mother made to send him to one of the two elementary schools in Philadelphia at the time when integrated schools were first being experimented with. Through numerous anecdotal experiences of his elementary and secondary school education, Abdus Sabur asserts that African American children have been "systematically conditioned" to see themselves as inferior to their White classmates (Abdus Sabur 2005, 4). He goes on to explain, however, that attending schools where African American teachers and students comprised the majority were no better. He remembers that "[a]lthough there were sincere dedicated teachers at the local high school, there were also those that systematically perpetuated the process of social partitioning" (Abdus Sabur 2005, 4). Such perpetuation of race and class bias included teachers, both Black and White, that held low expectations for Black students, lack of positive reinforcement of ethnic and cultural contributions to society, and an inherent belief that students of color were incapable of any academic rigor.

In schools that were integrated, Black children were systematically excluded from extracurricular activities. They would either not get access to opportunities such as musical instruments or would have access to swimming pools only on Friday afternoons, before the water would be drained, for example (Douglas 2005, 123–66). The impetus for such racial segregation was deep-rooted. Among school administrators, teachers, and parents, it was widely held that Black children were naturally less capable, deficient, and more prone to retardation. Measuring the intelligence of students who had only been formally schooled for a handful of sporadic months confirmed these beliefs. Undoing such an intense indoctrination of inequality arguably required a relative amount of oppositional thought. What Elijah Muhammad instituted, therefore, was a vigorous process of re- education that relied on psychologically retraining the mind to think in ways that were, arguably, absurdly radical. His approach employed a combination of what Alastair Bonnett categorizes as psychological and radical anti-racism. The following section will delve into how Elijah Muhammad systematically re-taught and reinforced a positive self-image to alter the psyche of a nation. Using Bonnett's example, Elijah Muhammad, like Franz Fanon, achieved this while justifying radical, including violent, means if necessary (Bonnett 2000, 90–106).

Systematically Re-Educating a Nation: Beginnings of the University of Islam Schools

The Nation of Islam, along with the many other forms of "Black Religion" that evolved in the United States in the early 20th century was, in the words of Sherman Jackson, "a pragmatic, folk-oriented, holy protest against anti-black racism" (Jackson 2005, 4). The teachings of the NOI were a radical medley of mythical beliefs. Some call them sensationalized, others say it was a strategic conflating of Biblical and Qur'anic teachings with a sense of the systematic disempowerment of an entire people that made the teachings of Fard Muhammad palatable. Fard Muhammad, founder of the NOI, claimed to be God in human form and introduced science-fiction-like teachings about a "mothership" that would eventually destroy all Caucasians because of their deviant nature (Islamic History Project Group 2006, 93). For a destitute people in search of hope, Fard Muhammad was a "savior."[9]

The NOI believed that God came in the form of a man, Fard Muhammad, and made Elijah Muhammad his messenger to raise the Black man through these teachings. Fard Muhammad first appeared in Detroit in July 1930. Lee argues that within the era of the Great Depression, the migration of a significant African American population from the rural South to urban cities in the north (Chicago, Detroit, and New York in particular) and the demise of earlier Black Nationalist religions, such as the Moorish Science Temple and Marcus Garvey's Universal Negro Improvement Association, created a space for the beginnings of the Nation of Islam (Lee 1988, 27–31). Their teachings appealed to the oppressed, as this appropriated form of Black Nationalist Islam demanded a strict moral code, industriousness, and independence intended on mentally resurrecting the way believers understood themselves (Curtis IV 2002a, 64).

The Nation of Islam's teachings altered the mainstream teachings of Islam in a number of fundamental ways. Firstly, God is espoused to be a man, Fard Muhammad, and Elijah Muhammad claimed to be his final messenger, whereas mainstream Islam teaches that the final prophet of Islam was Muhammad of 7th century Arabia. God should not be understood as a spiritual being with the promise of a spiritual hereafter, but as a living being whose promises were as tangible as his physical presence on earth (Lee 1988, 39). Fard's "visit" was, therefore, to awaken Black Americans to their status as the Chosen People of God and to inform them that the suffering they had endured had meaning (Lee 1988, 39). At least in the initial stages of the NOI, part of the process of giving meaning had to do with reconnecting with their historical roots. Conversion required believers to take on their "original name," which included an "X" as their last name, to rid themselves of their "slave names" (Marsh 1996, 40). This process reconnected believers with their original nationality, what Elijah Muhammad called "Asiatics," or descendants of the original Black nation of Asia (Marsh 1996, 40).

The second fundamental way in which the Nation of Islam altered the teachings of mainstream Islam was through an ideology of racial superiority propagating, most notably, that "the white man is the devil." Curtis argues that Elijah Muhammad promoted an "absolutist particularism" that espoused a "fire-and-brimstone approach to race relations" (Curtis 2002a, 64). Through a mythical tale of an evil scientist named Yakub, a descendant of the Tribe of Shabazz, the NOI taught that races were created through genetics and cross-breeding 6800 years ago. Yakub, out of vengeance for being exiled, created the White race, who were evil by nature and who were destined to rule the world until 1914. This Tribe of Shabazz was believed to include all those of African descent who were enslaved in America. Fard Muhammad and Elijah Muhammad were, therefore, sent to relocate these "lost" people who have now been "found" to an independent state (Marsh 1996, 41). Essential to the teachings of the NOI was complete separation, and if not in the form of a separate state, then they demanded equal rights to economic and social mobility within the existing state. As sensational as the myth of Yakub sounds, it followed the format and purpose of most mythologies in that it provided a framework and rationale for existence, a moral code, and a direction for the future. The myth, therefore, re-positioned believers as the original race, which by virtue raised their level of self-confidence (McCloud 2003, 108–9).

Fard's mythical teachings were to undo the wrongs that slavery had imposed on African Americans. There is much conjecture on the actual ethnic and religious origins of Fard Muhammad. He went by many names, and his own emergence and disappearance from America is contested. Suffice it to say that many of the followers of Warith Deen today do not discount the wisdom in the mythical teachings or the sensationalist ideas of race that both Fard Muhammad and Elijah Muhammad used to define the theology of the NOI. For those who have now found their way "back" to the universal teachings of Islam, it is widely held that the teachings of the NOI were a necessary precursor to bring the Black American out of the shackles of slavery. When asked about the teachings of Fard Muhammad, Warith Deen has said it was symbolism for the "darkness that plagued America" in the days of slavery and racial segregation (Islamic History Project Group 2006, 96). He has also said that if you read the signs and symbols of both Fard Muhammad and his own father, Elijah Muhammad, carefully, one would recognize that the NOI was always intended on being a transitory stage in eventually bringing the Black American to the universal teachings of Islam. There was nothing Islamic about the NOI's teachings of Black superiority or White inferiority, but it was a necessary stage in re-conceptualizing African American identity and potential.

Fard's occult teachings were also not the sole attempt at reshaping the minds of African Americans in the 1920s and 30s. The Moorish Science Temple, through the vision of Noble Drew Ali, and other movements, such as those led by Marcus Garvey and Father Divine, also espoused similar attempts. It is widely held that like Drew Ali, Marcus Garvey was also highly influenced by Islam. Garvey lived in England between 1912 and 1916 and interacted with a pan-Islamist and pan-Africanist writer name Duse Muhammad Ali, who affected his thinking. Drew Ali's movement through the Moorish Science Temple established in 1913 encouraged Black Americans to resist American religious and cultural identity for an "Asiatic" one. And Garvey's Universal Negro Improvement Association encouraged the development of Black owned businesses and a re-identification with their African roots. Both movements struck a chord with Black Americans but came to untimely demises with the deportation of Garvey in 1927 and the death of Drew Ali in 1929. The void of both movements created fertile ground for Fard Muhammad and the NOI. In fact, many of the followers of Drew Ali and of Garvey soon found themselves to be followers of the NOI. Since Fard Muhammad's formal influence over the Nation of Islam, however, was limited, the real carriers of the NOI mission were Elijah and Clara Muhammad.

Clara Muhammad was born on November 2, 1899 in Georgia, where she married Elijah Poole in 1917. Elijah, two years older than Clara, began his life as a struggling sharecropper, dropping out of school after Grade 3 to help his family. From Macon County, Clara and Elijah moved to Detroit in 1923 in hopes of economic stability. It was there that the couple stumbled on Fard Muhammad, thought by the NOI to be God himself. It was upon meeting, hearing, and learning from Fard Muhammad that both Elijah and Clara embraced the teachings of the Nation of Islam in September 1931. Together the couple gained an increasing courage and conviction in the teachings of the NOI. Fard Muhammad would often teach the two privately in their home and encouraged a similar model for their children. It was by his example that Clara Muhammad decided to home school her children at a time when it was illegal to do so.

The first of such schools was established in the very home of the Honorable Elijah Muhammad. He inspired and empowered a people in search of liberation through knowledge. Elijah Muhammad said, "Educators should teach our people of the great history that was theirs before they were brought to America in shackles by slave masters. Our children should be trained in our own schools, not dropped into the schools of the enemy where they are taught that whites have been and forever will be world leaders" (Muhammad 1965, 48).

Fard Muhammad was intuitive and tactful in recognizing the importance of education as a mechanism for building a nation. The establishment of schools to re-educate converts but also to proactively educate children of converts defined his foresight. Racial pride was the core of the re-education process. Sentiments of "Black is beautiful" and Black Power were part of the initial reconceptualization of the curriculum (Ross 2003, 148). Ibrahim Shalaby argues that the crux of the UofI teachings was to reform and reinvent a Black identity for believers, one that challenges the perceptions and stereotypes that were commonly held of Black peoples (Shalaby 1967).

Warith Deen Mohammed recalled that the first school was directed and taught by his mother Clara Muhammad. The school was really the dining table of the Muhammad's residence, and its first students were Elijah and Clara's six children.

> [Her] own ideas, thoughts, and family history as well as Fard's teachings became sentences to be copied, word groups to be memorized, paragraphs that helped penmanship. While textbooks were not available, subjects still included the basics—reading, writing, arithmetic—as well as 'Temple History,' or the founding of the Nation of Islam and the myths about the origins of black people.
>
> (Ross 2003, 149)

Recognizing her limitations, Clara taught and administered the schools as best she could while the children were still young. Having only been formally educated to Grade 7, Clara was astute to pass on the responsibility to those better equipped to teach the Nation's children as soon as she could find believers to replace her (Ross 2003, 148; Lincoln 1962, 14).

University of Islam Schools

The University of Islam schools were a national movement within the Nation of Islam. Following the guidelines of Elijah Muhammad, believers were instructed to do things for themselves—for their own community—build their own schools, businesses, and any other services they would need. Elijah Muhammad's hope was that wherever the NOI had a presence, a community of believers, there would be a school to educate their children as well as adults.

By the fall of 1933, believers were instructed to remove their children from public schools and to enroll them in the UofI schools.[10] The locations of the schools varied from substandard and inadequate learning environments to viable educational facilities. Depending on the city, some schools were housed in a temple's prayer area and others in converted residences (Islamic History Project Group 2006, 124). In Paradise Valley, Detroit, alone, police raids estimated approximately 400 children being taught in UofI schools in 1934 (Evanzz 1999, 98). Recognizing the systematic removal of elementary school-aged children from Detroit public schools, the early UofI schools raised keen interest and fear among state school authorities. From its formal inception, the schools required security. The Nation's paramilitary arm, Fruit of Islam (FOI) and the Muslim Girls Training (MGT), had the role of monitoring children by accompanying them on school buses and standing guard outside of schools.

Referred to as the "cult school," located on 3408 Hasting Street in Detroit, the first UofI School was raided numerous times to arrest teachers and scrutinize curriculum. After a number of routine checks, school officials grew uncomfortable with the "dusty, cobwebbed, chamber of the cult, where colored children studied weird inscriptions under the shadow of a blood red flag with a white crescent and stars" (Bailey 1934, 1–3). Alarmed by the increasing number of "negroes" being removed from public schools, the school authorities demanded the UofI schools be investigated. Prosecutors claimed that the investigations were to assure that the school was adhering to state requirements for public and parochial schooling, but the investigation seemed by its description far more than routine police investigation. One news reporter described the investigation:

> A squad of police descended upon the place, and working swiftly, surrounded the building, blocked entrances, clipped telephone wires

to prevent word of their coming from being flashed in the "university" by a clever arrangement of warning buzzers, and proceeded to the second floor assembly room. . . . The raiders then made a systematic seizure of records, books and other data to be used as evidence.

(Bailey 1934, 1–3)

What they found were school textbooks with the Black Nationalist, racial superiority teachings of the Nation of Islam: that Muhammad killed 6 million Christians and put 90,000 heads in a hole and that the NOI had an army of 21 million trained soldiers to remove the "devils" from the earth. The intermittent raids only bolstered the conviction of the Fruit of Islam (FOI) that the White man would go to any lengths to keep the Black man uneducated.

Arrested on numerous occasions after raids and police station protests gone wrong, Elijah Muhammad fled to Chicago, afraid of further persecution (Evanzz 1999, 102). But this was just the beginning. The schools were now a foundational aspect of nation building. Schools began to meet state standards with respect to enrollment registers and curriculum, while Elijah Muhammad continued to advocate the tenets of the Nation. Although established as formal schools, most still lacked proper educational facilities or adequate funding to pay teachers. Police raids soon became negative publicity as state interventions continued to shut schools down. But NOI persisted. Riding the conviction of the cause, many of my own participants who taught in the schools said the NOI demanded a sense of commitment that outweighed mundane concerns such as remuneration.

With the exception of a few non-Muslims who were sympathetic to the cause, the vast majority of teachers were believers themselves. Often not certified educators, the early teachers at the UofI schools exhibited an unparalleled dedication to Elijah Muhammad's vision of a separate community. Many teachers worked for next to nothing. When Qadir Abdus Sabur began teaching at the UofI schools, he worked for an income well under the poverty line. With a family and the expenses that come along with maintaining a home, his dedication did not waver: "People were absolutely committed to the project even at the cost of their own family—it was a level of commitment that you will rarely see. . . ." And many were just beginning their careers while transitioning to a new consciousness. They taught and learned at the same time. Digging deep into history, Rafiq Iddin recalled that "We [believers in the NOI] didn't have a lot of people with degrees—we were higher people from within our own community—but they [teachers at the UofI schools] studied themselves and were creative with the lessons and we only focused on the younger grades at first so teachers didn't need a deep understanding" of academic subject areas. What they needed was a deep knowledge of themselves.

It was this determination that also attracted a new educated wave of Black Muslim converts to the NOI in the 1960s. Disillusioned with the

Civil Rights movement with the assassination of Martin Luther King, Jr., many of the converts to the NOI in the late 60s were educators by profession. Energized and committed, there was no doubt in the minds of these new converts of the need for the UofI schools during the Civil Rights era in America. Justifications came couched both in rhetoric common in the 1960s and direct statements: the fact was that African Americans were separate and unequal.

It was a combination of the energy of a new educated class and the turbulence of the 1960s that soon began to see plans put in place to extend the University of Islam schools into a community college. University campuses were becoming ever more hostile toward African Americans, while at the same time the Nation was now graduating stable student populations from their UofI schools. Although many of the young high school graduates had gained acceptance to prestigious universities, Elijah Muhammad insisted that the times required their own solutions. In 1963, Abdul Alim Shabazz was given the directive by Elijah Muhammad to establish the Nation's first college.

The college was to be a unique program that still taught the liberal arts as most colleges do, but would focus on essential knowledge and as a result quicken the process of education. Inspired by the words of Elijah Muhammad when he would often say, "teach them quickly but don't teach them lies," Shabazz and others developed a curriculum based on essential knowledge that aimed to graduate students in two years as opposed to the usual four-year baccalaureate. It took Shabazz ten years to put plans in place to begin what was a single trailer campus attached to the temple that he led. As the Nation spread and infrastructure fortified, most appointed ministers made education the backbone of their temple's activity. Having the UofI schools attached to the temples proved to be the saving grace for their existence. As the schools grew in size and influence, a greater public interest followed.

By 1970, major media outlets in urban cities were covering stories on the UofI schools. By the 1970s, UofI schools, similar to NOI temples, had spread all over the country. Estimates of the number of schools vary between 14 and 42 (Evanzz 1999, 153). Some were weekend programs, but many were full-time alternatives to public schools. The UofI in Washington, D.C., had grown at its peak to housing 412 students in the day school and 50 students in the college by the mid-1970s.

Along the vision of Abdul Alim Shabazz and inspired by Elijah Muhammad, the standard 13 years of schools (elementary, middle, and high school) was condensed to 9 levels of teaching that intended on sending students to college by the age of 14 or 15. Students would attend school year-round and could start as early as three and a half to four years of age.

By the late 1960s and into the 1970s, the potential and perception of the schools had evolved greatly. The philosophy of the schools had also become more finely developed, and the social and educational impact was evident. The schools were a definite reason for preventing young children from leading lives similar to their parents' before joining the NOI. The NOI had a major effect on turning around the lives of many African Americans from a life of crime and drugs to self-discipline and moral uprightness. Similarly, the intent of the UofI schools was to impact children with a code of behavior from an even younger age. Young girls dressed in white scarves and long skirts, and boys trained in a militaristic style, for their "regular exercises" were expected to raise their level of self-awareness and self-dignity. In the words of Louis Farrakhan, torchbearer of the NOI today, defining the difference of their educational experience from that of others, he told a group of young elementary boys, "You have been trained to see what others don't see and to ask why while others ask what."[11] The training was intense, both structurally and in terms of curriculum. Children attended the schools 50 weeks out of the year, which consisted of a three-hour, four-day week. The fifth day was reserved for recreation and social activities. One teacher described the philosophy, saying: "We eliminate the sport, the play, the rest periods, the snack periods, the free periods, all of these which give the children nothing."[12] No lunch or recess periods were allotted. Boys and girls were also segregated to avoid being distracted, at least while learning. By this time, many of the schools had reached a level of noted excellence. There were more qualified educators who had converted to the NOI in the late 1960s who brought a new professionalism to the schools. In 1970, a district superintendent in Harlem praised the local UofI School for its modern facilities, at par curriculum, and a teaching staff that held B.A.s and master's degrees in the subject areas that they taught.[13]

By the 1970s, the schools had begun to place a large emphasis on imparting daily Muslim duties, teaching Arabic, observance of strict dietary laws, and character development. On character development, students were formally graded on aspects of their personal behavior such as: courtesy, cooperation, cleanliness, self-control, and conduct.[14] In terms of the formal curriculum, much time was spent on what Elijah Muhammad preached to be the "knowledge of self" (Muhammad 1965, Chapter 23). Knowledge of self included formal lessons on the history of the Black nation, knowledge of civilizations of man and the universe, and all sciences. Of course, these bodies of content were framed from within the teachings of the Nation of Islam's worldview based upon the teachings of Spook theology.[15]

The UofI schools also emphasized a strong academic education along Elijah Muhammad's teachings of "do for self." He said, "Since our being brought in chains to the shores of America, our brain power, labor, skills, talent and wealth have been taken, given, and spent toward building and adding to the civilization of another people. It is time for you and me, the so-called Negroes, to start doing for ourselves" (Muhammad 1965,

Chapters 37 and 56). Doing for self along with moral behavior together shaped the educational vision that Elijah Muhammad exhibited in the schools. Informational material of Detroit's University of Islam stated that "public schools are 'blackboard jungles' over-ridden with juvenile delinquents who smoke cigarettes, marijuana, chew tobacco, drink alcoholics [sic], curse, fight, and murder."[16] What some scholars have labeled the NOI's form of Black Puritanism, Elijah Muhammad's vision sought to vociferously transform believers with a sense of self-respect and responsibility.

The Educational Vision of Elijah Muhammad

The education provided by the UofI schools and NOI temples entailed education for both children and adults. Elijah Muhammad put "a massive adult education program in motion. And young men, old men, and women, learned how to read and write by being integrated into the NOI," according to Rafiq Iddin. To become a believer, one had to be able to read and write. That was the bar that Elijah Muhammad set for new converts. It was a no nonsense way of demanding utter commitment to re-educating a nation. To become a member of the NOI, one had to write a personal letter to Elijah Muhammad. That is how he empowered the illiterate and distraught. And then all believers were offered classes that were set up to provide necessary career and social skills. Abdul Alim Shabazz explained, "and they were educated people because they knew knowledge of God, knowledge of themselves, and the knowledge of others. Those were primary subjects that had to be learned by the student and that knowledge permeated everything we studied."

There was consensus among my participants that the re-education was intended to bring about the self-development and self-reliance of a people that have been historically subjected to forced inferiority. Elijah Muhammad taught African Americans to think differently about themselves. He empowered believers, made them feel adequate, equal, if not superior through a process of re-education and dispelling untruths. He challenged the perceptions that Blacks are inherently lazy, less capable, or intellectually deficient. Most importantly, he challenged believers to push themselves toward professional and intellectual pursuits.

In the NOI, schools served as vehicles of empowerment. But for a community of believers that were largely uneducated and had limited formal schooling experience, Elijah Muhammad made the concept of schooling accessible to them. He taught that schools were everywhere, and everybody who lives is being schooled because life is school. At home, on the street, buying groceries, playing with friends, working, and every other mundane activity became an educative experience for believers. Making believers feel that learning can happen anywhere and everywhere attracted those who had negative formal schooling experiences. Then, when Elijah Muhammad introduced formal lessons through the Muslim Girls Training (MGT) the General Civilization Class (GCC), a class for the FOI (Fruit of Islam) and the Junior FOI, believers felt a sense of self-empowerment that regular schooling experiences could not convey. More importantly, through teaching that life is school, Elijah Muhammad involved everyone in the process of education and re-education, not limiting schools to school-aged children. Everyone from mothers nursing at home to fathers working in the day and preaching by night were involved in schooling (Abdus Sabur and Abdus Sabur 2000, 27–8).

Abdul Alim Shabazz explained that among Elijah Muhammad's foundational teachings was "Islam is mathematics and mathematics is Islam." Appropriating mathematics, Elijah Muhammad exhibited his reliance on historical Muslim contributions. Shabazz explained that the significance of this teaching is instructive of the development of his vision. Islam, like mathematics, must be decoded, grappled with, and understood deeply. It is complex and yet based on foundational principles—simple truths. Within it is a unity that expands and contracts toward a multiplicity and back to its original essence. Its secret resides in those who reflect. For Abdul Alim Shabazz, who was highly influenced by this statement, it became his battle cry. An esteemed professor of mathematics himself, this teaching in particular bore an in-depth connection to Elijah Muhammad: "I listened to his mind, the wisdom he was teaching, I understood, I grabbed the books of the life of the Prophet Muhammad and the Qur'an, and I studied these books and the more I studied, the more I understood the reality of what the Hon. Elijah Muhammad was trying to do for his people." For Shabazz, the analogy described the essence of education. You could not separate the teaching of academic subject matter from the lessons of life. Islam is life—a way of life, of living—and he taught that through the logic of mathematics.

Since his conversion in 1960, Shabazz embedded the wisdom of Elijah Muhammad into his own university teaching. He "taught that no matter how abstruse or opaque a mathematical equation is, it comes from life and it can be applied to life." When teaching at Atlanta University in the late 1950s and early 60s, he developed math clubs to inspire African Americans to learn math. From his perspective, students yearned for his approach to mathematics because it made sense. Malcolm X, a close friend of Abdul Alim Shabazz, was invited to speak to the math club: "[Malcolm] would speak to standing room only crowds when he spoke about the pyramids and the sphinx—spellbinding. This is the beauty of Islam, the beauty of mathematics, the beauty of life itself."

Daa'iyah Abdur Rashid recounted that Elijah Muhammad's conviction in the power of mathematics was contagious. Daa'iyah told me the story of one of her mentors, Sister Nuurah, an elementary school teacher in the early days of the NOI. Sister Nuurah was inspired by Elijah Muhammad's words that if a child can master mathematics, he can learn anything. Elijah Muhammad told this to Sister Nuurah at dinner one night, and she tried it out in her Grade 1 classroom in a Detroit public school. Using Elijah Muhammad's wisdom, she went to her class, removed all the other books, and began teaching reading, writing, spelling, and all other subjects from math books only. By the end of the year, she said that the principal double promoted all her students to Grade 3. What Sister Nuurah found was not so much the success of a single class in learning to read through math, but the potential for the unity of learning that Elijah Muhammad advocated. The reliance on a single science from which all knowledge stems is a core element in the teachings of the NOI.

Elijah Muhammad's emphasis on mathematics came from his knowledge of Muslim civilizations of the past. He sought to connect the simplicity and yet profoundness of the concept of *tawhid* (Oneness of God) with an emphasis on mathematics as was common in classical Muslim scholarship.[17] Elijah Muhammad's emphasis on mathematics also spoke to the importance of business development and financial self-reliance. Nurturing the practical side of daily life interactions that encouraged believers to be thrifty with their wealth illustrated that his message was for both the educated and the lay. The teachings of Elijah Muhammad were teachings for life. He emphasized sacrifice, struggle, and empowerment. Knowledge was all that they needed for empowerment, but it came with struggle and sacrifice.

According to all of my participants, these teachings about the origin of man and the potential of the Black man in particular were elevating. It was dramatically effective in reviving the down-trodden and subjugated ex-slave descendants in America. For many, it gave them a new hope, an aspiration. Rafiq Iddin said it clearly: "America was doing us a disservice and we thought it was absolutely necessary that we had to do things ourselves. We needed to take things into our own hands. We felt that public schools were mis-educating us so we began hiring our own teachers and taking our children out of the public schools."

As Edward Curtis argues, Elijah Muhammad sought to "civilize" the Black body (Curtis 2005, 97). Aside from his sensationalistic theology, Elijah Muhammad pieced together basic, fundamental tenets of moral behavior from disparate faith traditions. He used both Islamic and Christian teachings together along with his own religious ideology to nurture self-respect for the Black body. He associated civilized behavior "with values of thrift, sexual propriety, industriousness, and temperance." (Curtis 2005, 97). Men were commanded to treat women believers with the utmost respect, hold doors for them, speak to them with respect, and be responsible for the household income. Women were equally taught conservative values of homemaking. MGT classes included sewing, cooking, and maintaining homes. Women were taught that the breakdown of the family was a result of women in the workforce. These conservative teachings were indeed transformational for many. In the voices of Curtis' oral history, he found many women praising the regimentation of the NOI. The teachings of Elijah Muhammad, they said, civilized African Americans and liberated them from a psyche of inferiority. Through a re-education of the Black man, Elijah Muhammad sought to dignify African Americans. Believing men in suits and bowties and women with their head covered and donning long dresses challenged the values of American relativism both inwardly and outwardly. UofI schools, MGT, and FOI training taught believers how to eat, act, walk, talk, and live.

The legacy of the early UofI schools should not, however, be simply understood as a form of racial protest similar to the rise of Afrocentric discourse, the Black Power movement, and the Civil Rights era of the 1960s. As Austin says, "scholars need to remember that the organization [NOI] began in 1930 and not 1950 or 1960." To attempt to understand the NOI simply for its protest of racial inequality denies the movement's ability to inspire and transform a nation through an inherently religious discourse.

Although much of the curriculum remained state-sanctioned, the appendage of religious teachings, moral commandments, and Arabic language remained religious in nature and not Afrocentric necessarily (Austin 1997, 39). It was not until the 1960s when the schools adopted a more explicit curriculum of Afrocentrism as an additional marker of identity, but that did not remove the focus of Black Religion. Even the protection of the Black body was an inherently religious act. Having the FOI and MGT inspect school children upon arrival for cleanliness, uniform, and to ensure that they did not bring inappropriate things to school (candy, magazines, etc.) was not "a celebration of what they perceived as blackness but a move away from blackness" (Austin 1997, 41). The NOI in many ways appropriated particular aspects of the Islamic tradition to protest stereotypical Black behavior and the ideology of White superiority that contributed to it.

In so doing, however, the teachings of Elijah Muhammad seemed contradictory. Between Black empowerment and yet a distaste for Afrocentricity, and between White hate and the adoption of White middle-class values, Elijah Muhammad truly instigated a distinct ideology.[18] The NOI's protest was complicated, though, because they generally accepted what were considered White, middle-class Protestant values of economic self-sufficiency, heterosexuality, and concerns for modest diet, dress, and frugal spending (Curtis 2005, 9). Within the NOI, all of these values were couched in language which aligned them with Islamic teachings. The "Islamization" of White, middle-class values "challenged the cultural and ideological foundations of the American nation-state, its social structures, and its dominant religious foundations" (Curtis 2005, 9). The education of believers emphasized moral habits aimed at challenging Black stereotypes over gaining academic credentials. Laziness was counteracted with strict discipline, dirtiness with regular inspections, and promiscuity with teachings of self-restraint and self-respect (Austin 1997, 41).

What Elijah Muhammad achieved in 45 years of leadership cannot be undermined in the history of Islam in America or for the history of Islamic schooling. Between nurturing Black consciousness, challenging inferiority, and embedding these within a unique religious discourse, he engendered an immense commitment to protest.

Losing Conviction in the Nation

By the 1960s, Elijah Muhammad himself had begun loosening his commitment to Black exclusivity in the NOI and broadening his connection with the Muslim world. In 1959, he performed his first Hajj to the holy city of Mecca and began to allow the teaching of Arabic in the UofI schools by Arabs who were outside the fold of the NOI. Rafiq Iddin said that select Arabs were known to have had a substantial impact on the upbringing on Elijah Muhammad's children. Access to Arabic and the Qur'an, along with the recognition of mainstream Islamic beliefs during the last decade of the old NOI,[19] served as the basis for notable ministers in the NOI like Malcolm X and Warith Deen Mohammed to question the legitimacy of the NOI's doctrines.

Warith Deen Mohammed had moved toward orthodoxy well before his father's death in 1975. Having performed his first Hajj in 1967, he had already fallen out of favor with many of the NOI's faithful. Having traveled the Muslim world and experienced orthodox Islam, Warith Deen Mohammed brought with him teachings of mainstream Islamic beliefs which needed to be silenced. At the command of his father, Warith Deen was thrown out of the NOI three times for heresy. In an interview with Steven Barboza, Warith Deen Mohammed said that the NOI had been losing touch with reality for a while: "I feel they were always losing contact with reality and the nature of the teachings especially the theological teachings, or the mythical teachings" (Barboza 1993, 97). Teachings that God is a man in the form of Fard Muhammad, the mythology of "tricknology,"[20] and the origin of the tribe of Shabazz being from space were systematically challenged by Warith Deen Mohammed.

Imam Warith Deen recalls that he began questioning the teachings of the NOI as early as his teens:

> As I grew as a young man, and I got in my teens—at fifteen, sixteen—I started to wonder why this man looking so white [referring to a picture of Fard Muhammad hanging on a wall at home as a child] was supposed to be black and a black god. I started to see similarity between the way Jesus is portrayed in Christianity and the way he [Fard Muhammad] was portrayed. Maybe the Qur'an had started to influence my thinking without me knowing.
>
> (quoted in Barboza 1993, 100)

The belief in racial superiority that Elijah Muhammad instituted was among the fundamental contentions that most believers challenged after performing the pilgrimage of Hajj and experiencing the practice of an orthodox Islam theoretically void of racial hierarchies and distinctions. Malcolm X popularized this sentiment in his letters to his wife from Mecca on his pilgrimage in 1964 (Haley 1965, 339–42). Similarly, Imam Warith Deen grew uncomfortable with the theology of the NOI but never strayed too far. Jackson (2005) argues that although Warith Deen had fallen out of favor with his father on three occasions and gone as far as temporarily establishing his own organization, the Afro-Descendent Upliftment Society, he remained committed to the potential of the NOI. Never quite fully convinced, it was not until 1975 that Warith Deen had the opportunity to re-envision the NOI while still maintaining its organizational structure.

Death of Elijah Muhammad: Transitioning a Nation

At the passing of Elijah Muhammad in 1975 after the passing of his wife, Clara Muhammad, three years earlier, the passion, conviction, and sacrifice that once defined a program of re-education of a subjugated people evolved once again. The death of Elijah Muhammad marked the end of what Sherman Jackson coined the First Resurrection and the beginning of the Second (Jackson 2005, 4–5).

The death of Elijah Muhammad came on the eve of Savior's Day, the birthday of Fard Muhammad. In emotional turmoil, believers worried with great intensity about the future of the Nation and its leadership. Closing his address on that day, Imam Warith Deen (Wallace Deen at the time) quoted the words of his father to give reassurance but more importantly to hint at redirection. He said:

> The Honorable Elijah Muhammad says 'I have Supreme Wisdom from Almighty God.' And all of us are men and women of knowledge, so when the strong gust of wind, coming from the forces of emotion, comes against this house, the windows stay intact, the shade doesn't even waver, the curtain's at the window—though the window be up—won't even be moved by the winds of emotion, simply because this house is built on strength—Divine strength.
> (Abdullah et al. 1995, 10–1)

Warith Deen's choice of closing words were not arbitrary. On a day when the NOI needed direction and a day that he began to formally shift that direction, the final emphasis of the NOI being built on Divine strength was purposeful in legitimizing that shift. He strategically employed those of his father's teachings that supported the evolution of the NOI's beliefs toward mainstream Islamic teachings.

Believers were taught to continue to respect the sacrifices and the vision of the NOI. The work of Elijah Muhammad and the NOI was a necessary step in the evolution of the community to regain their sense of self. Warith Deen did not preach hate or remorse toward Fard Muhammad or toward his father, but rather praised them for the much-needed awakening required for the NOI to have reached this current stage of clarity and understanding of "true" Islam. As he reflected, he said, "Perhaps I redefined his role." The role of Elijah Muhammad was one of a social reformer who inspired the downtrodden to believe in themselves, and so few would question his sincerity. Warith Deen's rationale for his father's teachings of hate through a pseudo Islamic theology is that

> He was ignorant and misinformed, and when I say ignorant, I'm not saying it in the ugly sense. I'm saying that he didn't know world religions or anything. He came from the South with no high school education, and he had no way of knowing what the Islamic world believed in or what it didn't believe in.
>
> (quoted in Barboza 1993, 99)

The new direction that Warith Deen then proposed was a return to Islam's universal teachings practiced by Muslims worldwide. In defense of the NOI's appropriation of Islamic beliefs, Jackson (2005) contends that even in the earliest periods of Islamic history, the enterprise of religious conversion often required an altering of religious tenets to validate a people's past and understand new directions: "This is often a messy undertaking that entails numerous misses (at least from the standpoint of orthodoxy) en-route to complete assimilation" (2005, 46). The sensationalist, "doctrinal excesses, omissions, and blasphemies" that Fard Muhammad and Elijah Muhammad created out of Black Religion and Sunni Islam were arguably necessary in positioning and popularizing the potential for Islam among African Americans. Claiming that God was a man, a Black man whose roots could be traced back to a tribe from Mecca, Saudi Arabia, grounded the unorthodoxy of the NOI. To then indoctrinate racial superiority and an inherent evil nature of Europeans, let alone Spook theology, made prominent believers in the NOI question the tenets of faith. It became clear that veering away from orthodox Islam would be unsustainable.

From Black to "Bilalian:" Shifting Discourses From Race to Mainstream Islam

Within the first years of his leadership, Warith Deen Mohammed began to dismantle his father's tenets and realign with the mainstream Islamic tradition. He welcomed Whites into the organization, encouraged patriotism, encouraged believers to adopt names with Islamic significance as he did himself, made temples into mosques, ministers into Imams, and instituted prayers in Arabic (Hasan 1998). Organizationally, he also made critical changes to how the NOI was administered in order to create more local control and possibly less opportunity for internal corruption. The Fruit of Islam, the NOI's security arm, was disbanded. Imam Warith Deen also capped ministers' salaries and ended the forced institution of charity dues.

Likely his most radical departure was the removal of the concept of the superiority of one race over another. Recognizing the universality of the religion of Islam, Imam Warith Deen emphasized the importance of equality of races, evidenced in such Qur'anic passages as the following famous verses:

> O mankind! We created you from a single (pair) Of a male and female
> And made you into nations and tribes, that you may know one another
> Not that you may despise one another.
> Verily the most honored of you in the sight of God is (he who is) the most righteous of you
> And God has full knowledge of and is well acquainted with all things.
> (Qur'an 49–13)

Preaching racial equality, however, risked the loss of a distinct African American agenda and also would forfeit the legacy of the NOI. Imam Warith Deen inspired believers by positioning the NOI's trajectory within the history of Islam. He employed the historical narrative of Islam's first Black Muslim, Bilal Ibn Rabah, to maintain a sense of racial identity within a global Muslim brotherhood. On Savior's Day 1976, in front of an audience of 80,000 nationwide, Imam Warith Deen continued his strategic bridging of the old and the new directions. He said that Fard Muhammad was not misguiding but skillful in bringing the "Bilalian community" to where they are now. He also emphasized that Fard Muhammad knew of the Orthodox Muslim community, about Allah and the Qur'an, but the Bilalian community was not ready to accept that message:

> Master Fard Muhammad discovered that what was absent in the Bilalian community was material . . . you cannot teach the 'heavens' to a society that has not yet been formed in the earth. You have to teach them the earth first. That was the wisdom (the key) that Master Fard Muhammad discovered. . . . Today we have arrived at our goal and the trip has been successful. The great plan achieved what it was designed to achieve.
> (Abdullah et al. 1995, 14)

The story of Bilal Ibn Rabah, an Ethiopian slave brought to Arabia and freed by the Prophet Muhammad in the 7th century A.D., provided a framework for transition. Highlighting the esteem that Bilal had among the early Muslim community with the honor of being the *mu'adhdhin* (popularly spelt *muezzin*) or caller to prayer, it situated African American Muslims within Islam's historical narrative (Mamiya 1982). Formerly considered a part of the mythical Tribe of Shabazz, Bilal's story gave members of the old NOI a sense of legitimacy. It also justified the need to connect to the mainstream practices of Islam as contained in the Qur'an and Prophetic Tradition (Sunnah) and interpreted throughout the centuries by Islam's vast juridical traditions (Jackson 2005, 82).

Un-Racializing Protest

The shift from Black to Bilalian, which in itself was a short-lived concept, and Warith Deen Mohammed's transition from the NOI to mainstream Islam in general had a number of adverse affects that shaped the plight of the UofI schools.

Dismantling essential aspects of the Nation's hierarchical structure with the intent of promoting both racial and class based equality by virtue also systematically removed the urgency of protest. By opening their doors to races of every sort and being willing to work with a broader range of activist groups, including African American groups previously considered "Uncle Toms,"[21] now meant that their guard could be let down. At the same time, reconnecting with the practices of mainstream Islam required a process of unlearning and re-learning the tenets of Islam. The combination of dismantling hierarchy and putting in place high expectations for a re-education was a difficult transition for believers who were still riding the energy of the Civil Rights era.

For many who lived through the tumultuous era of abject racism in America, activism and protest defined their existence. Abdul Alim Shabazz, for example, who began teaching mathematics at Cornell University in 1955, represents the protest of revolution that defined the era as well as the commitment that Elijah Muhammad inspired. From short snippets of his life in book chapters and articles to his own writings,[22] and with my own personal conversation with him, I realized that his conviction is contagious. Every university that he taught at, he recalled students were revolutionized in their thinking. Students would yearn to come to the blackboard (a privilege at the time) to grapple with mathematical equations. They protested in libraries by standing and reading where they were denied the right to sign out books. Coming from an era where it was normative to have crosses burned at his doorstep because he was an educated Black man reinforced the teachings of Elijah Muhammad in relation to power, privilege, education, and the need to do for self. In my interview with him, he described these days as the

> [E]arly days of my learning that the Powers that Be did not want our youth to be taught in a way that would cause them to think about

their circumstances and condition and learn how they could improve their own circumstances. It was my students that initiated the sit in struggle in Atlanta, Georgia, that brought about the destruction of Jim Crow in the South, Atlanta in particular.

For Shabazz, like others in the NOI, these occurrences only reaffirmed their struggle and their conviction in the teachings of Elijah Muhammad. Understanding the "knowledge of themselves," who they are as a people, their history became ever more important. Under the new leadership of Warith Deen Mohammed, however, to remove this urgency for an education based on struggle, protest, and redemption created major schisms within the community.

Within the realm of the UofI schools, Imam Warith Deen had to make strategic decisions for the sake of the community that were often unpopular amongst varying factions. These were times of tenuous leadership that had to be handled assertively and yet delicately. For reasons beyond this historical narrative, the likes of instrumental educators within the NOI, such as Abdul Alim Shabazz and his aspirations of establishing sites for higher education, were derailed. Shifted from being the National Director of Education to the Director of Adult Education within months of the death of Elijah Muhammad directly affected the energy that could be placed on the educational initiatives. By this time, the NOI had been officially renamed to the World Community of Islam in the West (WCIW), along with other major name changes, such as the *Muhammad Speaks* newspaper became the *Bilalian News*. As the Director of Adult Education, Shabazz wrote a weekly column for the *Bilalian News*, grappling with the vision of Islamic education for the WCIW. In 1977, under the leadership of Imam Warith Deen and inspired by the teachings of Elijah Muhammad, Shabazz's educational columns were reworked and published in book form as *The Fundamentals of Islamic Education*. During the inner reworking within the WCIW, the work of those like Dr. Shabazz, who were passionate about the state of education, continued to be sidetracked. In 1979, he shifted responsibilities once again to be Imam of the Councils. By 1982, when the WCIW made yet another shift in direction and aims through renaming itself the American Muslim Mission (AMM), tensions of difference and disagreement within the community affected individual commitment. Abdul Alim Shabazz eventually traveled to Saudi Arabia that same year to teach at the world renowned Umm ul Qura University while the transition within the NOI settled down. In many ways, the departure of Abdul Alim Shabazz marked the dwindling of energy around educational initiatives inspired by Elijah Muhammad as the NOI knew it.

For many believers themselves, the changes left them in a state of disillusionment, still in shock that Elijah Muhammad had passed. Warith Deen Mohammed's push toward prayer over politics also disenfranchised some. Zakiyyah Muhammad, a cornerstone in the re-envisioning of the Clara Muhammad schools (CMS) curriculum, recounts, "They weren't doing anything. Praying five times a day and reading the Koran wasn't enough. I wanted to be involved in making life better for Black people." Previously in the NOI, the emphasis was different. Rafiq Iddin recalls that "we prayed and we learned to pray but our emphasis wasn't on prayer; it was on getting out of the situation we were in." The new tides of change depoliticized the project toward spiritual growth and civic duty. It reflected Imam Warith Deen's conviction in correcting misinformed religious practices by moving closer to the teachings of mainstream Islam. For some, the change was drastic. Removing the seats out of temples and teaching believers to bow their heads to the ground in submission, realigning the month of Ramadan according to the lunar calendar, and most importantly re-learning the reality of God's true nature characterized the learning required of believers.

Between re-learning faith and a radically different approach toward civic integration, Warith Deen Mohammed's "changes caused dissension, particularly among hard-nosed nationalists for whom rallying round the flag would have felt as perverse as buddying up to Jim Crow" (Barboza 1993, 96). Warith Deen's emphasis on building relationships with organizations and people external to his community was another major point of departure. For many even from within the community, Warith Deen Mohammed's Patriotism Act served as a major defection from the teachings of his father. Integrating with Whites and accepting all people as equal was more a matter of time and reflection in order to cultivate understanding. But a shift toward allegiance to America proved to be a major point of disagreement for believers. Some say it began the day Warith Deen Mohammed walked across a stage carrying an American flag in 1976. He urged believers to recognize and celebrate the contributions, sacrifices, and history of African Americans not only in terms of their African heritage but also of their American heritage. His philosophy advocated that believers celebrate the opportunities of the land they inhabit, which does not by any means silence their struggle for justice. Warith Deen Mohammed's push for patriotism represents not only a remarkable transformation from the teachings of his father, but helps his community situate themselves within a distinctly African American Muslim identity (Terry 2002). On the other hand, such a fundamental departure early in his leadership also soon split the community. Initially, most of the believers remained on board with the vision of Warith Deen Mohammed, if hesitatingly. It was not until 1977 when Abdul Haleem Farrakhan returned to his original name of Louis and reestablished the NOI with its image of man as God and its paramilitary hierarchy that dissension became public.[23] The plan of transition for Warith Deen Mohammed was, therefore, far from well orchestrated. By shifting away from the urgency of protest, he lost many believers in the process, but also had to regain and re-inspire commitment through new directions informed by mainstream Islam. In the following chapter, I will turn my focus to how these new directions established by Warith Deen Mohammed played out in the realm of schooling. Repositioning his community with the global Muslim community and de-racializing the agenda of the NOI came with their own challenges in restructuring the UofI schools.

Notes

1. Jim Crow laws were the enactment of American civil law that espoused a "separate but equal" line of protest. Practiced between 1876 and 1965, these laws segregated schools, restaurants, restrooms, and other public spaces. The term Jim Crow itself represented the stereotypical behavior of Black Americans that reinforced their presumed inferiority. Through popular culture, most notably in stage plays, the term became widespread.
2. The Nation of Islam was preceded by other pseudo Islamic movements intended on empowering African Americans, such as the Moorish Science Temple led by Noble Drew Ali. The Moorish Science Temple was founded in the early 1900s and became popular in Chicago by the 1920s. Founded and led by Noble Drew Ali, the movement attempted to make a historical link between African Americans and their lineage to the North African Moors, hence an Islamic ancestry. Combining elements of Islamic theology along with Christian, Aboriginal, and mystic spirituality, Drew Ali developed his own religion to address America's legacy of White racial superiority.
3. Elijah Muhammad and by virtue the Nation of Islam were vehemently against the integrationist aspirations (even if partial in the case of DuBois) of the National Association for the Advancement of Colored People (NAACP) and the stance of notable civil rights activists such as W.E.B. DuBois and later Martin Luther King, Jr.
4. I employ Jackson's conceptualization of Black religion because it serves as an effective framework to understand the NOI's distinct religious ideology—not simply a racial one—and to explain why immigrant Muslims, who became a major stakeholder in American Islam after the transition, found it difficult to accept the community of Imam Warith Deen Mohammed.
5. Sherman Jackson, *Islam and the Blackamerican: Looking Toward the Third Resurrection* (New York: Oxford University Press, 2005), 24–25. In his conception of Black Religion, Jackson argues that it is not a synonym for "African-American religion," which is often employed as a catchphrase for all forms of Black religious denominations in America. Black religion is but one form, or denomination, amongst other religious orientations that are distinctly Black and American. Other forms of religiosity or at least spirituality, such as Black power, Black consciousness (including Afrocentricity as articulated by Molefi Asante), and Black theology, e.g. Black Pentecostalism, have been inherently passive and conforming. From these examples, Jackson argues that "waging war against white supremacy and anti-black racism has not been an integral feature of *all* religion among Blackamericans. As such, 'Black Religion' and 'African-American Religion' must be understood to connote two distinct, though interrelated, realities in Blackamerican life" (Jackson, *Islam and the Blackamerican*, 30).
6. At times I employ Sherman Jackson's use of the Blackamerican as opposed to African American. The term Blackamerican (all one word), he argues,

connotes something distinctly different from Black Africans who are able to trace their historical ancestry to Africa. Blackamericans, on the other hand, are not simply displaced people. The term Blackamerican allows for the historical legacy of American colonialism and subjugation of Black peoples to come to the fore. It is this latter experience that has intrinsically shaped the experience of Blackamericans as both distinctly Black and American. By reconceptualizing the experience of the widely used term "African American," the need to establish forms of Black religion (further discussed in subsequent chapters of this book) become evident in the experience of Blackamericans. While recognizing the distinction, I personally use the term interchangeably dependent on the context of the writing.

7. The framework of mapping the history of Blackamericans under three "resurrections" is developed in Jackson, *Islam and the Blackamerican*, 5–6.
8. The landmark case of *Brown v. Board of Education* in 1954 officially ended racial segregation in American public schools. The case of Oliver Brown and the over 200 plaintiffs of the case was not the first attempt to legally challenge school segregation. The NAACP had numerous previous attempts that failed since their inception. The victory of the Brown case, however, set the precedent for numerous other race based forms of discrimination and eventually served as the basis for the Civil Rights movement.
9. Savior's Day is annual celebration in the NOI that signifies the coming of W.D. Fard Muhammad. The commemorative day still continues under the leadership of Imam Warith Deen Mohammed but has been given new significance through renaming it "Saviors Day," i.e. removing the apostrophe to suggest that he alone was not the only savior.
10. The actual start year has varied depending on the source. Some scholars have said 1934 (Hakim Rashid and Zakiyyah Muhammad), and others have said the first school was established as early as 1932. Because the first school was located in the home of Elijah and Clara Muhammad and was not formally registered, it is difficult to be completely accurate.
11. Lesly Jones, "Muslim Teaching Makes Impact on Harlem," *New York Amsterdam News*, August 29, 1970, 1 and 43. Retrieved from ProQuest Historical Newspapers New York Amsterdam News: 1922–1993.
12. Atlanta Daily World, "To Be Heard on National TV," April 21, 1970. Retrieved from ProQuest Historical Newspapers Atlanta Daily World, 1931–2003.
13. Jones, "Muslim Teaching Makes Impact on Harlem," 1 and 43.
14. "Muhammad University of Islam Actual Report Card for 1971–1972 School Year in Detroit." Retrieved from www.muhammadspeaks.com/reportcard.html. Accessed on February 23, 2008.
15. Spook theology teaches that the devil (the White man) was taught by his father, Yakub, 6,000 years ago that God is not a man but rather a spook (spirit). The reality of God's existence, whether as a man or as a spiritual being, was intended to be a point of contestation between the "great arch deceivers" (the White race) and the rest of humanity. The belief grounding the NOI's theology is that God has always been present in the form of a man and that the Supreme God has appeared in the form of Fard Muhammad with the infinite wisdom to bring about change, cited in *Message to the Blackman in America* by Elijah Muhammad, Chapter 5: "The Origin of God as a Spirit and Not a Man"). It was claimed that the knowledge of God's being had never been known to people until the coming of Fard Muhammad and, therefore, the Blackman had been blessed with the opportunity to teach the truth and raise themselves out of their condition.

16. "Detroit's University of Islam." Reprinted from *Salaam Newspaper*, July 1960. Retrieved from www.muhammadspeaks.com/reportcard.html. Accessed on February 23, 2008.
17. Part of the lessons in the University of Islam schools were logical fallacies that had to be memorized. In my interview with Bilal Ajieb, former member of the NOI, he recounted some of the rhythmic lessons that were taught in the UofI schools.
18. The way in which Afrocentricity has been articulated and the re-education which it aspires to as a movement are in contradistinction to the aims of the NOI. According to Asante, "Afrocentricity proposes a cultural reconstruction that incorporates the African perspective as a part of an entire human transformation . . ." (Molefi K. Asante, *The Afrocentric Idea* (Philadelphia, Temple University Press, 1987), 5). She continues, stating that the "Afrocentric analysis reestablishes the centrality of the ancient Kemetic (Egyptian) civilization and the Nile Valley cultural complex as points of reference for an African perspective in much the same way as Greece and Rome serve as reference points for the European world" (Asante, *The Afrocentric Idea*, 9). Besides the NOI's concocted mythology of the Tribe of Shabazz, unlike the Afrocentric idea that Asante and others have articulated, Elijah Muhammad never tried to connect the Nation of Islam to Islam's African heritage, which has numerous palpable elements (see Jackson, *Islam and the Blackamerican*, 38–42. Also see Edward Curtis, *Islam in Black America: Identity, Liberation, and Difference in African-American Islamic Thought* (Albany: State University of New York Press, 2002), 73.
19. I refer to the NOI under Elijah Muhammad as the "old NOI" in order to make a distinction between what the world knew of the NOI during Elijah Muhammad separate from its revival under Louis Farrakhan in 1977. The resurrection of the NOI under Louis Farrakhan is in many ways a conflation of both teachings of Elijah Muhammad along with a much greater reliance on Sunni Islam, and therefore requires a distinction.
20. One of the core teachings of Fard Muhammad was that of a "science of deception," or "tricknology," which held that thousands of years ago the White race had been grafted from the Black race through gene manipulation. The theory served to justify the supremacy of the Black race and the inherent evil of the White race. For a more detailed discussion, see Karl Evanzz, *The Messenger: The Rise and Fall of Elijah Muhammad* (New York: Pantheon Books, 1999), 75.
21. Uncle Tom is a pejorative term commonly used in the pre-Civil Rights era in the United States to describe African Americans perceived to be behaving in a subservient manner to Whites in positions of authority.
22. See Steven Barboza, *American Jihad: Islam after Malcolm X* (New York: Doubleday, 1993), 294–299; Also see Abdul Alim Shabazz, *Fundamentals of Islamic Education* (NOI). The copy I had access to was a draft manuscript of the text written in the early 1980s. A photocopy was mailed to me by Abdul Alim Shabazz from his personal archives because the book itself has been out of print for many years and he did not want to part with his only copy.
23. McCloud notes that by the late 1980s, Louis Farrakhan also began to move the Nation toward mainstream Islam while maintaining an emphasis on addressing the needs of Black Americans. And by 2000, both Imam Warith Deen and Imam Farrakhan have begun to reconcile differences for the sake of the larger Black American community. See: Aminah Beverly McCloud, "Blackness in the Nation of Islam." In *Religion and the Creation of Race and Ethnicity: An Introduction*, edited by Craig Prentiss (New York: New York University, 2003), 101–110.

References

Abdullah, M., Bilal, W., Muhammad, F., Waheed, A.H., and Zambezi, S. *Evolution of a Community*. Chicago: Warith Deen Muhammad Publications, 1995.

Abdus Sabur, Qadir. *Evolution of a Curriculum Framework: A Collection of Research Articles and Essays on the Education of Muslim Children in the West*. Richmond, VA: Dar Abdul Rahman Publishing, 2005.

Abdus Sabur, Qadir and Abdus Sabur, Beverly. *Developing Muslim School Curricula*. Richmond, VA: Muslim Teachers College, 2000.

Asante, Molefi, K. *Afrocentricity: The Theory of Social Change*. Chicago: African American Images, 2003.

Austin, Algernon. *Achieving Blackness: Race, Black Nationalism, and Afrocentrism in the Twentieth Century*. New York: New York University Press, 2006.

Austin, Allan. *African Muslims in Antebellum America: Transatlantic Stories and Spiritual Struggles*. New York: Routledge, 1997.

Bailey, R.H. "400 Youths at Cult School." *Atlanta Daily World*, April 24, 1934, pp. 1, 3. Retrieved from ProQuest Historical Newspapers Atlanta Daily World, 1931–2003.

Barboza, Steven. *American Jihad: Islam After Malcolm X*. New York: Doubleday, 1993.

Bonnett, Alastair. *Anti-Racism*. London and New York: Routledge, 2000.

Curtis IV, Edward. *Islam in Black America: Identity, Liberation, and Difference in African-American Islamic Thought*. Albany: State University of New York Press, 2002a.

Curtis IV, Edward. "African-American Islamization Reconsidered: Black History Narratives and Muslim Identity." *Journal of American Academy of Religion* 73 (2005): 659–684.

Dannin, Robert. *Black Pilgrimage to Islam*. New York: Oxford University Press, 2002.

Diouf, Sylviane A. *Servants of Allah: African Muslims Enslaved in the Americas*. New York: New York University Press, 1998.

Douglas, Davison. *Jim Crow Moves North: The Battle Over Northern School Segregation 1865–1954*. New York: Cambridge University Press, 2005.

Du Bois, W.E.B. "Does the Negro Need Separate Schools?" *The Journal of Negro Education* 4 no. 3 (July 1935): 328–335.

Essien-Udom, Essien Udosen. *Black Nationalism: The Rise of the Black Muslims in the U.S.A.* Harmondsworth: Penguin, 1966.

Evanzz, Karl. *The Messenger: The Rise and Fall of Elijah Muhammad*. New York: Patheon Books, 1999.

Gaddis, John. *The Landscape of History: How Historians Map the Past*. New York: Oxford University Press, 2002.

Haley, Alex. *The Autobiography of Malcolm X*. New York: Grove Press, 1965.

Hasan, Abdul-Majid Karim. *Reflections on the Islamic Teachings of Imam W. Deen Mohammed*. Jersey City, NJ: New Mind Productions Inc., 1998.

Islamic History Project Group. *A History of Muslim African Americans*. Calumet City, IL: WDM Publications, 2006.

Jackson, Sherman. *Islam and the Blackamerican: Looking Toward the Third Resurrection*. New York: Oxford University Press, 2005.

Lee, Martha. *The Nation of Islam: An American Millenarian Movement* (Lewiston/Queenston: The Edwin Mellen Press, 1988), pp. 27–31.

Lincoln, C. Eric. *The Black Muslims in America*. Boston: Beacon Press, 1962.

Mamiya, Lawrence. "From Black to Bilalian: The Evolution of a Movement." *Journal for the Scientific Study of Religion* 21, no. 2 (1982): 138–152.

Marsh, Clifton E. *From Black Muslims to Muslims: The Resurrection, Transformation, and Change of the Lost-Found Nation of Islam in America 1930–1995*. London: The Scarecrow Press, Inc., 1996.

McCloud, Aminah Beverly. "Islam in America: The Mosaic." In *Religion and Immigration: Christian, Jewish, and Muslim Experiences in the United States*, edited by Yvonne Y. Haddad, Jane I. Smith, and John L. Esposito. New York: Altamira Press, 2003.

Muhammad, Elijah. *Message to the Blackman in America*. Chicago: Secretarius Memps, 1965.

Patterson, James T. *Brown v. Board of Education: A Civil Rights Milestone and Its Troubled Legacy*. New York: Oxford University Press, 2001.

Pitre, Abul. *The Educational Philosophy of Elijah Muhammad: Education for a New World*. Lanham, MD: University Press of America, 2008.

Rashed, Ayesha Nadirah. "The Role of the Muslim School as an Alternative to Special Education for Bilalian Children Labeled as Deviant." PhD Diss., University of Michigan, 1977.

Ross, Rosetta E. *Witnessing and Testifying: Black Women, Religion, and Civil Rights*. Minneapolis: Fortress Press, 2003.

Shalaby, Ibrahim. "The Role of the School in Cultural Renewal and Identity Development in the Nation of Islam in America." PhD Diss., University of Arizona, 1967.

Terry, Don. "W.D. Mohammed: A Leap of Faith." *Chicago Tribune*, October 20, 2002. Retrieved from www.chicagotribune.com.

Wilson, Anna Victoria and Segall, William. *Oh, Do I Remember! Experiences of Teachers During the Desegregation of Austin's Schools, 1964–1971*. New York: State University of New York Press, 2001.

Zine, Jasmin. "Creating Faith-Centered Space for Anti-Racist Feminism: Reflections from a Muslim Scholar Activist." *Journal of Feminist Studies in Religion* 20, no. 2 (Fall 2004).

3 Preservation
Preserving Islamic Identity: Indigenous and Immigrant Muslim Educators Meet

By the time Warith Deen Mohammed had taken on the leadership of the Nation of Islam (NOI) in 1975, immigrant Muslims, mostly from parts of Africa, the Middle East, and Southeast Asia, had established themselves in major cities in North America. The challenges for Warith Deen Mohammed in transitioning his community toward orthodox Islam were complex. Re-teaching a faith that African American Muslims formerly under the leadership of his father thought they knew was one major task. The other task was to unite his community with their global Muslim brethren who recently immigrated to America. Together, these two tasks intertwined in the realm of schooling and can tell a rich history of growth, collaboration, and tensions between the Clara Muhammad schools (CMS) and immigrant established Islamic schools in North America.

For the community of Warith Deen Mohammed, the priorities and practices set forth by his father were undergoing a strategic overhaul. Muslims under his leadership were now encouraged to integrate with public institutions and both benefit from and contribute to their local communities. For many African American Muslims, formerly part of the NOI, this meant they could send their children to public schools—and they did. As a result of the transition from the University of Islam (UofI) schools under the NOI to the CMS under Warith Deen Mohammed, many of the schools shut down, and others dwindled in their enrollment. For those educators who remained committed to the CMS, the vision evolved from a re-education of Black identity to a curriculum that would preserve the orthodox Islamic identity of their children.

Overlapping the same time period (late 1960s to late 1970s), immigrant Muslims were beginning to establish organizational support structures to practice and preserve their own faith. The Muslim Students' Association (MSA), mosques, and Islamic schools are examples of such supports. Arguably, both of the latter (mosques and schools) evolved out of the networks established at university campuses across the country through MSAs. The ideological underpinnings of the MSA provide insight into the early aims and objectives for Islamic schools as well.

The aim of this chapter is not only to trace the re-envisioning of the CMS and the growth of immigrant established schools but more importantly to trace how these two communities collaborated. Collaborations most notably through the Council of Islamic Schools in North America (CISNA) describe the inevitable differences in objectives, histories, and ideologies that shape the growth of Islamic schools and how Islamic schools are catalytic sites for intercultural and interracial community development.

From Black Religion to Post-Colonial Religion

Through the oral histories of my participants, three findings inform the analysis and structure of this chapter. Firstly, Warith Deen Mohammed's shift from protest to integration had a direct effect on the urgency and level of sacrifice believers were willing to commit to the development of CMS. For many African American Muslims who were accustomed to the importance of addressing racial inequality under Elijah Muhammad, teaching and learning an Islamic identity that was largely defined by religious observance over social injustice was deemed overly apologetic.

Secondly, similar sentiments of preserving an Islamic identity were taken up by immigrant Muslims but for different reasons. For African American Muslims formerly a part of the NOI, schools were outlets to learn (some would say "re-learn") Islam. For the immigrant Muslims who came from countries where Islam had already been passed on generationally, Islamic schools served to protect and preserve faith in their children growing up in secular foreign lands. The form that Islamic schools would initially take, however, was influenced by the experience of the post-colonial period that most immigrants endured. Early Islamic schools by and large grafted Islamic teachings as separate subjects onto an existing public school curriculum similar to convent schools in colonized countries back home.

Thirdly, when the two communities, indigenous and immigrant, began to formally collaborate to enhance the quality of Islamic schools, their potential was hindered by two points of contention: 1) authority over the Islamic tradition and 2) issues of difference in relation to race and class.

With the influx of Sunni Muslims through immigration post-1965, the landscape of Islam in America shifted from what Sherman Jackson (2005) calls Black Religion to post-colonial religion. In the previous chapter I employed the concept of Black Religion to explain how the NOI was an indigenous, distinctly American phenomenon that appropriated Islam to empower a segment of the African American population. Embedded within Black Religion was a commitment to both resistance and liberation on the basis of anti-Black racism. But Black Religion likely never intended on "coming over" to Islam proper until Warith Deen

Mohammed assumed leadership of the NOI. At this juncture of transition, his new direction toward universal Islam inherently meant forfeiting both Black Religion and its driving pledge to protest, and, in so doing, initially succumbing to the whims of a new religious force in America, namely post-colonial religion.

As much as immigrant Muslims presumed to bring a pure and unadulterated form of Islam to America, Jackson (2005) argues that immigrants were no less informed by the historical and contextual influences that amalgamated Islamic, Third World, and Western ideas and values as much as Black Religion was informed by racial segregation. Distinct from the experience of the NOI and the leadership of Warith Deen Mohammed, post-colonial religion was equally influenced by both Whiteness and Western-ness.

The aims of post-colonial religion are twofold and yet interconnected in a somewhat contradictory way. The first response is a reactionary aspiration for redemption and the second an attempt to justify integration. Jackson (2005) describes the two responses as:

> [T]hat inner voice that incessantly highlights the disparity between a fallen present and a powerful and glorious past. Post Colonial religion seeks first and foremost to reverse the sociocultural and psychological influences of the West, either by seizing political power as a means of redirecting society or through an ideological rejection of all perceived influences of the West. Where these options are deemed undesirable or unattainable, the influence of the West is essentially overcome by denying the alien provenance of would-be Western influences, affirming in the process the complete compatibility between Islam and the dominant culture in the West.
>
> (Jackson 2005, 77–8)

The first response is an ideological rejection which in many ways has been articulated in revivalist discourses across the Muslim world, most emphatically in the 1950s and 1960s.[1] Seeking to redeem the cultural and intellectual prowess that Islamic civilizations once held centuries back, Jackson (2005) argues that immigrants introduced the "West" as the new counter-category. Not entirely opposed to the privileges that "Whiteness" affords, immigrant Muslims reframed the agenda for American Islam away from issues of racial discrimination and toward the global ideology of secularism that was institutionalized by colonialism in the Muslim world.

The second response of affirming complete compatibility between Islam and the West is, arguably, the immigrant Muslim justification for the privileges they gained through post-colonialism. Through the experience of colonization, "educated classes in the Muslim world evolved into some of the biggest defenders of the dominant culture in the West and the harshest critics of those aspects of Islam deemed offensive by that culture" (Jackson 2005, 79). The influence of post-colonial education (learning English and Western norms for example) gave many early immigrants, most of whom belonged to educated classes back home, a sense of superiority and relative ease in integration. However, both the access to Western education that post-colonialism awarded to some immigrant Muslims and, for some, their ability to articulate an ideological rejection of Western-ness distanced them from Black American Muslims.

The shift from the driving force of Black Religion to post-colonial religion removed the voice of authority that Black Americans once held and stunted the potential collaboration between the indigenous and immigrant American Muslim communities. The assumption that the history of the Muslim world was more important not only silenced the histories of African American Islam but concentrated the American Muslim agenda solely on "reversing the losses inflicted *upon the Muslim world* . . . under the influence of Post Colonial Religion . . ." (Jackson 2005, 78; his emphasis). The social and political agenda of Black Religion that sought to address inner city issues of police brutality, joblessness, urban violence, single parentage, and the drug-prison complex were also replaced with a new agenda based on the plight of the *ummah* in Palestine, Kashmir, and Afghanistan (Jackson 2005, 73). The shift inherently demarcated issues that affected indigenous Muslims as less important, but also established immigrant Islam as the sole voice of authority of not only Islamic tradition but Islam in America.

In the realm of Islamic schooling, the findings of this chapter reinforce that the historical influences of post-colonial religion deeply inform the aims of education for both the indigenous and immigrant communities. In order to counter the secular influence of the West, immigrant established Islamic schools sought to preserve and protect religious and cultural identities without forfeiting the Western cultural nuances adopted through generations of colonial education. For immigrant established Islamic schools, this meant adopting and maintaining conventional educational practices common in Western education. The shift toward preservation, however, left schools under Warith Deen Mohammed's leadership neither here nor there. Stuck between preserving a newly adopted identity and attempting to prove their own credibility to a community who had already assumed it in many ways stunted the early potential for Islamic schools in America.

Pioneering Voices of Islamic School Growth

In this chapter, many of my research participants who speak to the experiences of the transition to CMS are among those mentioned in the previous chapter on the UofI schools. Zakiyyah Muhammad, Qadir Abdus Sabur, and Bilal Ajieb are all African American Muslims who initially came to Islam through Elijah Muhammad and transitioned along with Warith Deen Mohammed. Their experiences and narratives are especially important because all three of them have collaborated at a national level with immigrant Muslims on the enhancement of Islamic schools in America. Each of them has also administered immigrant established Islamic schools at some point in their professional career, or, in the case of Qadir Abdus Sabur, initiated a joint venture between the indigenous and immigrant communities in Richmond, Virginia to establish a school. Having participants that were able to speak to both the indigenous and immigrant experience therefore deepened the narrative.

As honored as I am to have met and/or spoken to the individuals mentioned earlier, I am equally indebted to those who have worked tirelessly to establish Islamic schools from within the immigrant community as well. Meeting and speaking with each of them has revealed a unique story.

The snowball of meeting participants began in 2006 when I had begun to map out my study. I presented a paper at the Islamic Education in America Conference held at Georgetown University in April 2006. There, for the first time, I met Dawud Tauhidi, who came to me after my presentation and discussed the interconnectedness of our work. I then learned about his Tarbiyah Project, one of a handful of unique curriculum frameworks for Islamic schools, and his initiation of Crescent Academy, an Islamic school in Canton, Michigan since 1985, as well as his involvement with the Council of Islamic Schools in North America (CISNA) since the 1980s. Dawud is unique because as a White convert to Islam, he challenges my dichotomy of indigenous and immigrant Muslims and yet is able to speak to both through his involvement. Dawud is also among the few Muslim educators who pursued doctoral studies specifically in the area of an Islamic philosophy of education. My interview with Dawud in the winter of 2008 provided an opportunity to speak about philosophical issues in relation to curriculum development as well as sit in on a number of elementary classes and watch the curriculum in action.

A week after the *Islamic Education in America* conference in Washington, D.C., I presented a paper at the 7th Annual ISNA Education Forum in Chicago. Here my research began to evolve as I met a number of others that are widely held to be pioneers of Islamic education in North America. Most notably amongst these people are Sheikh Abdalla Idris Ali, who established the first Islamic school in Canada, the present-day ISNA school in Mississauga, Ontario. He also served as the chair of CISNA for a period of time and as the president of the Islamic Society of North America (ISNA), the largest national Muslim organization in North America. As a youth growing up in Toronto, I recall listening to

Sheikh Abdalla Idris give Friday sermons and lectures at fundraising dinners in the 1980s, but I never had the chance to formally meet him. I formally met him for the first time at the ISNA Education Forum in 2006, and then early in 2008 when I was ready to gather my data, he invited me to Kansas City, where he and his family reside, to spend a week with him, interview him, and scavenge through his personal archives on Islamic education. With the utmost hospitality, as is custom for the Sudanese, I learned from the daily routine, etiquette, and personal generosity and sacrifice of Sheikh Abdalla that is indicative of an Islamic education. Although much of the data I gathered is well beyond the scope of this research, through Sheikh Abdalla, I was able to gain a comparative view into the Canadian and American experience of establishing Islamic schools that reaches back to the 1970s and extends to today.

Presenting at the ISNA Education Forum numerous times since 2006, I have been able to meet a number of other Islamic school pioneers as well. Dr. Seema Imam, who formerly served as the principal of one of the earliest Islamic schools in the United States, challenges my strict dichotomy of indigenous/immigrant as a White convert to Islam but principal of an Islamic school that caters largely to immigrant students. Dr. Tasneema Ghazi is another pioneer who immigrated from India in the 1960s to pursue higher education and, along with her husband, developed IQRA, the first formal Islamic school curriculum initiative. And lastly, Salahuddin Abdul Kareem is among my most unique voices because he speaks of the experience of African American Muslims in the United States who came directly into orthodox Islam and not through the Nation of Islam. His experience, similar to Seema Imam's, complicates the narrative of Islamic school growth.

In the following section, I will continue the historical narrative from the mid-1970s, where I left off in the previous chapter on the Clara Muhammad schools. The focus will, however, shift to how Imam Warith Deen altered the schools through his own vision of Islamic education in America over the following decade. The chapter will then spiral back to the mid-1960s in order to introduce the arrival of immigrant Muslims. The establishment of the Muslim Students' Association (MSA) on university campuses during that period served as a catalyst for the growth of weekend Islamic schools initially and, later, the birth of the first full-time schools within immigrant circles in the late 1970s. Into the 1980s, once both communities had established Islamic schools in major urban cities, a push for collaboration takes shape. I close this chapter with the rise and decline to dormancy of CISNA. The last section explores the ideological tensions that have stifled the potential collaboration between the indigenous and immigrant communities with respect to Islamic schools while at the same time new networks of hope have blossomed to achieve a common vision.

The Indigenous Experience

Making the Transition

In his string of name and label changes when transitioning from the NOI to a community under mainstream Islamic teachings, changing the name of the schools was equally necessary. Rafiq Iddin told me that Imam Warith Deen was a man about truth and reality and quite simply, the name University of Islam (UofI) was misleading. So along with other changes, the schools too had to be renamed.

Renaming the UofI schools after his mother, Sister Clara Muhammad, was by no means arbitrary. After decades of reverence for his father, Imam Warith Deen consciously renamed the community's consortium of schools after his mother, celebrated as the first educator of the NOI (Marsh 1996, 168). The oft-narrated story about her recalls the time when the authorities came to her door after they became aware that she had pulled her children out of public school and was home schooling them. To the demands of the authorities, she vociferously responded, "I'll be deader than a doorknob before I send my children to your school." Speaking out against the authorities in Michigan in the 1930s, a time when it remained illegal for children to be home schooled, illustrated the level of conviction that the NOI held for separate schools. In addition, at the time that she opted to pull her children out of public schools, she was solely running the household while the Honorable Elijah Muhammad served a jail term. Her insistence on educating her children about their heritage and their potential was largely her own.[2] As Safiyyah Shahid told me, Clara Muhammad "stood up, she stood up for education, Islamic education and because of her stand, her dignified way of carrying herself, and how she not only taught her children but also the children of others, admiration for her and her courage, moved the Imam to name the schools after her instead of himself." As much as the name change was meant to represent both a reality and the strength of Clara Muhammad, it also represented a change in founding principles. Along the shift toward universal Islam and the belief of racial equality in particular, the CMS were now open to students of all races and cultures, emphasized compatibility between an Islamic and American identity, and by virtue of both of these, principles of universal Islam as interpreted by Imam Warith Deen himself.

Vision of Imam Warith Deen Mohammed

The educational vision of Imam Warith Deen aimed to achieve two things: firstly, to establish the primacy of the Qur'an, and secondly, to maintain the work ethic that defined the NOI. The first major departure in the vision of Imam Warith Deen's educational philosophy and even for his vision for community development was the reinstatement of the Qur'an as the source for guidance and example. Turning directly to the Qur'an defined the re-education for the entire community, who, under the leadership of the Hon. Elijah Muhammad, were by and large not encouraged to read its wisdom nor grapple with the relevance of its teachings. For Imam Warith Deen, the Qur'an served as the exemplar par excellence, and every aspect of daily life is aligned with the teachings of the Qur'an. For the CMS and teachers, this meant re-envisioning curriculum, pedagogy, and administration. The transition did not come easy for all believers, though. Turning to the Qur'an and the Prophetic tradition as sole sources of guidance also meant that Imam Warith Deen officially replaced his father's authority and by virtue his own role as the primary source of guidance.

In many ways, Imam Warith Deen was seamless in aligning the teachings of the NOI with Qur'anic principles. This meant gradually altering the beliefs of an entire community. It was not as drastic as an overnight transformation per se, but more so an extension and elaboration on the teachings of the NOI. The plight of Black American Muslims remained consistent but could now be understood as part of the larger framework of marginalized peoples worldwide.

Shifting to the teachings of the Qur'an with regards to prayer, fasting, and the other foundational beliefs of mainstream Islam were similarly a gradual transition of alignment. Aligning with universal principles of brotherhood and innate goodness of all mankind was not a far stretch for some believers. Given that both Malcolm X and Warith Deen Mohammed had questioned and been reprimanded for challenging the teachings of the NOI in the 1960s, it was not uncommon for new converts to the NOI to have had access to both perspectives. For educators like Qadir Abdus Sabur and Abdul Alim Shabazz, the shift in leadership did not affect their teaching approach from the UofI to the CMS largely because they had already engaged with the Qur'an while under the NOI, as I alluded to earlier. It was common knowledge under the NOI that Hon. Elijah Muhammad did not encourage accessing the Qur'an. But many believers, who came into the NOI in its final years, came in with an open curiosity. When asked about how his own teaching shifted between the UofI schools to the CMS, Qadir Abdus Sabur said:

> My teaching really didn't change. Because when I became a Muslim in 1971, I got in touch with the Qur'an right then. I got in touch with a brother who [quoted a verse from the Qur'an that says] *'you know when you read the Qur'an you see people in it'* so even though we weren't encouraged to read the Qur'an in the NOI—I did—I read it every day. I read it in great detail. My classes didn't really change that much. So, when I was teaching math and science I was using examples from the Qur'an and some people had difficulties with it 'cause I was like a salmon swimming upstream.

Within a few years and by the time Imam Warith Deen became leader of the community in 1975, Qadir Abdus Sabur was not alone in swimming upstream.

For the majority of educators who had not read the Qur'an, however, Imam Warith Deen's shift toward the orthodox teachings of Islam was difficult to grasp initially. The transition meant a third element to an already complex identity for believers. Pushed and pulled between the multiple identities of being American, of African heritage, and Muslim attached them to national, indigenous, and global communities that weave together cultural, racial, and religious affiliations (Nuruddin 1998). In the words of Safiyyah Shahid,

> [I]t is a challenge for us to really try to reshape and reinvent and really *invent* and create our own perspective based on Qur'anic knowledge so it is not easy . . . everybody doesn't have the vision, and really it's up to the leader to forge that path—and we're doing that every day. We are examining our practices and develop the criteria of what an Islamic school should look like. And it changes over time, you know as our understandings develop so I can't say that our school is there 100%.

In trying to forge this new path and define Islamic education in a way that speaks to the experiences and needs of the African American Muslim community, Imam Warith Deen still maintained particular sentiments related to work ethics espoused by his father and shed others to raise the academic standards of the schools.

With the shift toward traditional Islamic concepts, language, and ethos, Imam Warith Deen urged the community's educators to revive these schools with a freshness and energy that would strive for excellence in every facet. Rafiq Iddin reflected, "He [Imam Warith Deen] told us that our schools needed to be the best in the country and that we needed to rally around the schools and raise the quality of them." Keeping with the values of the White protestant ethic as espoused by his father, the CMS were to mirror elite private American schools. As early as 1976, a reevaluation process of the schools was underway. Schools were to move from masjid buildings and into school buildings that were conducive for learning equipped with gymnasiums, libraries, and labs. Teachers were also reevaluated and a more rigorous attempt was made to hire qualified, state certified teachers.

In this move toward the formal institutionalization of their schools, however, the concern over finances (as expected) needed to be addressed. The community could no longer be insular and expect that funds would be raised from within the community only if the schools were to compete at a national level. Nor was Imam Warith Deen's aim to keep the community separated from fellow Americans. It was high time to shift toward inter-reliance, dialogue, and service. Rafiq Iddin told me that for the schools, this meant that administrators and directors had more opportunities to learn from and access educational trends, research, subsidies, and resources:

> Once he [Imam Warith Deen] came into office, a lot of the things that were available to private schools he allowed us to seek—we were to go into society and whatever we were entitled to as citizens he encouraged us to get our fair share of things—so we were able to get more resources for our schools and students—apply for scholarships, funding, transportation, he allowed us to get more support for our schools.

Collaborating with and accessing services, expertise, and funds from non-NOI sources, including those from ethnically diverse organizations, was a major departure from the principles of the Hon. Elijah Muhammad. Foundational to Imam Warith Deen's view was an insistence on patriotism and recognition of citizen responsibilities toward American people as a whole. He emphasized that the plight of African Americans must continue for prosperity but must be sought under the Constitution of the United States and the rights granted by it (Hasan 1998, 20). To augment his push toward integration and universality, on July 4, 1979, "New World Patriotism Day" was initiated by Imam Warith Deen with a parade and public address in Chicago's Grant Park. The commemorative day symbolized Imam Warith Deen's commitment to ingraining a sense of Muslim-American dignity. It represented a major shift from the teachings of his father and the new direction of the American Muslim Mission (AMM). He instructed believers to be Muslims first but to equally recognize their responsibilities as civil society actors in American society. They should be politically active, economically contributive, and socially integrated. He encouraged them to no longer envision themselves as an independent community in America but rather an interdependent community with America. This drastically altered the curriculum of schools as well. Clara Muhammad schools were now able to access public grants and services available to independent schools. They began interacting through dialogue and community service with their local communities, and a sense of civic responsibility slowly began to develop amongst them as a result.

Imam Warith Deen continued to exhibit his commitment to the growth of the schools by attending fundraising dinners across the country to inspire his community to support the schools. In his push to build community partnerships and collaborations, benefit dinners under his new vision often also honored the sacrifices of people outside his community. The likes of Rev. Jesse Jackson, Jean Hutson, and Thomas Moore, for example, were honored at the benefit dinner to kick off the opening of Harlem's Clara Muhammad school in 1979.[3] Such an attempt at building bridges across racial and religious lines defined Imam Warith Deen's openness and sincere willingness to combine the work of his community with the struggle of all American people.

The new direction of community partnerships, reliance on public resources and support, and the onus of active civic engagement shaped the vision of the CMS away from an emphasis on race to one of responsibility. By the late 1970s, the CMS had already begun to take shape along Imam Warith Deen's new vision. Some schools, like Pittsburgh's CMS, for example, made a relatively smooth transition from its UofI roots. Established in 1972 under the NOI and renamed and re-envisioned in 1975, the school's philosophy was clear as to what was going to stay and what had to go. Shedding its reputation as the Black Nationalist Muslim religion of America, the education director of the Pittsburgh CMS said soon after the transition that "As far as we're concerned racism is a dead dog. It doesn't even matter. We're taking a step into the universal." What remained within the framework of the universal teachings of Islam was an emphasis on self-help and understanding the Black Muslim experience in America.[4]

A Difficult Transition

There has undoubtedly been a decline in the CMS over the years and especially since the transition. The exact percentage of the decline has been difficult to determine because some schools reverted back to the UofI schools under the leadership of Louis Farrakhan when he revived the Nation in 1977. Other schools were shut down by Imam Warith Deen himself at the time of the transition for the sake of economic viability and strategic localized control.[5] And still others simply began to wane over the years as the community of Imam Mohammed re-envisioned itself. When I spoke with Rafiq Iddin, who served in different capacities at the CMS in Philadelphia, which was shut down for many years and is currently being revived, he said that each school struggled in its own way. Some schools had to reduce the number of grades they offered, while others shut down completely, mainly because of the lack of funds. Catering largely to inner city families, paying for an education required major sacrifices both from the parents and the teachers. Teachers would often work for less than half of what they would get paid teaching in a public school, and parents would pay whatever they could, which never adequately covered the expenses of running a school. Financial viability continued to be a struggle, and for many believers, the motivation that once drove them lost its urgency. When I asked Rafiq Iddin about the urgency for their own schools, he said, "Yeah, it's not there." And then he explained:

> Educators sacrificed their careers for the Nation because of the firm belief that there was no other option. Parents sacrificed their lifestyles

to keep their children out of public schools. But times changed and along with it the commitment did for some as well.

When we were under the Hon Elijah Muhammad we were at war with America. . . . Then when Imam Warith Deen Mohammed came in he said we are not at war anymore and we need to use our citizenship—there is no excuse for us—our religion is universal—this was his approach—he transformed our thinking from militancy to becoming an integral, meaningful part of where we were at. But during that transition everybody didn't understand it that clear—some of it was lost in translation—transition.

Especially during the early days of transition, some strongly felt that Imam Warith Deen's strategy was soft, apologetic, and regressive. For his supporters, however, it was strategic and a wise shift toward universality. As criticized and celebrated as his decisions were, they still strayed far from what his father built a national community on. For the schools, as for the community, this meant a period of flux.

Zakiyyah Muhammad, who came into the NOI in the late '60s and began teaching in the UofI schools from the early '70s, saw the schools stumble during the transition. Depending on the city, she said, schools were shut down, while others remained open with little difficulty. Each individual community had a unique experience, and within communities, the transition created a rift in some and solidarity in others. The school in New York, for example, shut down for a year while the community leaders gathered themselves and attempted to make sense of a new direction in relation to the Qur'an and Sunnah. In the interim, parents who felt strongly about the importance of separate schools and keeping their children from the public schools educated their children at home. Others who were not fully convinced of the importance of separate schools used the transition as an opportunity to transition out of the UofI/CMS altogether. The transition proved difficult for many of the adult believers to grapple with. After years of ingrained conviction in the beliefs of the Hon. Elijah Muhammad, to see the Nation shift its priorities and foundational principles dislocated many believers as well. With reference to the schools, this meant that during the transition, parents who initially put their children into the public schools temporarily ended up making that decision permanent. The shift from Black Nationalism to Qur'an and Sunnah removed the anger, passion, and conviction that deflated the commitment of many. Many believers who had recently converted to the NOI and now were in the midst of a transition did not see this coming and felt Imam Warith Deen was, in the words of Bilal Ajieb, "flipping the script on them." Going from "Black to Bilalian,"[6] as discussed earlier, in an attempt to unite with the global Muslim community yet maintain distinction was too much integration all at once for some.

Zakiyyah Muhammad and Rafiq Iddin told me that as a result of making the schools optional, many believers also felt confident enough to be critical of the schools in relation to finances and quality. Believers now questioned whether the CMS could meet the educational needs of their children with such limited resources—a notion that was not heard of when the schools represented struggle and sacrifice. Given the authority to do so, parents now asserted that these schools did not look like schools in the traditional sense with bright, shiny classrooms, large gymnasiums, science labs, and the like. It suddenly became increasingly difficult to convince parents of the unique aspects of the curriculum and school ethos now that the urgency of absolute separation from the larger American communities had faded.

Although race was deemphasized and universal Islamic principles came to the fore under Imam Warith Deen's vision, he maintained his father's insistence on self-empowerment. Establishing schools had always been a means to an end within the larger framework of community building for both father and son. The essence of Imam Warith Deen's vision, therefore, remained consistent with that of his father's position of "to do for self." His primary concern carried on from his father has undoubtedly been the establishment of business investments along this principle. The vast majority of his public lectures emphasized business management, self-entrepreneurship, and encouragement to become a self-reliant community. In a recorded interview, Imam Warith Deen retold the story of his father, who led by example and started his own business by becoming a butcher, for which he had no prior experience, only an inner drive to work for himself.[7] The aspiration for self-reliance served as the catalyst for the earliest UofI schools and continues to the present day with the Clara Muhammad schools. The vision remains grounded on the same principles: "do for self" and impart an education that teaches about God, self, and other.

The other major challenge posed to the community by the transition of schools came from within. As Imam Warith Deen re-envisioned the Nation under the universal principles of Islam, he by virtue set a high learning curve for existing Imams in the community. Imams (previously known as Ministers under the NOI) held a great sense of authority that was given to them by the Hon. Elijah Muhammad. Under Imam Warith Deen, however, the transition meant that Imams now had to re-educate and realign themselves with a new vision. Dr. Zakiyyah Muhammad recollected that in this process of re-education, Imams who once held authority now were leveled with many of the lay believers in terms of their Islamic knowledge. For schools, and specifically around imparting curriculum, this meant that some teachers and principals felt they had equal if not a greater grasp on the universal principles of Islam than the Imams did, which created a power struggle from within. Having educators who were in some cases professors of education who also had a working knowledge of Arabic and Qur'anic concepts meant that the need for Imams to guide curriculum development diminished in particular schools. Replacing the hierarchical structure in relation to knowledge control that defined the NOI was disconcerting most commonly for those who held positions of power, but it was empowering for others who now had an equal stake in the community.

When Imam Warith Deen decentralized the community in 1985 and gave local Imams authority over their own communities, the process left a sense of emptiness for many. Dr. Qadir Abdus Sabur recounted that day in Cleveland, Ohio, when Imam Warith Deen met with 100 Imams nationwide to explain his rationale. Many of the Imams felt shaken, and in response, Imam Warith Deen said, "some of you think that we are disbanding our association but if you go where the Qur'an is taking you then you'll find me there." Those words have resonated with Qadir Abdus Sabur until this day. In his own words, he said, "That statement has guided me and has been responsible for why I feel so strongly about education." For Qadir Abdus Sabur, that statement redirected him to where he needed to turn for inspiration in curriculum development, toward which he and his wife aspired. Curriculum initiatives shifted from the personal teachings of the Hon. Elijah Muhammad to those of the Qur'an. Imam Warith Deen served more as an inspiration for turning toward the Qur'an in developing school curricula than for his own particular teachings. He inspired a community of educators to rethink their school missions and visions and to actively redevelop an indigenous Black American Muslim model of schooling. When he said that the "challenge for the Muslim educator is to become responsible for extracting from the Qur'an and the life of the Prophet Muhammad the natural and proper basis for looking at the world," he inspired educators like Dr. Daaiyah Saleem and others to organize an ad hoc committee to develop teaching resources through a Qur'anic worldview.

The push to master the Qur'an and integrate its wisdom in the curriculum for CMS raised questions of credibility and authenticity when immigrant Muslims became an integral part of the North American landscape. Having emigrated from countries where the language of the Qur'an and embodiment of the tenets of the Islamic tradition was part and parcel of cultural identity, recent immigrants were by and large uneasy with the historical trajectory by which the community of Imam Warith Deen came to orthodox Islam. Many immigrants felt that Imam Warith Deen had not gone far enough in transforming his community and shedding the teachings of his father. To gain a deeper sense of this perspective, I will now spiral back to the 1960s and attempt to trace the growth of the immigrant Muslim community in North America.

The Immigrant Experience

Coming to North America

Unlike the experience of African American Muslims in the United States, whose history can be traced back to the earliest European settlement, the

Middle East and South Asian Muslim presence in Canada and the United States is a more recent phenomenon. It was not until the policy of immigration was widened primarily for higher education in the 1960s and '70s that the presence of immigrant Muslims was felt. Although there were pockets of Muslim communities who had migrated as early as the mid-19th century to rural parts of the Canadian prairies[8] or served as dockworkers in Detroit,[9] I have not come across evidence that aspirations of establishing faith-based schools had crossed the minds of these early immigrants. As a result, I begin the narrative of Islamic schools established by immigrant Muslims both in Canada and the United States in the 1960s and '70s.

By the 1960s, North America began to attract foreign nationals from around the world to come and study in North American universities. Many of these students who initially came on student visas opted to make North America their home after graduation. The vast majority of these immigrants came from the educated elite of their home country or were at least privileged enough that they could gather enough money to find a way to North America. All the participants that I interviewed who immigrated to both Canada and the United States confirm this characterization. M.D. Khalid, early administrator of Canada's first Islamic school, recalls that "it all really started when Muslim immigrants began coming for graduate studies." Most settled into the larger urban cities and often at very prestigious educational institutions. Tasneema Ghazi and her husband, Abidullah Ghazi, founders of the first immigrant Muslim Islamic school curriculum initiative, came to the Boston area in 1967, for example. Abidullah completed his master's at the London School of Economics and then pursued a doctorate at Harvard University on a full scholarship, while Tasneema taught in the Boston public school system initially and later pursued a doctorate herself. Similarly, M.D. Khalid first immigrated to Vancouver, Canada, to complete his master's in economics in 1970 before relocating to Toronto in 1975. And it was in 1977 that M.D. Khalid met Sheikh Abdalla Idris, founder of the first Islamic school in Canada, who had recently emigrated from Sudan to pursue a doctorate in political science at the University of Toronto. The level of education of this wave of Muslim immigrants had a major impact on the socio-political presence of Muslims in North America. Many found secure employment in government, academia, and other influential posts.

Haddad (2002) distinguishes between the Muslim immigrants who came to North America before the 1960s and those who came after. The Muslims who came before, she insists, were more willing to adapt to the new culture and were content with keeping their own faith practice within the confines of their homes and small mosques. The immigrants who came after the 1960s, however, carried a very different attitude and intellectual capital than their predecessors. Haddad (2002) argues,

The more recent immigrants are neither poor nor uneducated; on the contrary, they represent the best-educated elite of the Muslim world who see themselves as helping develop America's leadership in medicine, technology, and education. They have been influenced by a different socialization process, and while they appreciate, enjoy, and have helped create America's technology, they want no part in what they see as its concomitant social and spiritual problems. Confident that Islam has a solution to America's ills, they have no patience for the kind of accommodation that they see as compromising the true Islamic way.

(22)

Although the intent for many immigrants was to eventually return back home and assist in the structural redevelopment of their own countries, it soon became evident to many who were politically active of the potential for change that America, in particular, offered. Tasneema Ghazi recalls that after she and her husband both earned their doctorates, they wanted to return to Pakistan and help improve the education system there. But they realized that the task of teaching Islam was equally important, if not more urgent, in North America, where there were fewer qualified and committed individuals to do religious work.

Early immigrants sought to achieve two things: establish a distinct American Muslim presence in North America and to actively support political tensions back home that were often intertwined with U.S. foreign policy. McCloud (2006) asserts that those who immigrated in the 1960s and earlier had a different integration experience from those who came during the 1970s and later. Early immigrants were few and far between, so their plight was defined by the plight of the indigenous Muslims already in North America. For the second, more robust wave of Muslim immigrants, the experience of migrating was one of establishing cultural enclaves of their own while remaining concerned about the plight of their families back home.

The goals for these waves of immigrant Muslims were very different from the indigenous African American Muslim experience. As ethnically and linguistically diverse as they were, they were not affected by, and could not relate to, the racial discrimination and subjugation that had been and continues to be experienced by their African American Muslim brethren. Nor could this wave of immigrants relate to the issues of class that has been imposed on African Americans. For the South Asian and Arab Muslim immigrants, their socioeconomic and educational privileges awarded them the ability to network, mobilize, and establish Muslim organizations far more effectively. The challenge for immigrant Muslims was relatively less affected by issues of race or class but rather affected by the extent to which religious and cultural traditions ought to be preserved.

Esposito (2000) asks the vital question to Muslim immigrants who have come to America: "will they remain Muslims *in* America or become

American Muslims?" (3). This crisis of identity has characterized Muslim immigrants caught between the religious and cultural tradition from back home and the new cultures of North America. Tasneema Ghazi recalls from her earliest days in Boston that one would find Muslims changing their names to fit in. One would come across Muslims who shed their given names for the sake of ease in integration.

Haddad (2002) argues that the process of colonization and neo-colonization has shaped the way in which Muslim immigrants have defined their identities in North America. She says that many Muslim immigrants increasingly "see their marginalized situation as deliberate and specific, the product of longstanding tendencies in American society to fear and distrust Islam." For the immigrant Muslim, the task of shaping an American Muslim identity has been twofold: how to nurture the faith and values of their forefathers while integrating socially and economically with the dominant structures of North American society as equal players.

To ensure that new immigrants would not lose attachment to their religious identity and values, some young Muslim intellectuals began to organize themselves both socially and politically into networks called the Muslim Students' Association (MSA). The MSA began to spread to individual university campuses across the United States and Canada and served students on campus with congregational prayers, study circles, and political activism around issues that were affecting the Muslim world. The struggle in Afghanistan against the Russians in the late 1970s, the Iranian Revolution in 1979, and the Iran-Iraq war from 1980–88 all served as major political fronts that focused the MSA's energies and united Muslim immigrants. The MSA from its inception served as a vehicle to activate and develop a sense of cultural solidarity among diasporic immigrants. But its aspiration was distinctly selective in relation to how it would engage civically. Mattson (2003) argues the MSA advocated a paradigm of selective engagement where civil rights and socioeconomic privileges were largely used to address religious and cultural community concerns over national civic issues. The following section will further explain how the paradigm of selective engagement shaped Muslim organizational structures like the MSA.

I feel the history of the MSA is vital for this narrative on Islamic schools for two reasons: firstly, those who espoused the need for Islamic schools were founding members of the MSA, and secondly, because the MSA spanned both Canada and the United States, its work explains why I seemingly conflate the Canadian and American immigrant experiences in establishing Islamic schools.

Muslim Student's Association: Mobilizing and Organizing on Campus

By the testament of my participants reflecting on 40 years of Islamic work in North America, there was agreement that the work of the MSA was pioneering in establishing an American Muslim identity. These young and educated Muslim immigrants like Ahmed Sakr and Ahmed Totonji were among the first to encourage American Muslims to adopt an American ideal of citizenship without forfeiting concerns over the plight of the global Muslim community.

Preceding the establishment of the Muslim Students' Association in 1963 was the Federation of Islamic Associations (FIA), established in 1952 as the International Muslim Society, and then renamed a year later. The FIA began in Cedar Rapids, Iowa, with a core group of Muslims whose families had immigrated in the early 20th century. By the 1950s, these Muslims were already second-generation immigrants and had largely assimilated into American society. Although still intent on building community, some activities of the FIA, such as mixed social dances, were deemed to be un-Islamic by those who established the MSA a decade later. The FIAs' focus on education conferences was welcomed by the MSA, but the ideological rift on Islamic practices kept the two national organizations divided until the FIA eventually disbanded.

Many of the early MSA executives were active in the work of Islamic organizations even before the MSA. Ahmed Totonji, for example, who came to America through a stint in the UK, was instrumental in establishing the Muslim Students Society in England and Ireland, the United Muslim Student Organization of Europe (UMSO), and the Federation of Students Islamic Societies of the UK all in the early 1960s. In January 1963, Ahmed Sakr, Ahmed Totonji, Fazil Abadi, and Faisal Muqawwi, among others, all recent immigrants and graduate students, gathered at the University of Illinois at Urbana Champaign to formally establish the Muslim Student's Association. The committee developed a working constitution and a set a date for the first national convention to be held on Labor Day weekend in September 1963. The mission of the MSA was to establish chapters on university campuses across the country to teach, practice, and propagate Islam.

The main objective of the MSA was to preserve religious identity in America. The aim was to unite disparate peoples who had emigrated from various parts of the Muslim world under the banner of Islam. Preservation of identity meant specifically that the "MSA was formed out of necessity—the necessity to organize the Jum'ah [Friday] prayers when mosques were rare or non-existent, for *zabiha* [halal] food when all they could eat were vegetables, and for a way to educate others about Islam" (Ali 2003, 24). The MSA initiated numerous community outreach strategies that included a newsletter which later became *Islamic Horizons* magazine, the Eid Card Project, professional organizations such as the Association of Muslim Social Scientists (AMSS), and much more.

Most MSA participants were male bachelors, and for those who were married, their wives largely stayed at home. As early as 1969, the all-male MSA decision making body was diversified with women who actively participated in event planning and committee decisions. Had it not been for the involvement of women into the MSA, the concern for Islamic education and schooling may have taken a lot longer to become a part of MSA work.

Thinking About the Future: The Beginnings of Islamic School Initiatives

As families were established and male bachelors found wives either back home or in many cases married North American converts, the considerations of children and family needs began to take shape within MSA circles. The Muslim Women's Auxiliary Committee, which was the women's voice of the MSA, along with the MSA proper, first started with youth camps to nurture Islamic values and positive relationship building among youth. To complement the camps, the women's committee also began establishing weekend schools and children's programs at the annual conventions. By the early 1970s, they began to foresee a potential for full-time schools as children came of age in substantial numbers. Freda Shamma, an American convert and professor of education, spearheaded an education committee to map out these ideas:

> The women were the first to start planning for an Islamic school. At the time, constructing *masjids* was the main priority of the Muslim communities and the MSA. As the communities solidified, the next step was establishing Islamic centers. However, during the Muslim Women's Auxiliary Committee annual seminars, women were planning for their children's education.

In my interviews with Dr. Freda Shamma, she reminded me that it was not as simple as it sounds. Even though Islamic education was on the agenda of every year's annual MSA conference, "there was a lot of talk and not a lot of movement." There were always a consistent eight to ten people at the roundtable on education, but few were willing to follow through on directions forward. Either because of the time commitment required or not fully recognizing the urgency, or because many simply were not sure that America would be their permanent home, the ability to harness energy for community based projects was difficult.

M.D. Khalid, who settled in Toronto, and Tasneema Ghazi, who settled in Chicago, shared similar sentiments. They both recalled that initially most immigrant Muslims came to Canada and the United States to gain a North American university education, which they had every intent on taking back home. Dr. Tasneema vividly recollected her days living on campus at Harvard while her husband studied. She would visit the Center for Study of World Religions and discuss the education of her children with Christian and Jewish scholars there. Speaking of 1965–66, she recalls that "[a]t Harvard there was a movement about what to do with our children around Islamic education." The other Muslim mothers living on campus would try to teach their children a little Qur'an and Arabic at home. So taking the advice of her husband's colleagues, Tasneema and Abidullah decided to systematize a formal Islamic education program for children through a Sunday school model in 1968.

Simply having a Sunday school in major cities where Muslim immigrants resided was not the only goal. For the Ghazis, what was important was a curriculum. With the assistance of Jewish and Christian scholars at Harvard, the Ghazis began the first curriculum development project to serve Islamic schooling. The need for curricula in that early period was urgent. Tasneema recalls that Sunday schools in the late 1960s and early 1970s were starting up very fast. The Ghazis housed their first Sunday school on campus at Harvard, which served their own children and those of others studying and living in the Boston area.

Tasneema recognized that their Sunday school initiative in Boston may not have been the only one or necessarily the first. As early as 1958, a young Muslim couple, Marghoob and Iffat Qureshi of northern California, had also started an annual week-long youth camp to bring together Muslim families and teach Islamic values. Similarly, Dr. Osman Ahmed, who voluntarily managed the MSA headquarters in the late 1960s along with his wife, are credited with starting the MSA's first weekend school in the mid-1960s in Gary, Indiana (*Islamic Horizons Magazine* 2003, 44–9). The Muslim Community Center (MCC) in Chicago, among the eldest mosques in the country, had also established a Sunday school in and around the same time. Dr. Seema Imam, a White Muslim convert and professor of education from the Chicago area, recalls her early experience teaching in immigrant established weekend Islamic schools since the 1970s. She described weekend and summer schools in the mid-1970s as very busy and with Muslim children ranging from elementary ages to high school students. Married to an immigrant Muslim herself and having started a family, Seema recognized the urgency of such education programs but also saw it as a way for her to gain more knowledge about Islam. She recollected, "I was impressed that they [referring to the immigrant Muslim community] allowed me to teach and was very excited to learn about Islam and to be a Muslim and kids were definitely in need."

During the same time in the mid-1970s, Muslim immigrants in major urban cities in Canada were also beginning to recognize the need for Islamic educational programs for their children. Sheikh Abdalla Idris, who emigrated from Sudan to pursue a doctorate at the University of Toronto, remembers the early days at Toronto's first mosque, Jame Mosque. It was in the late 1970s when the Imam of Jame Mosque approached Abdalla Idris and asked him to get involved with their existing evening and weekend school in the mosque. The evening and weekend classes at the time were held in the basement of the mosque. Lighting was minimal, resources were limited, and space was cluttered, but the demand for teaching children of newly arrived immigrants the Qur'an and religious observances was growing rapidly. Abdalla Idris's commitment to education and passion for teaching quickly became apparent to the mosque's board of directors, so they made him the Educational Director.

In his new role, Abdalla Idris astutely used the rights awarded to new immigrants in Canada under the multiculturalism policy[10] to expand Islamic educational programs in Toronto. The Ministry of Education at the time would fund educational programs that taught multicultural languages under the Heritage Language Program.[11] To take advantage of the language program, Abdalla Idris combined the teaching of Arabic through the Heritage Language Program grant along with an Islamic studies portion to develop a summer school program for Muslim children. The Ministry would pay for teachers, materials, and building rentals to cover two and a half hours of Arabic instruction that would be open to all but mainly attended by Muslim children, and Jame Mosque would then rent out the same building for the rest of the afternoon to provide two and a half hours of Islamic studies instruction, which they would oversee. The summer school program took the weekend and evening classes to a much higher level of professionalism and exposure. Within a year, Abdalla Idris was overseeing three sites for these programs in the east, west, and central areas of Toronto. What soon became an annual summer program in Toronto also set the stage for a full-time Islamic school. Through the summer programs, Abdalla Idris had developed a network of interested parents, teachers, and superintendents, not to mention a long waiting list of students.

For many early Muslims, both in the United States and in Canada, it was from this early experience with weekend schools and summer programs that the idea of a full-time Islamic school evolved. From the experience of Seema Imam in Chicago and Abdalla Idris in Toronto, establishing full-time schools seemed like the next logical step forward. Seema recalled the impact those years of teaching at Chicago weekend Islamic school programs had on her with respect to the potential for growth:

> It's amazing that from that experience I began to say, okay I have an undergraduate degree in teaching and now I have a child and I want good Islamic education. And I started talking about lesson plans and I started talking about Islamic schools, thinking about why the Catholic schools were full-time [and] why are we just doing weekend schools?

For most early pioneers of Islamic schooling, Seema's rationale seemed obvious. If we have successful weekend school programs and a growing demand, why not develop day schools similar to those of other faiths, they asked. It was a question that led to the inevitable.

First Full-Time Islamic Schools in Canada

Within the MSA's community planning initiatives was a committee set up to focus on the educational needs of Muslim children. The educational committee was comprised of some of the MSA's key pioneers: Dr. Muhammad Ismail, Dr. Talat Sultan, Dr. Mahmoud Rashdan, Dr. Sha'ban Ismail, and Dr. Nimat Barzangi, all professors of education. By the mid-1970s, the education committee envisioned expanding weekend and evening Islamic education programs into full-time schools. They envisioned two pilot projects: one in Toronto and the other in Chicago. The Toronto pilot project is the present-day ISNA School located in Mississauga, Ontario, which was initially directed by Sheikh Abdalla Idris; and the Chicago pilot project is the present day Universal School located in Bridgeview, Illinois, that Dr. Seema Imam administered in its early years.

Expanding to a full-time school in Toronto was greatly assisted by the successful summer school programs that were already in place. Sheikh Abdalla recalled that when Muhammad Ismail and Talat Sultan came to Toronto to propose the pilot project to him, they were very impressed by the network of educators and committed parents that had already been established to the extent that they asked him to join the education committee even as a non-educator by training. To ensure the viability of the Toronto pilot project and determine the amount of seed money that would be granted, the MSA education committee suggested conducting a survey to gauge the level of interest of Muslim parents. The survey was designed to gather data about how many parents were interested in sending their children to an Islamic school, how many teachers were willing to teach in one, and what sorts of concerns, questions, and hesitations parents had. They administered the survey on an Eid day, when the gathering of Muslims would be at its potential maximum. With 1,500 questionnaires in hand, naysayers told Sheikh Abdalla, who was also giving the Eid day sermon, that he would not get more than 200 surveys returned. From his memory, he got close to 500. But in the words of Sheikh Abdalla, "that's when we found divergent opinions about what parents wanted out of the school." Parents fell into four categories, he said. The South Asians were split within themselves as well. Some leaned toward traditional *madaris*, where the Qur'an would be memorized and Muslim legal scholars would be raised. Other South Asians feared exactly that form of traditionalism and either sent their children to Catholic schools for the discipline and presumed rigor or wanted Islamic schools to mirror elite private schools similar to "back home." Still others wanted a combination of the two—an Islamization of Knowledge model, which will be discussed further in the next chapter. And lastly, a great majority said, "let's start a school, put all the subjects we have, and see where it takes us," which is the stance that Sheikh Abdalla also agreed with. Between outright resistance and embrace were those, like Sheikh Abdalla, who opted to selectively engage. Just what that level of selective engagement would look like remained initially unclear.

Although I have found differences with respect to formal start dates, including contradictory statistics at the Ministry of Education in Toronto,[12] from Sheikh Abdalla's recollection, the school began formally in 1982 in the basement of Jame Mosque with about 50 students. He described the basement as dusty, dim, and roach infested; certainly not a conducive learning environment for young children. With continued fundraising efforts and additional seed money from ISNA (formed in 1982), the school was able to afford a proper school building by 1985. The shift was not easy, though. When he spoke about the importance of the school to raise funds at the Friday *khutba* (sermon), people would yell out in anger. He recalls:

> The community was split. At that time the Subcontinent [South Asian] Muslim community didn't want to have an Islamic school because they used to think of the *madrassa* and schools for the orphans, you know, people voiced it, we don't want this. If we have these types of schools our children will be *mullas* [conservative religious leaders] and won't be academics and so on. That was there at that time. So, we struggled with people from the inside and the outside.

The voices of resistance from within the community were those that feared Islamic schools would isolate rather than integrate their children as Muslims in Canada. Establishing separate schools was tantamount to forfeiting the very privileges that colonial schooling awarded the colonized: habits of high culture and language. Islamic schools, they feared, would reinforce the very religious and cultural practices that would highlight their differentness.

From outside the community, there was also resistance when the new building was purchased in a residential area of Mississauga, Ontario. Some residents of the area petitioned the building being used for religious schooling, claiming that the school would bring traffic and noise to the quiet residential streets. Eventually, the deal did go through for the purchase of the school building, but a week before the school was to shift from Jame Mosque to the new building, it had been broken into and vandalized. Sheikh Abdalla described how water fountains, toilets, mirrors, and windows were smashed throughout the building. The resistance came more from public neighbors than from a government level, M.D. Khalid, who was also involved with the school as a member of the parents' committee and treasurer since the early days, recalled.

Some Muslims from within the community also tried to purchase the intended school building before those lobbying for the school could. Sheikh Abdalla estimates that there were roughly 30 families that were initially committed to the idea of an Islamic school at the time. There were many more that attended out of circumstance, he said, but few that really wholeheartedly believed in the project. The others were those who either lived through some form of discrimination, their children were discriminated against, or they were indifferent and felt it was worth a try. Although there was great dedication on the part of the early teachers, the ISNA school was the first of its kind in the country, and many parents remained skeptical even after enrolling their children. Some parents, Sheikh Abdalla told me, who were keen on ensuring their children would become professional doctors, engineers, and lawyers, would remove their children at the beginning of Grade 7. It became a trend, he said. "They were concerned that their children might not have the skills and experience to do well in public high schools, so some of them pulled their children out in Grade 7 to give them a year or two to integrate into the public system before high school—to adapt. They started doubting the Islamic school." For many of Toronto's South Asian Muslim community, the mentality was still informed by their own schooling experiences in post-colonial education systems—convent schools and English-medium British schools that reduced religion to its rudiments, what Zine describes as the "colonial classroom." These classrooms are unadorned, controlled with a strict code of behavior, and limited to rote instruction (Zine 2008, 288–94). Despite teaching styles that mirrored those of colonial schools, Islamic schools in North America continued to grow among the immigrant community.

Sheikh Abdalla recalls that, in the beginning, the demand exceeded what the school could offer. With the intent of adding additional grades every year, the new ISNA school did not have the capacity to accommodate the number of parents who wanted to enroll their children. He recalled one parent who found out that the classes were filled for the year simply decided to start her own. That initiative is the present day IQRA school located in Mississauga, Ontario. Many schools during the period opened up in and around Toronto either because ISNA was unable to meet the community's growing needs or because the distance of travel for those who lived in other suburbs of Toronto was too far. Similarly, other urban cities in Canada, namely, Vancouver, Calgary, Ottawa, and Montreal, began Islamic schools as early as the mid-1980s.[13] Sheikh Abdalla would often be called to most, if not all, the new school projects around the continent (including the United States) to serve as an education consultant. Most often he would be flown in to speak to prospective parents in the community about the importance of Islamic education and to fundraise for the new school. "That's partly why I left Toronto, because I was exhausted. I used to travel every weekend across the United States and Canada to speak to communities, and I was teaching and acting as the principal of ISNA School. It was very tiring." Combined with being overworked, it was a promise of calmness and the ability to focus on national projects related to Islamic schooling that convinced Sheikh Abdalla to eventually move with his family to Kansas City.

Every school initiative has been led by the energy and vision of a handful, if not a single person. In the case of the first full-time school in Toronto, the role of Sheikh Abdalla Idris is immeasurable. Both the people I interviewed and those who declined to be interviewed did so with the insistence that I would be best served to interview Sheikh Abdalla. Indeed, prior to moving to the United States in the 1990s and since, his impact on providing direction and vision for Islamic schooling in the United States was just as important. His narrative, along with the role of MSA/ISNA in establishing the first pilot school in Toronto, ties the Canadian and American experiences together. Initially called the Islamic Community School, only to later come under the formal auspices of ISNA, the first school in Toronto, arguably, served as a successful model for immigrant established Islamic schools across Canada and the United States.

First Full-Time Islamic Schools (Immigrant Established) in the United States

Outside the MSA/ISNA pilot project initiatives, arguably, the first immigrant Islamic school was the Al-Aqsa school in Bridgeview, Illinois. Established in the mid-1970s, Al-Aqsa is an all-girls high school founded by an early Palestinian immigrant community. The fact that Al-Aqsa has, since its inception, been geared solely for Muslim girls and focused on high school aged students is very telling of the perceptions of the early Muslim immigrants and their objectives in establishing Islamic schools. Dr. Tasneema Ghazi told me that "if you were here in the 1960s, you'd understand." It was a time of great change in American society. African Americans were protesting for Civil Rights, women struggled for equality, and many emphatically disagreed with American foreign policy to the point where, in the words of Tasneema Ghazi, "souls wanted to be free." Tasneema was someone who, while at Harvard, regularly attended the meetings of the Black Panther Party and the meetings of the women's liberation groups. As a South Asian Muslim woman, this was well outside the norm. For many Muslim immigrants, these outward expressions of protest and rebellion represented chaos—a chaos they feared would destabilize family values. Freeing the souls for most new immigrants was the one aspect of American culture which they most feared. Tasneema recalls that "the dating, they couldn't reconcile, the dress [revealing clothes], the language [swearing], they couldn't reconcile. It's a shock, it's a very different thing. . . . So immigrants got very scared and schools were a way to protect their children."

From the analysis of Loukia Sarroub (2005), early Muslim immigrants were sojourners.[14] Sarroub conducted a study of Yemeni Muslim immigrants in Dearborn, Michigan, and their struggle to balance their religious, cultural, and ethnic identities as young Yemeni women with their own individual conceptions of American-ness while attending public schools. Sarroub found that children of immigrant families have the difficult task of straddling two worlds, "the literate world of school and the home world of religious and cultural values where text (Qur'an) sanctions behavior, certain language use, disposition, and cultural norms" (2005, 22). Although her work focuses on public school experiences, her research reveals the sentiments common among Arab families in relation to protecting the reputation and upbringing of their girls especially. The wave of immigrants who came after the late 1970s were generally less educated and economically stable, which Sarroub found engendered a greater skepticism of integrating into and adopting American lifestyles. In Dearborn, Michigan, where Sarroub conducted her study and where the largest Arab population outside of the Middle East resides, she found, for example, that among observant Arab Muslim families, adolescent boys could often be found working far from home. But the "girls were rarely allowed to distance themselves from the home or to be seen in public working . . . because public notice could ultimately lead to gossip and the loss of their good reputations . . ." (2005, 25). The importance of protecting young Muslim girls from Western cultural influences is a sentiment that heavily influenced the decision to establish early Islamic schools as well.

Seema Imam concurred that the earliest schools were established to protect and nurture the "pious Muslim girl" (Zine 2008, 210). Seema Imam told me that the real shift from weekend school programs to full-time Islamic schools did not take place until the mid-1980s, by which time most immigrants who came in the early wave had now decided on staying. She said that in that first decade of immigrant Islamic schooling from the mid-1970s to the mid-1980s, "the few people who decided to establish schools were establishing them to find a way to keep their kids out of mainstream culture and keep their girls out of trouble. You know, protection, because they recognized some of the issues that they were facing." Such "protection" of the pious Muslim girl is often an overemphasis of extrinsic elements of faith, such as dress and gender appropriate behavior, of which the latter is often more culturally determined than religious (Zine 2008). These are often more conservative, patriarchal, cultural interpretations of faith practice espoused by early immigrants who fear assimilation into opposing cultural practices. Such "public performance of piety," in the words of Zine (2008), is often exhibited through "maintaining specific dress codes, such as the *hijab* [headscarf] and *jilbab* [long overcoat] from the time of puberty, shying away from the use of makeup for nail polish, and avoiding all unnecessary contact with boys." (210–211).

Growing Pains of Early Schools: Lack of Planning and Direction

Most schools opened with a limited sense of direction, specifically in relation to educational philosophy, that would shape unique pedagogical practices. During the early stages of Islamic school growth, administrators were often more concerned about logistical issues over pedagogical ones. After teaching in Chicago public schools for over 15 years, Seema Imam reflected that when she first decided to shift to teaching in Islamic schools in the mid-1970s, it was shocking to see the lack of educational expertise being employed to make decisions. "[T]here was nobody talking about curriculum for the school or a governance plan or rules and regulations. There was just no discussion about that, I was like you open the school and let the kids come in. It just seemed like it hadn't been planned at all." Part of the reason for the lack of planning was that for many early immigrants, these schools still remained temporary solutions until they would take their children back home. The commitment, financial resources, and expertise that were poured into the early schools were therefore limited. When Seema accepted her first principal post at Universal School, for example, she recalls being ridiculed for attempting to uphold a sense of professionalism, "I insisted on a contract and a secretary, and they laughed at me." She asked for a five-year contract for a sense of job security, but then another member on the board asked her "you want a secretary AND a contract?" (emphasis hers).

Finding qualified Muslim teachers who were willing to sacrifice a respectable salary and standard school working conditions was also a next to impossible task in early Islamic schools. That is partly why many of those most concerned and involved with Islamic schooling in America have not been trained educators per se. Islamic schools often carried; and in many ways still do carry, the stigma of substandard education. Parents who did support the school often did so for their own particular ends. In some cases, parents felt that Islamic schools would be able to give their children Muslim values that they themselves did not have time to nurture at home. Others prized the autonomy of private schools to shape and alter both curriculum and policy to suit their requests. In many ways, such perceptions were existent in the immigrant schools more than in indigenous Islamic schools. Public schools defined the standard, and private schools defined excellence. Islamic schools were as a result a default option that few families actually supported. Among those who did support the schools there existed little background in educational standards: "You could see board members or donors making specific changes related to the needs of their children, including giving credits to their kids who hadn't done a course. And they didn't understand credits and courses" (Seema Imam). The learning curve for most immigrant parents to a foreign system of education, along with ingrained expectations of highly regimented schools back home, made the initial beginnings of Islamic schooling more complex. Parents pushed and pulled the schools in multiple directions in relation to the academic, religious, and civic aims of schools. It was, quite simply, a cacophony of voices that shaped the early Islamic school experience.

Preservation of Identity: Ideology of Early Islamic Schools

From among Muslim parents that supported early Islamic schools, there remained a divergence of rationale. Almost all of my participants at one point in our interviews attempted to give me a sense of the varying categories. Firstly, there were those parents who were weary of the public system. They had either had a negative experience of social or cultural discrimination or were taught curricular outcomes that misrepresented Islam and Muslims. These were often the obvious controversial issues that arise between faith-observant families and the public school curriculum:

1. Teaching evolutionary theory versus teaching Creationism and/or Intelligent Design;
2. Teaching sex education, the acceptability of promiscuity, and pre-marriage relationships;
3. Celebrating Christmas with carols, pageants, and ceremonies;
4. Students wanting to research religious figures and prophets;
5. Religiously based school clubs where religious worship takes place within schools albeit during lunch or after school;
6. Teaching religious perspectives in civics classes;
7. Schools that teach tolerance and inclusion of homosexual lifestyle choices;
8. Religiously motivated inspirational speeches at school events;
9. Religious books, including the Bible, Torah, and Qur'an in the school library and classroom bookshelves for reading during spare time;
10. Classroom textbooks that misconstrue religious worldviews (Greenawalt 2004, 1–3).

In the words of M.D. Khalid, who enrolled his children in Islamic school from the time they were ready to attend, "The fear is that if you throw them [our children] out [into public schools] without the proper guidance about the religion, they might completely get lost, lose their culture, their religion." He told me that "in those days," back in the 1970s and 1980s, religion was still formally part of the public school curriculum. The Lord's Prayer, celebrating Christmas, and Good Friday remained an integral part of the curriculum. He felt that weekend schools and evening religion classes could not suffice to balance the Christian influenced public school curriculum. The school ethos and values, he felt, would confuse children and hinder their ability to discern what they were taught in school in relation to the faith of their forefathers. What he and others wanted was for Islamic religious observances such as prayer, fasting, and daily etiquette to be taught along with knowledge of the Qur'an and Islamic beliefs.

Secondly, there were those parents who were especially concerned about issues of marriage, promiscuity, and the protection of their girls in particular, as discussed in the case of the Al-Aqsa School. In her interviews within the Jewish community, for example, Lois Sweet (1997) explains the extended purpose of faith-based schooling as a deterrent from inter-marriages. She found that parents want to often shield their children from inter-religious and inter-cultural marriages. One of the ways of ensuring children do not marry outside of the fold is to provide greater opportunities for interaction within their own faith and community.

Thirdly, there were those who were simply afraid of the unknown. Because many Muslims are new to the country and continue to be so through immigration, many come "here and they come with a fear: What are they going to face? They have problems of language, problems of communication, problems of culture. And then they go to a public school, they are looked at as strangers. And many times, that demoralizes the children" (Sweet 1997, 75). Part of the unknown is also what Seema Imam asserted as the "public curriculum." "The media is a public curriculum," she said, and the whole world has been taught untruths about the global Muslim community, its history, beliefs, and impact on world civilizations. Islamic schools, therefore, serve to "go against the grain" and "empower" young Muslim Americans who are fed the public curriculum every day. Global conflicts that involved Muslim populations always had a direct effect on the choice immigrant parents made with respect to schooling, Seema insisted. As a principal during the era of the First Gulf War and the Bosnian genocide, she remembers that many families who immigrated during that period came directly to Universal School, "they didn't even consider the public school." The American public perception of Muslims during times of heightened global conflict worried some Muslim parents.

There were also those who came because of family pressure or expectations that either through mixed marriages or elders insisting that the children receive an Islamic education. Salahuddin Abdul Kareem called this "spousal arrangement," where immigrant men from Iran, in his experience in Washington D.C., married White converts who knew the American school system and "had their bumps and bruises with America as well," so they could relate to the project of Islamic schooling. And then there were those who wanted to keep the tradition of their elders alive. These people often came from countries where Islam has had a long history, a national pride, and honor that future generations would never dream of disbanding openly. For them, whether they were from India or Iraq, it was about keeping the memory of Islam alive through their children. They "could recall that grandpa was a *hafiz* of Qur'an and grandma used to teach me the ethics of Islam, and now I am in America and I don't want to evaporate all those memories. I don't want to lose all that too soon. So, I am gonna give it a try" (Salahuddin Abdul Karim).

Lastly, there were those parents who wanted to send their children to private schools and found Islamic schools more economically viable in relation to well established private institutions. These parents insisted on maintaining high academic standards and determined the success of the school by its ability to produce students who would gain entrance to elite university programs: "For us, secular education is very important, but so is religious education. We don't want to be deficient in regards to secular education but at the same time we want our children to have their moral code" (M.D. Khalid) Although the number of parents who fell in the final category were fewest in number, they represent the voices that were arguably most invested in creating a vision for the future. Like many of the voices who have contributed to this narrative, Islamic schools were intended to nurture faith-centeredness while not forfeiting the highest academic ideals.

Unlike the indigenous Black American experience, where the vision for separate schools was informed by a concerted movement of protest, part of the variance of voices that existed within the immigrant Muslim community is a result of the absence of such a binding communal vision.

From Protest to Preservation: Islamic Schools a Harder Sell to Immigrants Than Indigenous Muslims

The difference in intentions between the indigenous and immigrant Muslim communities for establishing Islamic schools had great variance. Salahuddin Abdul Kareem, an African American Muslim convert who worked with and administered Islamic schools within both communities, vividly described the distinction: for the immigrant Muslim, "coming from what they would say was the decadence of their own homelands to an America where you have concrete sidewalks and escalators and elevators and nice apartments and condos and you can get a car through financing, you don't need much money. America for them was like an oasis of possibility." I found all of my African American participants echo similar sentiments about the perception of superiority that immigrant Muslims held of America upon arrival and the low opinion of African Americans. Salahuddin continues to describe what he and other African American Muslims felt the immigrant Muslim community thought of them:

> [A]nd the Black, so called Black Muslim, African American Muslim, disenfranchised Muslim, or the less productive, less achieving Muslim was a like this strange creature who failed to realize that America was like this heaven on earth. Why aren't you taking advantage of all

these gifts? You're not a Pakistani, or Bangladeshi, or Iraqi who just got off the plane with mud still on their shoes from walking down an unpaved street in some village. You're in the good old America. So why do you want to have a school in a basement with limited lighting and old books, and uncertified teachers, when right around the corner you have this school with air conditioning and a big gym? What are you guys talking about? You must be out of your mind. In their minds, it was like you don't want to get in a car, you want to ride a camel again. It was a step backward for them.

Salahuddin's recollection and anger with the immigrant community's inability to see the importance of Islamic schools comes from years of tireless efforts in the Washington, D.C., area during the late 1970s and early 1980s to collaborate in establishing the first school there. Although there were initiatives similar to what he had envisioned sprouting up in Chicago and Toronto at the same time, his sentiments illustrate that there were indeed individuals within pockets of communities all over the continent who recognized the importance of Islamic schools, but there was also great resistance. As harsh or biased as Salahuddin's perspective may come across, his emotion is not unfounded. Sheikh Abdalla Idris himself noted that among the early immigrant Muslims, "There were very few people that saw the Islamic school as a vehicle that would take them and their family toward Allah." The immigrant perception largely shaped the need to integrate and assimilate culturally, economically, politically, and socially. To stand out, "do for self" or protest was a revivalist sentiment that was only held by a handful. For the vast majority, separate schools that teach religion conjured images of schooling that were outdated.

Many immigrant parents perceived the role of early Islamic schools as reform schools. It was difficult to turn students away because school enrollment numbers were necessary to maintain the upkeep of schools, but at the same time, this particular group of parents sent their children more as a dire last resort to "save their children" than to learn about the faith. As principals, Dr. Seema Imam and Sheikh Abdalla Idris recounted that these parents were often easier to identify because they would most often register their children during the school year as opposed to over the summer. Their children would begin the school year in public schools and would either be expelled or be partaking in social activities which the parents felt strongly against (commonly dating and smoking), which led parents to turn to an Islamic school. Islamic schools as reform schools also has a place in the colonial experience. Similar to the traditional *madaris*, early Islamic schools served, for some parents, as dumping grounds of the wayward. Children who portrayed little hope of academic success would often be turned over to the religious leadership to reform them and make something of them.

Between being perceived as reform schools and preserving the pious Muslim girl, early immigrant established Islamic schools had an equally difficult initiation. School visionaries and pioneers had particular aims in mind that often reflected preserving a religious and cultural identity, while parents brought with them contradicting images of what an Islamic school meant. Unlike the community of Imam Warith Deen, immigrant Muslims also had the internal challenge of navigating between cultural, ethnic, and ideological differences based on where in the Muslim world they immigrated from.

Continent-wide organizational structures such as the MSA and ISNA were intended to bring together Muslims on common issues related to the global *ummah* and local community building, such as establishing mosques and schools. Annual conferences became places for collaboration and agenda setting that were to meet the needs of the North American Muslim population. These needs, however, were never fully inclusive of the range of voices across the North American Muslim population. Arguably, the voices of indigenous Muslims, particularly those from the community of Imam Warith Deen, have been historically underrepresented when setting national agendas for Muslims in America. In relation to Islamic schools in particular, it was not until the joint establishment of the Council of Islamic Schools in North America (CISNA) in the early 1990s that formal collaboration and inherent tensions between the immigrant and indigenous community demarcated distinct visions of Islamic education.

Collaboration and Tension Between the Indigenous and Immigrant Communities: Finding Common Ground for the Common Purpose of Islamic Education

The history of Islamic schools in North America that I have articulated thus far has occurred in two distinct, largely separate umbrella communities: indigenous and immigrant. It would be inaccurate for me, however, to deny collaborations, and at the same time, tensions between the two communities, for that is where I feel the richness in this narrative truly begins. Although there were certainly collaborations between immigrant Muslims and the Nation of Islam on an informal, unorganized level, it was not until the death of Elijah Muhammad and the leadership of Imam Warith Deen Mohammed to align his father's community with the orthodox Muslim community that formal collaborative initiatives began.

As Islamic schools fluctuated in number and size throughout the 1980s and 1990s, it became increasingly important to establish support structures for the schools. Given that the Clara Muhammad schools have a longer history and were more established structurally, they were the first to begin annual education conferences, which have been held since the early 1980s. The conferences served as forums for teacher training, discussions around curriculum development, school philosophy, and school networking. On the other hand, although the MSA/ISNA had annual national conferences on general topics related to Islam in America since the 1960s, it was not until the late 1980s that ISNA established a Department of Education within their organizational structure to support the growth of immigrant established Islamic schools. It was at this time in the late 1980s that conversations around a joint organization specifically to meet the needs of Islamic schools began. The struggle to initiate and maintain the Council of Islamic Schools in North America (CISNA) illuminates the historical, contextual, and ideological distinctions that have shaped the visions of Islamic schools. To build toward the establishment of CISNA, I will first outline some of the organizational supports initiated within the indigenous and immigrant communities separately.

Organizational Structure of the Clara Muhammad Schools

Under the leadership of Imam Warith Deen, both the community structure and the schools have become decentralized. For curriculum, teacher, and school development, this has also meant less authoritative direction from the leader of the community and more initiative and direction from the educators themselves. Under the NOI, schools were administered nationally with respect to what was taught. Since the re-envisioning of the NOI schools into the CMS, curriculum planning initiatives have been more ad hoc, inspired and supported by Imam Warith Deen, and as a result often exhibited unique approaches from school to school.

Aside from formal decentralization of community leadership, particular support structures have kept the collaboration of CMS alive. National education conferences, for example, brought together teachers, principals, and Imams from within the community to map out the direction forward for the schools. The themes of these conferences ranged across curriculum development, issues of finance and fundraising, and tracking graduate success. The first of these conferences was held in Sedalia, Missouri, in 1982. It was at that Sedalia conference that many of my participants, including Dr. Zakiyyah Muhammad, Dr. Qadir Abdus Sabur, and Dr. Daaiyah Saleem, gained a sense of the roadmap ahead for Islamic schools in America. Zakiyyah Muhammad told me that that is where Imam Warith Deen Mohammed gave "the educators their task, and that task was to take the Qur'an, the Sunnah of the Prophet (peace be upon him), and the dictionary, and go into a room; take no psychology book, no sociology book and develop your curriculum from that. That was his charge to the Muslim educators in '82 in Sedalia." For all the participants of my study, it was this task of developing an indigenous Islamic education curriculum nuanced with the American experience that has informed the work forward.

In addition to national education conferences, there have been distinct attempts at collaboratively improving the state of CMS as well. The Muslim Teacher's College represents one such major initiative. The Muslim Teacher's Training College was established in Randolph, Virginia, in

October 1989 by Dr. Qadir Abdus Sabur. In 1992, the college opened its new campus, which consisted of 130 acres of land and five school buildings. The first freshman class started in 1993–94, and Imam Warith Deen was awarded an honorary doctorate from the college the same year. Balancing between periods of activity and dormancy, the college has been the host of educational workshops, conferences, and bachelor's and master's degrees in education over the past 20 years.

Other similar initiatives include an education committee that was established by Imam Warith Deen to advance the education in CMS. This committee continues to be active with quarterly meetings from both academics and educators from within the community who are working on a curriculum that builds on Islamic principles. The intent of this initiative is to eventually develop an entire curriculum for Grades 1 through 12 that integrates Islamic principles into every subject area. The curriculum committee achieved the "Clara Muhammad Curriculum Draft 1990," which has been used as the backbone for developing school curricula. Work on the draft was spearheaded by Dr. Zakiyyah Muhammad, who later established the Universal Institute in 1991 in California to find ways of putting Imam Warith Deen's educational vision into practice. In relation to practice, the establishment of the W.D. Mohammed High School in Atlanta, Georgia, around the same time has served to house and disseminate educational development for the CMS. The Atlanta school soon became known as the flagship school that represents the successes of the CMS system. Annual conferences were then combined with the annual summer graduation at W.D. Mohammed High, where Imam Warith Deen annually addressed educators, students, and parents on the importance of Islamic education.

From curriculum initiatives to a teachers' training college, the energy around educational development for CMS since the transition of the community was evident. These structures are important for two reasons. Firstly, it represents that Imam Warith Deen's commitment to education and the development of schools was unwavering. Despite the setbacks of transition, CMS and those who were instrumental in administering them remained committed not only to maintaining the schools but also to developing them through teacher training and curriculum development. The Qur'an-based approach that I will discuss in more detail in the following chapter is distinctly an American Muslim pedagogy that speaks to the religious and cultural needs of American Muslims.

By the early 1990s, therefore, the indigenous Muslim community had already gained expertise around establishing, administering, and shaping separate schools with an Islamic ethos. The second reason necessary to recognize the existing organizational structures, briefly outlined earlier, is to illuminate their expertise. As I turn toward the immigrant established schools and their organizational structures, particular tensions will become clearer.

Organizing Immigrant Established Islamic Schools Across the Country

Outside of IQRA's curriculum initiative since the 1960s, there were no formal organizational supports for immigrant established Islamic schools until the late 1980s. IQRA's work under the Ghazis was indeed pioneering in developing structured educational materials to teach Islamic studies to children in weekend and evening supplementary educational programs. And although IQRA materials have historically served as the core curricula in many full-time Islamic schools, the intent of IQRA has not been to serve as an initiative to bring together disparate schools and serve as a support structure.

There were also major international conferences on Islamic education during the same period that had a far greater global impact on the minds of Islamic school pioneers. The first of these conferences was the First World Conference on Islamic Education held in Mecca, Saudi Arabia, in 1977. Primarily in the Muslim world but concerned about the education of Muslim students both within and outside of the Muslim world, these conferences shaped in large part the direction of Islamic education for the end of the century. These world conferences have been held to address the state, curriculum, and approaches for Islamic schools in every aspect from elementary schools, Qur'anic schools, to higher education. Since the first conference in 1977, subsequent conferences on Islamic education have been held in Islamabad (1980), Dhaka (1981), Jakarta (1982), and Cairo (1987).

As a result of these conferences and the need to create an organization that would carry the recommendations beyond theory into the future, the International Board of Educational Research and Resources (IBERR) was established. Initiated by Yusuf Islam (formerly Cat Stevens), a major early advocate of Islamic schooling in the United Kingdom, major Muslim educational visionaries from around the world were gathered to establish IBERR. Among the international representation on IBERR's board membership are the founding visionaries of immigrant Islamic schools in America: Sheikh Abdalla Idris, Dr. Abdulla, and Dr. Tasneema Ghazi, as well as representation from America's first major Muslim think tank, the IIIT, with Dr. Abdul Hamid Abu Sulaiman.[15]

Contextually, however, these conferences were initiated as a reaction to the secularization of education in the Muslim world, not in North America. As instrumental as the world conferences on Islamic education were on shaping the agenda for immigrant established Islamic schools in North America, they remained limited in their ability to serve as collaborative supports for the given context. The outgrowth of IBERR discussed earlier was equally broad in its scope and unable to serve the immediate needs of schools currently being established. ISNA therefore served as the only national organization that had the potential of developing support systems for immigrant established Islamic schools in Canada and the United States, and their organizational focus did not direct them toward such structure until the late 1980s. It was around this time that ISNA finally decided to establish a Department of Education under their larger organizational structure. The Department's first task was to conduct a research study that would assess the needs of Islamic schools. It was at this juncture, when ISNA first decided to play a more formal role in the support and development of Islamic schools, that the narratives of the two communities intertwine.

Two Communities Meet: From the Ad Hoc Committee on Education to CISNA

By the late 1980s, initiatives to enhance the quality of Islamic schools began to go beyond loosely affiliated projects. By this time the Clara Muhammad schools had an established network of 38 schools (Rashid and Muhammad 1992), annual conferences, and were working toward a unified curriculum development initiative and teacher training college. The immigrant communities up to this point were still in the process of establishing schools and had not begun to consider collaborative structures. Although there were reportedly 49 immigrant Islamic schools in America by the late 1980s, they were established by local, individual initiatives and not networked nationally in any way (ISNA 1989). Between the two communities there remained no formal collaboration to address the educational needs of Muslim children together. In 1989, this was to change.

In 1989, ISNA's Department of Education conducted a study of Islamic schools across the United States to assess both the needs and challenges faced by these schools. Entitled the "In-depth study of full-time Islamic schools in North America," it continues to serve as the only published study of its sort. The research team was led by ISNA's Director of the Islamic Schools Department, Dr. Sha'ban Muftah Ismail. The study looked at 49 Islamic schools across the United States and consisted of a survey questionnaire, qualitative interviews, and classroom observations (ISNA 1989).

The scope of the study, which was intended to be its strength, proved to be its greatest weakness. The study's 49 Islamic schools were all Islamic schools established within immigrant community circles. The study passively recognized the existence of the Clara Muhammad schools but did not endeavor to understand them. Later that year, when the study was launched, the divide between the immigrant and indigenous communities became openly apparent.

To launch ISNA's in-depth study of Islamic schools, a national conference was held in Indianapolis, Indiana, entitled Towards an Applied Islamic Educational Model in North America. At this conference, many administrators from the CMS were also invited and indeed attended. It was the diversity in attendance, however, that provided fertile ground for divergent perspectives in relation to the challenges of Islamic schooling to be heard. Sifting through Sheikh Abdalla Idris's personal archives, I was fortunate enough to relive these tensions through a copy of the conference video. The most interesting aspect of reliving this moment as a researcher was that I had the opportunity to see and hear the conviction, passion, and commitment expressed by many of my participants 30 years ago. At the conference in Indiana, after the findings of ISNA's in-depth study were presented and questions from the audience were welcomed, Dr. Qadir Abdus Sabur very calmly and articulately began to address the concerns of educators from among the CMS.

> We have to be concerned about the voices that are being represented. The composition of the body of experts needs to reflect the composition of the Muslims of America: scholars that were born and raised in America, who know the unique problems and circumstances of American experience.

The void of an indigenous American Muslim voice on the issues of schooling was a major area of contention. Educators from the CMS questioned how it was possible to conduct a study of Islamic schools in North America or plan to address the challenges faced by schools without depending on the wealth of experience and struggle that African American Muslims have endured. Abdus Sabur continued within his numerous rhetorical questions to ask how the experiences of those who have "scuffled" for Islam in America are not valued. In response to the numerous challenges listed by immigrant Islamic schools in the in-depth study, such as financial viability and parental support, Abdus Sabur said:

> These educators [from within the indigenous community] know what it's like to try to make the payroll when parents haven't paid tuition, when students haven't eaten breakfast, when the school has to be concerned about providing role models because there aren't any fathers at home. . . . Things that have come out in the study [referring to ISNA's In-Depth Study] were apparent to indigenous educators 10 years ago.

Others from the CMS expressed similar sentiments after Qadir Abdus Sabur. Many felt that the problems and challenges being experienced by immigrant established schools are things that the indigenous community has already worked out. Another CMS administrator, Ishaq Abdul Malik ul Mulk, stood up and added that these conversations about needing a curriculum and a philosophy of education are unnecessary. "We've [referring to CMS] had a curriculum for 15 years, I have a philosophy of education in my bag." What the educators from the CMS wanted out of this conference was collaboration between the indigenous and immigrant communities that would recognize and value the experiences and proficiency of the already well-functioning Clara Muhammad school system. Faheem Shuaibe, Director of the CMS in Oakland, California, said that we cannot learn from one another until we begin to respect and value one another. When I spoke with Sheikh Abdalla Idris about the validity of these complaints, he concurred. He said that it is not an intellectual jealousy that has kept our communities apart but denial of the intrinsic value of each other.

The consensus reached at the end of the national conference in Indiana was the establishment of an "ad hoc" committee representative of both communities that would analyze the issues raised at the conference and map out a way forward. Two years later, in May 1991, the ad hoc Committee on Islamic Education reconvened, this time in Detroit, a more neutral city away from the ISNA headquarters located in Indiana. At this meeting, key educators, administrators, and Islamic school pioneers from both immigrant and indigenous communities, including most of the participants of this study, decided on establishing a national organization to oversee and support the growth of Islamic schools. This organization was envisioned to bring together varying types of schools regardless of orientation, ideology, and/or organizational affiliation for the sake of a collective agenda: to improve the quality of Islamic schools. Members of the ad hoc committee came to a consensus to name the organization the Council of Islamic Schools in North America (CISNA). The acronym soon became another point of contention, however, because of its similarity to ISNA and the perception that CISNA was a subsidiary of ISNA.

From Dr. Zakiyyah Muhammad's recollection, the first challenge of CISNA was to determine who would be the overseer of the organization. ISNA wanted to bring CISNA formally under its umbrella, and members from the indigenous community insisted it remain independent. She recalled, "Then it got to be very political [and] it got down to a matter of resources." To do the work that CISNA had envisioned, the organization needed funding that only ISNA could really provide. There were several meetings, Zakiyyah Muhammad recalls, that members of the ad hoc committee, now officially named CISNA, attended in the early 1990s to conceptualize how all this was going to work. Within the first few months of envisioning the work of CISNA, it became apparent and inevitable that ISNA's financial support was required.

In order to overlook organizational affiliations and remain independent of individual organizational agendas, one of the first tasks of CISNA was to divide areas of educational development by individual expertise rather than by schools. Abdalla Idris, for example, oversaw the development of Arabic and Islamic studies curriculum, Tasneema Ghazi looked over curriculum development, Zakiyyah Muhammad had teacher development, and Bilal Ajieb had school evaluation and accreditation. The initial hope was to have a general assembly meeting every two years with all the member schools and regional workshops for schools quarterly across the country. By 1993, within two years of the establishment of CISNA, the members decided that the task they set out for themselves was overly idealistic. Given that all of these members, those listed previously and others, were currently administering Islamic schools, working tirelessly in their local communities, in addition to having families, to attempt the work outlined by CISNA on a voluntary basis was becoming increasingly difficult. Not to mention the amount of travel that was required by each member to attend meetings at CISNA's floating office that shifted from city to city. Then in 1993, CISNA decided to focus all of their energies on a single aspect of Islamic school development: accreditation. Bilal Ajieb led this initiative along with the members of CISNA over the next couple of years to develop a self-study manual that individual Islamic schools could use to gain state accreditation. It was a 200-page document that outlined how a school should develop everything from aims and objectives to curriculum frameworks to administrative policies for staff and students. Although there have been differences of opinion within the community of the benefit of formal accreditation, for those in favor, accreditation provided and continues to provide credibility amongst other private schools in America; but, more importantly, it pushes the schools themselves to develop time tested forms of administrative procedures.

By the late 1990s, the work of CISNA began to wane, at least from the perspective of national collaboration between the two communities. CISNA became more closely affiliated with the national agenda of ISNA, and many from within the indigenous community began to either establish their own initiatives or find new ways of collaboration. The decade or so of formal attempts to make CISNA an independent national education organization solely for the sake of serving Islamic schools was not entirely futile, though. Many of the early members of CISNA have maintained the hope of collaboration through more local initiatives as opposed to a national level. Zakiyyah Muhammad and Qadir Abdus Sabur, for example, both went on to establish local initiatives in their respective communities with the same commitment for collaboration. Zakiyyah Muhammad began the Universal Institute to train Islamic schools teachers in California, and Qadir Abdus Sabur initiated the first Islamic high school in Virginia that serves both the indigenous and immigrant communities. Abdalla Idris had shifted his attention initially from Toronto, then to CISNA, and then to his own initiative called the Council of Islamic Education in North America (CIENA), which focused on school accreditation and was housed in Kansas. And there are other organizations, such as the Bureau for Islamic and Arabic Education (B.I.A.E.) in California and the Islamic Schools League in North America located in Chicago, that also offer support services to Islamic schools that blossomed as a result of the vacuum left by CISNA.

Looking Back, Looking Forward

After tracing the growth of Islamic schools in the community of Imam Warith Deen and among communities within immigrant Muslim populations in both Canada and the United States, it has become increasingly apparent that the hope for collaborative educational initiatives between communities has been hindered by various forms of historical baggage. More importantly, through the attempts of collaboration, we are given access to the very different reasons that shape each community's purpose for establishing Islamic schools. The tensions and at times silent hostilities that shape the post-colonial experience for African American Muslims have been drastically different from the experience of Muslim immigrants who have come to America post-decolonization. The deep divide based on socioeconomic class that shaped the experiences of indigenous African American and immigrant Muslims differently was also evident in the sentiments expressed by Qadir Abdus Sabur and others during the Islamic education conference in 1989. Undoubtedly there were exceptions, but, generally, based on how Qadir Abdus Sabur characterized the indigenous experience of struggle against the odds of racial and economic subjugation, it was an experience to which much of the immigrant class could not relate.

The realities faced by CMS have to do with deeply rooted social inequities and the intersections of race and class in particular. When describing the plight of the indigenous African American Muslim struggle for education, Qadir Abdus Sabur cited the 1954 *Brown v. Board of Ed.* decision as a major marker of their educational history. "We are a people that were denied an education—we hid, we were beaten, killed, because we wanted an education and wanted to read. No one has the experience we have. No one denied you an education. You have people like us who were denied an education and we got it any way." The inability of the immigrant Muslim community to understand or accept the aims and objectives of the Clara Muhammad schools is largely because the immigrants cannot relate to the historical experience endured by the indigenous community. While the immigrant community is concerned about protecting the pious Muslim girl, the indigenous community rallies around inequitable opportunities—two very different concerns and an unwillingness in many ways of the immigrant community to appreciate the plight of the indigenous.

As discussed in the Introduction, most of the immigrant Muslims who came to Canada and the United States in the 1960s and '70s were among the privileged few who either came with academic credentials or on student visas to increase academic credentials. Within the first decade of this immigration wave, many who aspired to return home decided otherwise to settle in their new land and establish roots with secure employment, families, and homes, largely in urban suburbs. The general experience of immigrant Muslims was one of stark contrast to the indigenous Black Muslim population, who continue to struggle to gain political and social mobility. Although there were exceptions to the general experience in both cases, the sentiments of social hierarchy certainly affected the potential for community collaboration into the 1980s and, for some, right up until today.

At the 2007 Muslim Alliance of North America (MANA) conference held in Philadelphia, the sentiments of abandonment from the immigrant community were unambiguous. MANA was established to address the concerns of Muslims in inner cities—drugs, unemployment, violence, and the lack of educational opportunities and leadership training. Shaped by the theme of "State of the Blackamerican Muslim Community," the conference keynote lectures reinforced the divide that has historically, and, to an extent, continues to plague the immigrant and indigenous Muslim communities in America.

Dr. Amir al-Islam, Professor at Medgar Evans College in New York at the time, drew an analogy between his experience growing up in the segregated South to compare the Blackamerican Muslim community's experience as Muslims in America: "I wasn't about to get on the back of the bus in the south and then come to the back of the *masjid* in Islam—that's a reality." The most commonly held view among the Black American Muslim community has been a feeling of debasement and inequality both from within the larger Muslim community and from without—what Auston (2017) refers to as "being Black twice." He then recalled demonstrations that he and many others in the audience participated in to demand national Muslim organizations like the MSA be more representative of indigenous Muslim voices and experiences. That was the 1970s, and the MANA conference held in 2007 was based on a similar agenda. Black American Muslim communities have questioned the legitimacy of a national American Muslim organization, with particular reference to ISNA and its affiliates (MSA and CISNA), which disregard the unique concerns of indigenous Muslims. The purpose of MANA was to fill that void with an "attempt to forge . . . an urban, indigenous agenda, which addresses the concerns and issues of our inner-city communities . . ." (MANA 2007). These are concerns of poverty, incarceration, and inner-city education, which immigrant communities have relatively been spared from because of class differences. With a general higher level of education, greater per capita income, and community initiative financial support from overseas, the sacrifice for many immigrant communities has been minimal in comparison to their indigenous brothers and sisters. The concern for immigrant communities has, therefore, been their families back home. Whether it meant finding ways to bring the remaining family members to North America or to send monies back home to help often large extended families, the primary concern of immigrants has not been to address the needs of the North American Muslim community. For African American and other indigenous Muslim American converts, shifting resources and concerns toward a home they cannot relate to has created schisms. Raising financial aid for the ailing *ummah* in Afghanistan in the late 1970s, for example, had to be balanced with serving their own local community's needs. In Dr. Sherman Jackson's keynote at that MANA conference, he challenged, "All the immigrant communities can help their own community back home, but when we suddenly try to help our community and address the crack houses in our inner cities—we are Black nationalists—I am not saying we should separate from the global communities."

Tensions between the immigrant and indigenous Muslim communities have also been over authenticity of religious beliefs and practice. Having evolved from religious teachings under the NOI that contradicted the core principles of faith of orthodox Sunni Islam, many immigrant Muslim communities challenged whether Imam Warith Deen's transition to Sunni Islam was complete. Some of my participants have felt that his philosophy and teachings were still embedded in the teachings of his father, with the annual Saviors Day commemoration or the continued respect for the Honorable Elijah Muhammad. Others have argued that the Imam has gone too far from his father's teachings of community building because he disbanded the leadership structure of the community. For immigrant Muslims, it has largely been an area of ignorance in understanding the wisdom with which Imam Warith Deen transitioned an entire nation and yet maintained its credibility.

The lack of understanding has affected the school front in particular, with minimal networking between immigrant established Islamic schools and the Clara Muhammad schools. Few parents from either community considered sending their children to the other's schools. In Atlanta, where the immigrant community's Islamic school only goes to Grade 8, few parents see Warith Deen Mohammed High School as a viable option for their children. Safiyyah Shahid, principal at W.D. Mohammed High, told me that although she encourages collaboration and even conducts collaborative teacher training, many immigrant Muslim families continue to choose to send their children to public high schools or to home school as opposed to sending them to her school. In her own words, "I think what's happening there is the fact that we are primarily African American, that is an obstacle I believe, it's not stated, but I do think it's something that's there . . . there is a separation. . . . Whatever those cultural differences are they are there. It is unfortunate." Some, like Dr. Abdul Alim Shabazz, attribute these cultural differences to the larger meta-narrative of race. Dr. Shabazz told me that the tensions within the immigrant and indigenous Muslim communities is largely because the immigrants have been "fed the lie of White supremacy and Black inferiority like everyone else. The immigrants have been made to believe that Blacks are prone to criminality." Such sentiments were not uncommon among my participants. It was widely expressed from my African American Muslim participants that they felt abandoned by their immigrant brothers and sisters. Although at times the communities have been at odds, there are not only many exceptions to the general picture that I have painted but also relentless collaborations by the very people who expressed these sentiments to bring the larger Muslim American community together.

Notes

1. The ideology of revivalism most notably attributed to the likes of Hassan al-Banna, Seyyid Qutb, and Abul ala Mawdudi will be discussed in detail in Chapter 4, entitled "Pedagogy."
2. Until the last years of her life (d. 1972), Clara Muhammad remained an active critic of poor educational standards of public schools and an advocate for nurturing the intellectual capacities of Black children. She was supportive of educational endeavors that some UofI schools were putting in place that would begin teaching children formally from as early as two years of age, such as at the New York UofI. See Rosetta E. Ross, "Clara Muhammad: Supporting Movement Ideas Outside Its Mainstream," in *Witnessing and Testifying: Black Women, Religion, and Civil Rights* (Minneapolis: Fortress Press, 2003), 148–51. For a more in-depth study on Clara Muhammad, see also Ajile Rahman, "She Stood by His Side and at Times in His Stead: The Life and Legacy of Sister Clara Muhammad, First Lady of the NOI" (PhD Diss., Clark Atlanta University, 1999).
3. "Wallace Muhammad speaks in NYC," *New York Amsterdam News*, April 14, 1979, 35. Retrieved from ProQuest Historical Newspapers New York Amsterdam News: 1922–1999.
4. Gary Webster, "Focusing on Academic Basics Moral Training and Religion," *New Pittsburgh Courier*, May 5, 1979, 10. Retrieved from ProQuest Historical Newspapers Pittsburgh Courier: 1911–2002.
5. See, for example, the University of Islam school in Washington, D.C., and the first college as well that was directed by Abdul Alim Shabazz. Without much elaboration, he said that although the schools were flourishing, Imam Warith Deen had to strategically reposition key people within the Nation when he assumed leadership in order to be on top of community affairs. What this meant for many temples and schools were drastic, almost overnight closures.
6. "Black to Bilalian" was the battle cry or catchphrase that was popularized by Imam Warith Deen to explain to believers that they were trying to align themselves with orthodox Islamic tradition and history. Black represented the push for Afrocentricity and Black Nationalism that was espoused by his father. And "Bilal" was the first Black Muslim to have converted to Islam in Islamic history during the time of the Prophet Muhammad in 7th century Arabia. "Black to Bilalian" therefore represented a shift back toward Islam's roots while maintaining the individuality of the Blackness.
7. *An Interview with Warith Deen Muhammad*, VHS, directed by James Briggs Murray (New York: Schomburg Center for Research in Black Culture, May 21, 1983).
8. Daood Hassan Hamdani, "Muslim in the Canadian Mosaic," *Journal Institute of Muslim Minority Affairs* 5, no. 1 (1984): 8; Sheila McDonough and Homa Hoodfar, "Muslims in Canada: From Ethnic Groups to Religious

Community." In *Religion and Ethnicity in Canada*, edited by Paul Bramadat and David Seljak (Toronto: Pearson Canada, 2005), 136; See also Baha Abu Laban, *An Olive Branch on the Family Tree: The Arabs in Canada* (Toronto: McClelland and Stewart, 1980).
9. See Nabeel Abraham and Andrew Shryock, eds., *Arab Detroit: From the Margins to the Mainstream* (Detroit: Wayne State University Press, 2000); Michael Suleiman, ed., *Arabs in America: Building a New Future* (Philadelphia: Temple University Press, 1999); Umar Abd-Allah, *A Muslim in Victorian America: The Life of Alexander Russell Webb* (New York: Oxford University Press, 2006); Michael Koszegi and Gordon Melton, eds., *Islam in North America: A Sourcebook* (New York: Garland Publications, 1992); Yvonne Haddad and Jane Smith, eds., *Muslim Minorities in the West: Visible and Invisible* (Walnut Creek, CA: Altamira Press, 2002).
10. Pierre Trudeau's Liberal Party ushered in a Policy of Multiculturalism within Bilingual Framework on October 8, 1971. This policy is the precursor to the Multiculturalism Act of 1988. For immigrant Canadians, Trudeau's policy not only eased the immigration process but also made federal funds available for ethnic and cultural programs, including programs to teach and preserve ethnic (heritage) languages.
11. Among the government initiatives under the multiculturalism policy was the Heritage Language Program that provided funding for cultural groups (Portuguese, Maltese, Chinese, etc.) to teach evening and weekend classes to children and adults to preserve their heritage languages.
12. Statistics from the Private Schools Department of the Ministry of Education in Ontario has missing statistics with respect to start dates, enrollment numbers, staff records, and so on. When I spoke with their statistician in February 2007, he said it can vary due to either schools not providing data when requested or inspections of schools being conducted every other year. The start date for the ISNA school officially says 1986, according to Ministry statistics, but my participants have told me it was as early as 1978, and others have said 1982.
13. See individual websites for Islamic schools across Canada as well as Mohammed Nimer's *North American Muslim Guide*.
14. A sojourner is someone who stays attached to their ethnic, religious, home culture while simultaneously detached or isolated from the culture and practice of the host country.
15. The International Institute of Islamic Thought (IIIT) was established in 1981 in Pennsylvania. The organization was established as a non-profit, privately funded research institute to better understand questions related to social sciences and the Muslim community. The organization is particularly relevant to this study because of its collaboration with the work of ISNA, but more importantly because of its theory of Islamization that shaped much of its early research and publications. Both the IIIT and its conceptualization of Islamization of Knowledge will be further discussed in Chapter 4, "Pedagogy."

References

Abd-Allah, Umar. *A Muslim in Victorian America: The Life of Alexander Russell Webb*. New York: Oxford University Press, 2006.
Abraham, Nabeel and Shryock, Andrew, eds. *Arab Detroit: From the Margins to the Mainstream*. Detroit: Wayne State University Press, 2000.
Ali, Saba. "Building a Movement: A Woman's Work." *Islamic Horizons*, May/June 2003, pp. 16–24.

Auston, Donna. "Prayer, Protest, and Police Brutality: Black Muslim Spiritual Resistance in the Ferguson Era." *Transforming Anthropology* 25, no. 1 (2017): 11–22.
Esposito, John. "Introduction: Muslims in America or American Muslims?" In *Muslims on the Americanization Path?* edited by Yvonne Haddad and John Esposito. New York: Oxford University Press, 2000.
Greenawalt, Kent. *Does God Belong in Public Schools?* Princeton, NJ: Princeton University Press, 2004.
Haddad, Y., ed. *Muslims in the West: From Sojourners to Citizens.* New York: Oxford University Press, 2002.
Haddad, Yvonne and Smith, Jane, eds. *Muslim Minorities in the West: Visible and Invisible.* Walnut Creek, CA: Altamira Press, 2002.
Hamdani, Daood Hassan, "Muslim in the Canadian Mosaic." *Journal Institute of Muslim Minority Affairs* 5, no. 1 (1984).
Hasan, Abdul-Majid Karim. *Reflections on the Islamic Teachings of Imam W. Deen Mohammed.* Jersey City, NJ: New Mind Productions Inc., 1998.
Islamic Schools Department. *In Depth Study of Full-Time Islamic Schools in North America: Results and Analysis.* Plainfield, IN: The Islamic Society of North America, 1989.
Jackson, Sherman. *Islam and the Blackamerican: Looking Toward the Third Resurrection.* New York: Oxford University Press, 2005.
Koszegi, Michael and Melton, Gordon, eds. *Islam in North America: A Sourcebook.* New York: Garland Publications, 1992.
Marsh, Clifton E. *From Black Muslims to Muslims: The Resurrection, Transformation, and Change of the Lost-Found Nation of Islam in America 1930–1995.* London: The Scarecrow Press, Inc., 1996.
Mattson, Ingrid. "How Muslims Use Islamic Paradigms to Define America." In *Religion and Immigration: Christian, Jewish, and Muslim Experiences in the United States,* edited by Yvonne Y. Haddad, Jane I. Smith, and John L. Esposito. New York: Altamira Press, 2003.
McCloud, Aminah Beverly. *Transnational Muslims in American Society.* Gainesville: University Press of Florida, 2006.
McDonough, Sheila and Hoodfar, Homa. "Muslims in Canada: From Ethnic Groups to Religious Community." In *Religion and Ethnicity in Canada,* edited by Paul Bramadat and David Seljak. Toronto: Pearson Canada, 2005.
Nimer, Mohamed. "Introduction." In *Islamophobia and Anti-Americanism: Causes and Remedies,* edited by Mohamed Nimer. Beltsville, MD: Amana Publications, 2007.
Nuruddin, Yusuf. "African-American Muslims and the Question of Identity: Between Traditional Islam, African Heritage, and the American Way." In *Muslims on the Americanization Path?* edited by Yvonne Haddad and John Esposito. New York: Oxford University Press, 1998.
Rahman, Ajile. "She Stood by His Side and at Times in His Stead: The Life and Legacy of Sister Clara Muhammad, First Lady of the NOI." PhD Diss., Clark Atlanta University, 1999.
Rashid, Hakim and Muhammad, Zakiyyah. "The Sister Clara Muhammad Schools: Pioneers in the Development of Islamic Education in America." *The Journal of Negro Education* 61, no. 2 (1992): 178–185.
Ross, Rosetta E. *Witnessing and Testifying: Black Women, Religion, and Civil Rights.* Minneapolis: Fortress Press, 2003.

Sarroub, Loukia K. *All American Yemeni Girls: Being Muslim in a Public School.* Philadelphia: University of Pennsylvania Press, 2005.
Suleiman, Michael, ed. *Arabs in America: Building a New Future.* Philadelphia: Temple University Press, 1999.
Sweet, Lois, *God in the Classroom: The Controversial Issue of Religion in Canada's Schools.* Toronto: McClelland and Stewart, 1997.
Wahhaj, Siraj, "Welcome Letter." *Muslim Alliance of North America (MANA) Conference.* MANA Conference Program, Philadelphia, USA, November 2, 2007.
Zine, Jasmin. *Canadian Islamic Schools: Unraveling the Politics of Faith, Gender, Knowledge, and Identity.* Toronto, ON: University of Toronto Press, 2008.

4 Pedagogy
Models of Islamic Schooling Emerge

This chapter focuses on the theoretical development of Islamic education models in North America as opposed to the actual practice of individual schools. The intent was not to provide an ethnographic account of particular schools (Merry 2007; Zine 2008; Ahmed 2012) but to understand the broader vision of Islamic education from those who established and shaped the earliest Islamic schools in North America. I continue to focus primarily on Islamic schools established in the community of Imam Warith Deen (Sister Clara Muhammad schools) and those schools established by immigrant Muslims generally influenced by major national organizations: MSA, ISNA, IIIT, and the like. From these two umbrella communities, I trace the development of two very distinct models of Islamic education that emerged: 1) a Qur'an-based model of Islamic schooling in the CMS and 2) a model based on integration and Islamization among immigrant schooling circles. The chapter will close with how these two founding models have generated new directions for Islamic schooling in North America.

Two key findings will shape the chapter: firstly, many of the visionaries and Islamic school pioneers that I interviewed claimed that that they have developed or are working toward developing an Islamic philosophy of education that outlines an educational framework and curriculum based on Islamic principles—what I would refer to as an Islamic pedagogical model. The general public sentiment often exhibited about Islamic schools, however, is that Islamic schools lack a model, structure, and/or pedagogy (in the broader philosophical sense) that is unique from conventional pedagogical practices. After meeting with visionaries and pioneers in the field, I gained a deep appreciation that, although a work in progress, the past 30 years of Islamic school development have produced unique working models of an Islamic pedagogy, which I will attempt to outline in this chapter. Secondly, this chapter illustrates how the two distinct models of Islamic schooling are shaped by fundamental differences based on Islamic ideology and perspectives. From the voices of my participants, the vision of Imam Warith Deen was rooted in the plight of African American Muslims but equally an active response to the authoritarian structures of the NOI that stunted accessing the core sources of Islamic theology. The perspective that evolved from within his community combined a historical mistrust of the White establishment inherited from the NOI and an equal mistrust of an immigrant Islam. What evolved as a result was an ideology of empowerment based on a deep attachment to the Qur'an and Sunnah, primarily, and an embedded sense of American patriotism. This chapter will further explore how a Qur'an-based model of Islamic schooling grew out of these core tenets of Imam Warith Deen's ideology.

The immigrant experience has been starkly different. There have been two major influences in shaping immigrant established Islamic schools. Firstly, most immigrants were educated in post-colonial education systems, in the Middle East and South Asia, for example, where the demarcation of secular and religious subjects was a cornerstone. The vision of Islamic education, at least for the visionaries whom I interviewed, was often articulated as an anti-colonial response to the bifurcated and fragmented education system that was developed in the West and imposed through colonialism on many parts of the Muslim world. Secondly, the revivalist thought of Islamic modernism that arose as a result of colonialism influenced the rhetoric and rationale for Islamic schooling. Whether indigenous or immigrant, most of my participants were either involved in, influenced by, or at least aware of the Islamization of Knowledge movement rooted within the discourse of Islamic revivalism and popularized in the late 1970s after the First World Conference on Islamic Education in Mecca, 1977. The pioneers of the MSA and ISNA's Department of Education were all influenced by and have written about the importance of the Islamization project in academic journals. Indigenous Muslims instrumental in establishing the CMS, such as Zakiyyah Muhammad and Bilal Ajieb, also have either acknowledged the importance of the movement on education or, in the case of Bilal Ajieb, were directly involved with promoting the movement. As a result, the impact of the Islamization movement consciously, if not implicitly, has shaped the curriculum designs of Islamic schools in North America.

The analysis of this chapter would not be possible without the underlying framework of a critical faith-based epistemology (Zine 2008) that allows, firstly, for the recognition of the ways in which religions, religious worldviews, and religious education have all been sites of oppression through the establishment of dominant discourses of Eurocentrism. It is also at this historical stage of the development of Islamic schools that the push to re-center faith-based ways of knowing through the Qur'an and Prophetic tradition in particular were established. The Islamization of Knowledge movement and the Qur'an based curriculum framework of Imam Warith Deen's community are both attempts at challenging secular ways of knowing and teaching in schools. Lastly, Zine's framework is especially useful is creating a space for the multiple voices and ideological perspectives that exist within a particular Muslim sect.

The Islamization of Knowledge movement illustrates that there were discursive overlaps in ideological influences between the indigenous and immigrant Muslim experiences in establishing schools. The first half of the chapter will attempt to delve into these discursive overlaps and how they shaped educational thought between the two umbrella communities in North America. The second half of the chapter will focus specifically on how pedagogical practice is different between the two communities as a result of distinct historical, socio-political, and theological influences.

Conceptualizing Islamic Education

It is important to acknowledge that attempts to conceptualize Islamic education have been in phases. During the classical period, many treatises related to education were penned by the likes of Al Ghazali, Ibn Sahnun, and Ibn Khaldun (Cook and Malkāwī 2010; Gunther 2006).

During the Middle Ages, however, education was not considered an independent discipline in Islam or any other culture, for that matter. As a result, "educational science" or "educational philosophy" was never a separate discipline, and the pedagogical principles of a particular medieval scholar were never codified into a working pedagogy (Giladi 1987).

In post-colonial Muslim scholarship, other attempts were made, largely under the auspices of the Islamization of Knowledge movement, to re/define aims and objectives of Islamic education (Al-Attas 1979; Saqeb 2000; Mabud 2016) with a particular reactionary underpinning (Sahin 2018). Between these two de-contextualized articulations, current-day Islamic schools in the West have been challenged with trying to navigate what exactly is the "Islamic" in Islamic education/schools (Panjwani 2004; Lemu 2003). I rely on Nasr's (1987) concept of "sacred presence" to define what I refer to as the "Islamic" in Islamic education. Nasr argues that this sacred presence consists of the principles of the Islamic tradition and the spirit of the Qur'an. The principles of the Qur'an, he argues, have historically infused all aspects of learning, and it is the essence of what made Islamic civilization whole (Nasr 1987, 123). How these principles and concepts of Islam are interpreted and enacted in schools, is, in my opinion, the essence of Islamic schooling that allows for the richness of diversity and distinction. Schools that willingly label themselves as "Islamic" do so because they seek to connect to some semblance of the sacred presence in ways that are contextually relevant to the needs and aspirations of their institutions.

The Practice of Islamic Schooling in North America

As a result of the varied perspectives discussed earlier, what defines (and who defines) the purpose and potential of Islamic schooling is open for interpretation. Parents and educators who support Islamic schools

Pedagogy   115

often do so for their own particular ends or with their own particular conception in mind. And those from within North American Muslim communities who oppose Islamic schools equally have their own conception of what Islamic schools offer or do not offer. Among the common criticisms leveled at Islamic schools in North America are that there is no agreed upon sense of what an Islamic education entails, or that there is no unified theoretical vision of the aims and objectives that define Islamic education. For example, during my interviews, I made the distinction between teaching *about* Islam and teaching *Islamically* (or in other words an Islamic pedagogy), and the response I received from most of my participants echoed the words of Seema Imam, who responded saying, "No, I don't think people even now really know the difference." She then elaborated by explaining that most Islamic schools that began in the 1980s and 1990s really did so with little planning around distinct pedagogical concerns. She rhetorically then questioned the age-old concern: "So if you copy a public school, you have an Islamic school? What we really need are *Islamic* schools" (her emphasis).

In the history of Islamic school growth in North America, there have been numerous attempts at developing and defining a unique model of Islamic education through a curriculum. Early schools relied more heavily on existing public school curricula, with an appendage of Arabic and Islamic studies as single courses. Since then, a plethora of attempts and models of Islamic education have been under development. However, since most, if not all models remain a work in progress, it is not uncommon to find many Islamic schools today still functioning with the "appendage" model. In fact, most school administrators have come to define the uniqueness of their school through the additional Islamic studies courses offered along with a high level of academic success through state/province or even international standardized tests. The tireless efforts and debates of whether to "integrate" Islam with public school curriculum or "reframe" the entire curriculum itself from an Islamic perspective has been left to individual schools to work out.

I have had the absolute honor of meeting individuals whom I would refer to as visionaries of Islamic schooling in North America. All have been involved for several decades as teachers, administrators, principals, and professors, most of whom have a background in education, and many who crossed between the immigrant and indigenous school systems. Their contribution, commitment, and vision for the schools are far more refined than a disparate group of novice teachers in the field. Together they challenge the popular and anecdotal perception that there is no Islamic philosophy of education in North America. Attempts to define the vision and philosophy of Islamic schooling are far from complete, but in this chapter, I hope to illustrate that among these numerous initiatives of visionaries and pioneers whom I met, there have been a handful of important attempts to define an *Islamic* pedagogy. I concur that there is no single conception of an "Islamic" education/school (Panjwani 2004), but there are founding aims, objectives, and principles that inform the diverse methodologies used (Nasr 1987). Based on their ideological leanings or interpretations of the Islamic tradition, scholars, educators, and lay Muslims draw upon different aspects of their conception of Islamic education to nurture Muslim children toward the same end. The key here is that the end is the same—*taqwa* or God-consciousness (Abdus Sabur 2005, 84). What specifically each school emphasizes in the curriculum, how they pedagogically foster and assess learning, and what the institution looks and feels like all vary based on context, influence, and orientation. The following sections will delve deeper into how these variations in educational models are ideologically rooted.

Revivalist Ideology and the Rise of Islamic Schooling in the West

In the post-colonial era, numerous attempts to revive, redefine, and simply hold on to Islamic faith practice have been articulated. Terminologies and ideologies certainly overlap and transcend one another. Whether I speak in terms of revivalism, Islamism, modernism, fundamentalism, traditionalism, or the neo forms of each, there remain blurred trajectories. Such revivalist expressions of faith are anti-colonial manifestations against dominant forms of thinking that have marginalized the position, location, and history of colonized peoples (Dei and Kempf 2006, 3). It is important to recognize that the rhetoric, if not the wholehearted acceptance, of Islamic ideologies that grew out of the post-colonial experience has shaped the development of early Islamic schools in North America. The establishment of Islamic schools is an attempt to re-situate and re-centralize an Islamic epistemology (Zine 2008, 310–1). Although early Islamic schools were highly influenced by the colonial experience— namely the bifurcation of religious and secular—the rationale to establish schools remained anti-colonial. What I will attempt to elaborate in the following sections is a cursory overview of how Islamic revivalist movements, ideologies, and expressions of faith served as the fodder for the institutionalization of Islamic organizations in North America and, as a result, Islamic schools.

Beginnings of Revivalist Ideology

The development of contemporary Islamic ideologies took shape between the 1920s and 1940s. During the height of colonization, Muslim majority countries were reeling from inner confusion and a lack of direction that could neither fully explain how they befell such a circumstance nor how to overcome it. The reaction of Muslim scholars and activists alike was a response that fell along one of two general trajectories: to revive the pristine teachings of Islam in order to return to the long-held dominance of Muslim civilizations or to reform Islam in a way that masters and adapts to modern conditions and developments (Nasr 1987, 81; Rahnema 2005, xvl). Rahnema (2005) refers to the latter as a "backward-looking Islamic view in search of modernity." What developed through Mohammed 'Abduh and Rashid Rida in Egypt and Syria, respectively, formed the initial teachings of the *Salafiyyah* movement, which sought to revive the perfect harmony between humanism and rationalism through the purity of the essential Islamic sources (Rahnema 2005). Essential to the tenets of *Salafi* doctrine is a relative distaste for religious scholars (*ulama*) and their interpretations of Islamic sources. In place of scholarly interpretation, *Salafi* doctrine insists on the reinstatement and use of *ijtihad* (exercising independent reasoning in order to interpret religious texts).

Neofundamentalism, termed so by Jackson (2005) to reflect practices most commonly associated with the *Salafi* movement, serves as the other major ideological movement to have shaped the vision of Islamic schools in North America. The tenets of neofundamentalism are a rejection of the politicized agenda of Islamism, rejection of religious authority, and an attempt to purify and reform religious beliefs based on the purity of the "Golden Age" of Islam.[1] Religious practices that have been culturally influenced or exhibit any form of difference are relegated to forms of deviance, *bid'a* (unsanctioned innovation) (Kaloti 1974).

Hassan al-Banna, founder of the Egyptian Muslim Brotherhood (*al-Ikwan Muslimun*), further developed the thought of 'Abduh and Rida. Al-Banna, however, departed from the balance between Western modernism and reviving an Islamic ethos that defined the legacy of his predecessors. Instead, al-Banna proposed the establishment of an Islamic state that sought to cut off all Western influences. Al-Banna's ideology, shaped by an angry anti-colonialism, far exceeded the balance of Islam's teachings. His brand of revivalism was extreme yet palatable for Muslims living globally in an era caught between the rubble of a lost civilization and a new modernity. As Rehnema (2005) describes it, the era of "crisis of identity and faith created a belief vacuum, exposing Islam to a popularized discourse aimed at bringing a simplified version of traditional Islam to an anchoring position in the private and social life of Muslims" (xlviii). Al-Banna's version of Islam, as radical as it was, served as the catalyst for numerous ideologies that sought similar, often softer, rhetoric and programs that would intellectually define Muslim identity within a context of Western ascendancy. Abu'l A'la Mawdudi and Sayyid Qutb were two such outgrowths.

The relevance of the ideology of political Islam is necessary to accurately trace the historical narrative of Islamic schooling in North America. The tenets of such an ideology, which Jackson (2005) refers to as Islamism, are to reclaim political power, some would say through establishing an

Islamic state that would implement the Islamic ideal of everyday religious affairs. The influence of the major advocates of Islamism—Sayyid Qutb's Muslim Brotherhood (*Ikhwan al-muslimun*) and Abu'l A'la Mawdudi's Islamic Fellowship (*Jamaat-i-Islami*)—cannot be denied in their influence upon both early Muslim immigrants and indigenous African American Muslims in North America.

The latter revivalists (al-Banna, Mawdudi, Qutb) replaced the emphasis of *taqlid* (obedience to the views of religious leaders) with that of *ijtihad*. Their emphasis remained staunchly inward looking, exclusionist, and at times uncompromisingly critical. The general revivalist approach has three major elements:

1. Return to a strict application of the Qur'an and Sunnah;
2. Reinstating the institution of *ijtihad*; and
3. Reaffirmation of the potential and relevance of the Qur'anic message (Voll 1983, 35).

At the heart of ideological distinctions amongst Muslims is this issue of religious authority and interpretation (Hallaq 2001; Soroush 2006), which, although often confined to religious scholars, has also played a significant, albeit implicit, role in defining Islamic schooling.

Essential to the reform agenda of the Muslim Brotherhood and the teachings of Hasan al-Banna is to actively engage with core Islamic texts oneself and not fall prey to the religious edicts and interpretations of religious scholars. Direct access to sources is intended to allow for modern applications to changing circumstances. Calling for a strict application of the Qur'an and Sunnah and reinstating *ijtihad* has an inherent consequence. Rulings, scholarship, and authorities who have for centuries grappled with both general themes and specific circumstances regarding issues of faith and practice become optional, but no longer normative and binding. The *mujaddid* (renewer) "generally has claimed the right to make his own judgment based directly on an independent analysis of the Quran and the Sunna" (Voll 1983, 37). In an era when renewal has been most sought after, Muslims in America, both indigenous and immigrant, relied heavily on the ideological tenets of revivalism to shape and inspire their roles as Muslims in America.

Revivalist Ideology Comes to America

For African American Muslims, Hassan al-Banna, Sayyid Qutb, and Abu'l A'la Mawdudi[2] represented the inner and political struggle with which African Americans were all too familiar. It was a search for reclamation in an era already highly politicized by the Civil Rights movement in America. It was an era, as Salahuddeen Abdul Kareem described, known as "the decade following the decade of the Sixties."

The Sixties was our awakening for the African American to identity: Black pride, Panther Party, social activism, assassination of Dr. Martin Luther King, Jr., martyrdom on Malcolm X 1965—so in the early 1970s you have a lot awakening and a lot of social consciousness nationally and internationally. You had the rebellion against colonialism and African nations; I mean there was a lot of awakening. So, the Seventies was a period where a lot of things were opened up. The Sixties the barriers were knocked down. And the Seventies was the decade where you could pick and choose and decide where you want to go from here.

After the barriers of race had been institutionally defeated, many African American Muslims attached themselves to the global struggle felt by their Muslim brothers and sisters. Salahuddeen Abdul Kareem recalls that Muslims were united under the common plight at the time. African Americans related to the struggle of the Iranians, Afghanis, Pakistanis, and Syrians. As Salahuddeen reminisced about his early years as a Muslim, "When I first became Muslim, we were really hoping that *Ikhwan al—Muslimun* made it. It was the prayer of every African American Muslim. We made *du'a* [prayer] for them. Oh Allah let these people make it. These Egyptians, the beacons of culture, these educated people like Hassan al-Banna." Most African American Muslims, he recalled, were influenced by the scholarship of al-Banna, Qutb, and Maududi. Their politicized, anti-American, and revivalist teachings were highly influential to a people who were riding the energy of revolution. Sayyid Qutb's controversial yet deeply influential treatise, entitled *Milestones*, for example, served as the red book for revolution. In the words of Salahuddeen, "coming to Islam and reading Maududi and Qutb really resonated with our young spirit because in the backdrop of our conversion we were rejecting the ills and harms of Americanism and racism, and oppression; all of that is fresh in our minds and we hate it."

The impact of revivalism in its various shapes had also been an influence on immigrant Muslims in North America. Arguably, immigrants are the ones who brought the ideologies of struggle over with them and whose emphasis on the struggle "back home" in Muslim majority lands is what informed the early political activism of Muslims in North America. Tasneema Ghazi remembered that *Milestones* "was like a New York Times bestseller for American Muslims . . . people would fight for that book." For early Muslim immigrants in America, the work of Qutb and Maududi gave them the language, she says, for revolution and to "fight post-colonialism." The language of *jahiliyyah* (ignorance) reframed the power dynamic that had otherized Eastern peoples for so long. Qutb empowered Muslims by demanding they shed their imposed complex of inferiority and recognize the urgency for renewal of Islam through a renewed self-identity, political struggle, and institution building. The latter became the mainstay for immigrant Muslims who arrived to America with both intellectual privilege and the attachment to the global Muslim struggle of self-identity. The major Islamic organizations in North America discussed in the previous chapter, MSA, ISNA, and the community of Imam Warith Deen, were highly influenced by the ideology of revivalism (Johnson 1991, 112; Haddad 1983, 68).

The fundamental contention of Islamic revivalism is an anti-colonial response to the imposed secularization of the Muslim mind, which highly resonated with Muslims in North America. Revivalist ideology revolts against the dependence and domination of colonizers that were reinforced by a bifurcated education system. This education system, revivalists argue, groomed the Muslim intellectual elite to rule over the Muslim world void of an Islamic worldview. Langohr (n.d.) argues that colonial education in the Middle East and South Asia imposed a "Western-style education that was based on the conceptualization of religion as a discrete subject separate from and incapable of shedding reliable light upon worldly matters, and on the premise that it was mastery of these worldly matters, rather than piety and devotion, that would bring students success" (2). Colonial schools systematically relegated the teaching of religion to a "religion class," removing topics of morality, values, and scripture from classes on math, science, and language. The marginalization of religion in colonized societies bred revivalist thinking and used schooling as the primary vehicle for change (Ayalon and Wasserstein 2004).

Toward a Vision for Islamic Education in North America

Young Muslim intellectuals who had immigrated to the United States and Canada began to reflect more deeply and in concerted fashion over the revivalist thought that the previous generation had produced, particularly the activism of Qutb, Banna, and Mawdudi. Importantly, the revivalist response should not be misconstrued as "pathologically anti-Western." The revivalist resurgence was a call for reinstatement of balance and co-existence between the Muslim ways of knowing and the West as opposed to disempowerment and domination of one over the other (Ahmad 1983). These young Muslim immigrants in America questioned why the global revivalist movements appealed to the masses yet were unable to mobilize and carry-out systematic change. Between 1968 and 1977, numerous seminars were held in the United States and Canada to address the failure of Islamic reform movements. "It became evident that new effort is needed to reform the methodology of thought at its foundation.... The new reform effort should present a systematic and methodological approach to rebuild Islamic knowledge on the same firm foundation that supported Islamic Civilization in its first cycle" (Barzinji 1999, 18). This realization and call to action formed the vision of the Institute of Islamic Thought (IIIT), founded in 1981.

The growth of the IIIT, an educational think tank that sought to transform the natural, physical, and social science curriculum taught in universities across Muslim majority countries, is most often attributed to Dr. Ismail Faruqi. Faruqi, along with notables such as Seyyed Hossein Nasr and Naquib Al-Attas, represented the erudite, Western educated Muslim immigrant intellectuals who continue to shape the discourse of Islamic education. Faruqi (1921–1986) himself was a Palestinian American Muslim, Muslim activist, and among the handful of intellectual revivers of Islamic thought during the post-colonial period.

Grounded and passionate about both Arabism and an Islamic revival, Faruqi brought together the intellectual tradition of revivalist scholars (Esposito 1991; Shafiq 1994). He insisted that the decline and decay of Islamic civilizations is a result of leaving the practice of *ijtihad*. Like his predecessors, Faruqi sought to make the Islamic tradition relevant through individual reason. In addition to teaching at numerous universities, including the Department of Religion at Temple University until his death in 1986, Faruqi's most notable achievement was co-founding the IIIT and his conception of Islamization. He believed that the solution to Islam's revival is the Islamization of modern intellectual discourse in the political, social, and natural sciences.

The intellectual movement toward Islamization of Knowledge is a direct response to the impact of colonial systems of education. Ismail Faruqi said, "There can be no hope of a genuine revival of the *Ummah* unless the educational system is revamped and its faults are corrected. The present dualism in Muslim education, its bifurcation into an Islamic and a secular system must be abolished once and for all" (Khan 1999, 61). To correct this bifurcation and yet avoid simply reviving a tradition of the past, it is essential, he said, to raise Muslim intellectual thought "to compete with the emerging nations in sciences, arts, industry, and all the ingredients of modern life" (Barzinji 1999, 15). Faruqi encouraged immigrant Muslims to develop and adopt an Islamic ideology that could address the common sentiments of displacement and weakness that often overwhelmed people in a new land. He argued that Muslim immigrants are in America to contribute to this new land and not simply benefit from it. They should not feel guilty, therefore, of leaving the homeland and rising to a level of socioeconomic success here. The Islamic vision should be to use one's leverage and position to reform the ills of a new land with the love of God (Faruqi 1983).

The objective of the Islamization of Knowledge project was to deeply master the secular sciences and thereby transform them epistemologically with an Islamic worldview. The first tangible project of the IIIT was to develop university level textbooks for every discipline from an Islamic perspective. The intention has been to Islamize economics, finance, education, political science, philosophy, and psychology, with an inherent focus on the social sciences (Barzinji 1999). The fruits of the IIIT's activity have made a permanent mark through institutions of higher learning, most notably in Malaysia. As much as the Islamization of Knowledge project focused its energies on higher education, some of my participants said that it also deeply informed the vision of elementary and secondary Islamic schooling in North America.

It was not uncommon for me to ask my participants about the IIIT and the fathers of Islamization only to learn that they were colleagues at some point in their careers.

Tasneema Ghazi, founder of the first Islamic school curriculum project in America, for example, boasted of her and her husband's close relationship with both Ismail Faruqi and Seyyed Hossein Nasr. Speaking of the latter, she said, "He was a major influence on our lives." When I asked whether the Islamization movement influenced the development of IQRA curriculum materials, she acknowledged it as a "buzz" that had an impact. According to Sheikh Abdalla Idris, founder of the first Islamic school in Canada, it was on organizations like the IIIT, MSA, and ISNA to spark the idea and support the growth of the schools. Similarly, Salahuddeen Abdul Kareem concurred that Islamization may not have been the driving force per se for the Islamic school curriculum, largely because the writings of Faruqi and the IIIT were of an academic nature inaccessible often to lay educators, but the awareness of the concept of Islamization was something that Islamic school educators felt could be replicated at an elementary and secondary school level. For Zakiyyah Muhammad and Bilal Ajieb, instrumental in establishing and administering CMS and immigrant Islamic schools, the work of IIIT had a more direct impact on their educational outlook. Bilal Ajieb recalls the impact that people like the Malaysian American educator Dr. Naquib al-Attas, who completed a graduate degree in Islamic studies at McGill University in Canada, had on the beginnings of Islamization thought. Al-Attas's thought on Islamization first made its mark at the First World Conference on Islamic Education held in Mecca, Saudi Arabia, in 1977. He proposed a complete overhaul of the education systems in Muslim countries through the Islamization of curriculum, teacher training programs, and the establishment of Islamic universities that would implement such a model. For Bilal Ajieb, this shift to Islamization defined the new paradigm for Islamic education that educators like him had been waiting for. "It [Islamization of Knowledge] manifested itself mainly at the university, post-secondary level, but at the same time we were thinking about how to take these concepts and put them into a scope and sequence from PreK [Pre-Kindergarten]." Bilal Ajieb's conviction about developing a uniquely Islamic curriculum for Islamic schools informed his work with CISNA. Similarly, Zakiyyah Muhammad traces her first introduction to Islamization back to the 1977 conference as well. Soon after the establishment of the IIIT, Dr. Zakiyyah began working informally with the IIIT to spread the Islamization concept to Islamic schools. But as tremendous as the impact of Islamization was for educators like Dr. Zakiyyah, it still fell short of being truly "Islamic." The concept of "Islamizing" or integrating still assumed two separate spheres of knowledge that remain dichotomous. Highly influenced by the teachings of Imam Warith Deen, Zakiyyah Muhammad and other educators among the CMS system began to ideologically part with respect to educational approaches. In her words,

> The challenge is still about curricular development, not integrating. The languages we use: integrate Islam or inculcate Islam in the curriculum, that's not Islamic education. The Qur'an *is* the curriculum and what Imam Mohammed said, the challenge for Muslim educators, he said, 'Is to take the Qur'an and the model of the Prophet (*salalahu alayhi wa salim* [peace and blessings be upon him]) and put it in educational language.' That has been the challenge, the Qur'an is the curriculum. Now how do you translate that into curricular language? That's the challenge for the Muslim educators.

What soon began to take shape in the 1990s was a stark distinction in pedagogical approach at a very deep theoretical level between visionaries as a result of the Islamization of Knowledge project. Although the revivalist, at times radical, writings of Qutb, Banna, and Maududi have been highly influential both in MSA/ISNA circles and amongst the African American Muslim community, including the community of Imam Warith Deen, the two eventually began to part ways in how that influence was going to be actualized. Scholars of Muslims in America have said that ISNA largely remained on the Islamization bandwagon (Khan 1999, 63), while others have said that the community of Imam Warith Deen adopted the rhetoric of "Qur'anic centeredness" from Qutb and developed a distinct ideology that speaks to the African American experience (Haddad 1983, 68).

Imam Warith Deen Mohammed's Alternative Vision

> What Imam Mohammed helped us understand is that although that philosophy [Islamization] had a tremendous core truth in it, we did not agree with the notion of the word. The word really was limiting and it was also isolating us from perceiving Islam in a logical context. If you want to alarm people and make them think that you are selective and only for your own kind talk about Islamization of Knowledge. It really is a barrier that makes others feel that it all belongs to you and no one else. And because language is so critical, one of the real centerpieces of Imam Mohammed's *tafseers* and insight of the Qur'an is that language is critical and this is why if you listen to any lectures of Imam Mohammed's you hear a different kind of language. You don't hear the traditional nomenclature that many Muslim scholars make.
>
> (Zakiyyah Muhammad)

For educators like Dr. Zakiyyah Muhammad and others involved with the CMS, Imam Warith Deen cleared a new path for Muslims in America based on inclusive language. He employed a language that connected people to humanistic roots over ideological differences. The analogy that Zakiyyah Muhammad gave me was that Imam Warith Deen used the language of H2O, not of water or eau or aqua but a language whose universal properties everyone can relate to, and "that's what he has done with the Qur'an and the model of the Prophet Muhammad." Such an approach empowers as opposed to alienates people from Islam. In relation to education, Zakiyyah Muhammad then clarified Imam Warith Deen's stance on Islamization by recalling his words: "'you do not have to Islamize what is already Islamic.' He's saying that all knowledge is from Allah. It's already Islamic. So, we don't use the term Islamization in the development of the Clara Muhammad curricular anymore."

Imam Warith Deen's alternative vision for Muslims in America and for Islamic schooling is equally ideologically and contextually constructed by the forces of revivalism and modernism discussed earlier but unique in that it is far more difficult to attach him to a relatively simpler trajectory as in the case of MSA/ISNA/IIIT (Curtis 2006, 122). According to Jackson (2005), the legacy of Black racism in America helped sustain the community of Imam Warith Deen's strength and relevance until a significant immigrant Muslim population established themselves in North America. Until then, Black American Muslims who had largely found their own way back to Islam celebrated a "sense of *ownership*" as the authority of Islam in America (5). The shift in authority over the religious sources then turned to the immigrant, whose mastery over the Islamic tradition has been bred over centuries. Once a significant immigrant Muslim population settled in America, the basis of religious authority "shifts to the sources, authorities, and interpretative methodologies of historical Islam" (Jackson 2005, 4). Given the intellectual legacy of immigrant Muslims over these sources (Qur'an and the Islamic sciences), African American Muslims were left with a faith practice that was de-legitimized.

Although Imam Warith Deen attempted to validate the legitimacy of his community to both the local immigrant Muslim community in America as well as leaders in the Arab world in the early years of his transition, it was inevitable that a unique identity separate from external influence was required. Initially, as Curtis (2006) notes, Imam Warith Deen allied with the work of the MSA and even allowed perceptions within the immigrant community toward some of his transitions to direct his decisions. For example, in the late 1970s, through Imam Warith Deen's work with the MSA, he arranged to have a Medina-trained Sudanese sheikh lead his community in Chicago. Similarly, as discussed earlier, perceptions within immigrant circles of Imam Warith Deen's decision to define the direction of his community through the story of Bilal ibn Rabah, the first African Muslim convert during the earliest period of Islam, was short lived because of the perception that it would shift the emphasis away from the essential sources of Islam: the Qur'an and Prophetic way (Curtis 2006, 118–22).

The community of Imam Warith Deen has strategically dodged adopting the ideological leanings of any immigrant Muslim movements or thinkers that have influenced other African American Muslims. Rather, their aim has been to chart out a uniquely indigenous interpretation of Sunni Islam that is distinctly American. Although they place an inherent emphasis on understanding the core sources of the Islamic tradition (Qur'an and Sunnah), they are far from being ideologically consistent with the puritanical elements of Wahhabism or Salafism. Nor are they politically charged with the anti-American rhetoric of the Dar-al Islam movement that is highly influenced by the writings of Abu Ala Mawdudi. Bilal Ajieb clarified that within the community of Imam Warith Deen, they often will not even recognize themselves as Sunni because "it's such a loaded term. [Rather] we say we are people trying to follow the *uswa* (way) of the Prophet Muhammad (peace be upon him)."

The potential responses to vying for authority were twofold. The African American community could either attempt to master the Islamic tradition, which the immigrants already held sway over, or continue to hold fast to the plight of empowerment and self-determination of African American peoples that no one could take away. They chose the latter and, by default, "non-mastery of the Sunni Tradition" (Jackson 2005, 5). The community of Imam Warith Deen developed a sense that any attempt to align themselves with or to master the Islamic sciences would simply make them inferior, in relation to religious authority over Islam in America, to immigrant Muslims. Jackson (2005) argues that this

> fear of domination translated into a palpable diffidence if not aversion towards the traditional Islamic sciences. Thus, while the followers of Imam Warithuddin [Warith Deen] Muhammad remain today among the most accomplished in terms of secular education, they have had little or no representation among those recognized as being versed in the traditional Islamic religious sciences.
>
> (76)

This is why the Islamic schools established by immigrant Muslims largely adopted (even if subconsciously) the Islamization model of education, and in reaction, the community of Imam Warith Deen strives to develop their own unique model that emphasizes a personal connection with the Qur'an absent of external interpretation.

Two Overarching Models: Qur'an Based and Islamization

The following two sections will outline "models" of Islamic education that have been organically developed in North America in an attempt to define the "Islamic" in Islamic education. The models themselves not only illustrate the historical trajectory of Islamic schooling in North America but also contextualize the socio-political and intellectual influences that have affected the rise of the Islamic schools themselves. These models represent the culmination of larger national and international discourses on Islamization and a Qur'anic worldview that have been widely addressed in Muslim intellectual circles. They also symbolize both the collaboration and diversion among Islamic school pioneers and visionaries in North America. All of the individuals discussed have either collaborated formally on local or national educational initiatives or at the least have become familiar with other existing models before developing their own.

The two distinct Sunni Muslim umbrella communities who support Islamic schools arrived in North America through very different paths and have been influenced by equally unique Islamic ideologies. In the previous section, I have described how the ideology of Imam Warith Deen's community came to rely more heavily on the fundamental sources of Islam. Not quite the fifth *madhhab* (school of thought)[3] that he had once proposed, the approach of his community was essentially a distinct departure from existing ideologies that characterize the Muslim world. The importance placed on rationally understanding and implementing the teachings of the Qur'an and living the *'uswa* (way) of the Prophet Muhammad, I will argue, also shaped the distinct pedagogical practices of the Clara Muhammad schools. As a community who came to Islam arguably on their own, the struggle and search to derive inner meaning from the Qur'an is something they will not forfeit. Nor is the landscape of America foreign to them. For the indigenous Muslims who have looked to Imam Warith Deen for direction, then, the approach toward education has always been to deeply engage with the Qur'an through one's innate ability and to apply its teachings to their everyday lives.

Similarly, the post-colonial immigrant experience described earlier and the revivalist response that followed through the discourse of Islamization has uniquely influenced the curriculum of Islamic schools established by Muslim immigrants in Canada and the United States. Although the Islamization movement influenced both the indigenous and immigrant communities to an extent, the lasting impact of Islamization remains to shape the approach of immigrant established schools. However, unlike the community of Imam Warith Deen, which was far more centralized in the 1990s and continues to draw solidarity behind his vision, few immigrant Islamic schools would likely attribute their school design to the Islamization discourse largely because the rhetoric swirled more among academics than school principals. That said, I feel participants of this study concurred that Islamization rhetoric influenced their thinking while the earliest Islamic schools were being established. The Islamization approach transferred to K-12 schools sought to append, alter, and align secular, Eurocentric school curricula through an Islamic worldview with the integration of Islamic history, civilization, contributions, and ethics. At its core, the Islamization model is an integrative curricular model. The remainder of this chapter will turn its focus to how these separate histories and ideologies have shaped innovative models of Islamic schooling amidst similar aims.

Clara Muhammad Schools and a Qur'an Based Model

The development of a Qur'an based model for the consortium of Clara Muhammad schools is a pedagogy becoming. In its initial stage during the late 1970s and into the 1980s, the Islamization of Knowledge project influenced the curricular approaches even for CMS. However, as early as the Sedalia conference in 1982, when Imam Warith Deen insisted that educators in his community develop a unique educational model with nothing except the Qur'an and a dictionary, the roots of an indigenous Islamic pedagogy began to form. From the voices of the visionaries whom I met, the educational philosophy of the CMS is based on three overarching pedagogical principles: primacy of the Qur'an, nurturing *asabiyya*, and serving the *ummah*, which will be discussed in the following.

Qur'an is the Curriculum

The primacy and centrality that the CMS placed on the Qur'an as the curriculum is reflected in their aims, objectives, curriculum content, and in the instructional methods as well. Bilal Ajieb attested that the ability to even think differently is a result of the plight of African American Muslims. Inheriting the legacy of protest from the NOI, Ajieb asserts, "We knew how to challenge the public education system. We weren't worried about accreditation or anything like that. We were concerned about our own needs." Central to these needs was deeply engaging with the Qur'an, which the community had until then been misinformed about. Combined with Imam Warith Deen's new direction of patriotism, such longing to grapple with the Qur'an framed the aims and objectives of the community and as a result the schools as well.

Imam Warith Deen's emphasis on patriotism encouraged a new way of interacting with all that was accessible as Americans, including public schools. The approach for CMS was not to disregard conventional public school curricula but to seek to view it through a lens of the Qur'an. Such an approach does not then draw a dichotomy between knowledge that is secular and that which is Islamic. Rather, it begins with the premise that all knowledge is inherently from God and must be understood through the book of God. Curriculum in CMS begins with the Qur'an and teaches existing state curricula in a way where students gain an appreciation of

God's magnificence. Abdus Sabur defines the Qur'anic curriculum as the aggregate total of all activities, academic, social, and spiritual, in an educational setting that contributes to the Qur'anically guided intellectual development of individuals as they internalize their relationship with God and His purpose for their lives.

As discussed in the section on ideology, Imam Warith Deen's teachings encourage individuals to make sense of the Qur'an for themselves without a particular reliance upon the Qur'anic exegetical tradition. Such a stance is not only divergent ideologically from most of the other conservative and traditional Islamic ideologies, but also reframes the approach to Islamic education as a result. In the CMS's Statement of Philosophy, for example, it states:

> The aim of education must then be for our students (1) to use the **G-d given powers of judgment** to make their evaluation by **evidence of reason and inference**; and (2) because seeing is certainty for believing, examine reality with **their own eyes** using all the faculties of perception and the **best tools of rational science** that extend them; and (3) understand that beyond human understanding **there is absolute truth**, the only truth that is without error, the possession of G-d alone.
>
> (emphasis in bold added)[4]

The essence of Islamic education is to unravel and understand the absolute truth of our existence defined by God. But in the CMS's philosophy, it is to search for that truth without hindrance from external sources. Each individual is capable of attaining a sense of that absolute truth through their own volition, not needing any intermediary or external supports. Such a pedagogical approach is intended to empower and uplift a people who for decades were discouraged from self-exploration and self-definition under the NOI. Imam Warith Deen's approach has elements commonly associated with the *Salafiyya* movement described earlier and must be juxtaposed with traditional or classical Islam, which relies on wider Islamic legal and theological interpretive traditions. By distancing themselves from the mainstream Islamic tradition, Imam Warith Deen sought to empower believers in his community through self-interpretation and self-reliance on the Qur'an and Prophetic tradition. Imam Warith Deen's adoption of such a position has been instrumental in breaking from traditional practices and forging a distinct path forward.

The schools have also sought to define themselves distinctly from immigrant approaches to Islamic schooling. Reliance on scholarship that is inherently American as opposed to religious teachings and texts from abroad are one such attempt.[5] Along similar lines, a limited number of core Islamic texts are used by the teachers and the students as primers on Islam. The Clara Muhammad schools, and the community of Imam

Warith Deen in general, rely on a select few essential sources of Islam to gain their understanding of the faith: *The Holy Qur'an* (Yusuf Ali Translation), major *hadith* compilations, such as *Sahih Bukhari* and *Sahih Muslim*, "Alim: The Islamic Scholar" (multimedia software), a concordance of the Qur'an, an encyclopedia of Seerah, and other biographies of the Prophet, such as "The Sealed Nectar: A Biography of the Noble Prophet." All this, in addition to the Quranic *Tafsir* of Imam WD Mohammed, is embraced by the Islamic studies department of each school. The reliance on Imam Warith Deen's *tafsir* (interpretation) of the Qur'an serves as an inroad to the teachings of Islam through a lens that is both African and American. The focus on essential sources has led to what many scholars have called a Qur'anic framework. The late Dawud Tauhidi, a White American convert to Islam and director of the Tarbiyah Project, gave me an outsider's insight to such an approach. Referring to Imam Warith Deen's approach, Dawud said it is the approach most converts take, "It's a no brainer that they're going to use the Qur'an as their starting point. And with whatever limited conceptual skills—but the amazing thing about the Qur'an is that if you just keep reading it, even in English, that framework is being embedded . . . [the] frame of reference will be what has been etched into the mind."

Establishing the primacy of the Qur'an in all aspects of living may be the initial response of most converts, as Dawud Tauhidi attests, but few scholars have encouraged believers to use the Qur'an as a framework. Imam Warith Deen's insistence on the Qur'an as a framework for business, education, and civic responsibility has made the Qur'an truly a guide for everyday living. In a CMS publication speaking of the Qur'an as guidance, it says, "G-d establishes all the possibilities in human nature and the natural world of reality and gives Qur'anic guidance for establishing the complete human consciousness including reason."[6] For the CMS, this has meant charting an educational framework whose principles and practices are derived from Imam Warith Deen's interpretations of the Qur'an.

Nurturing *Asabiyya*: Cultural Awareness and Identity

The fundamental aims and objectives of the CMS reflect a stark similarity to those in Islamic education in general: to nurture well balanced Muslims who have an awareness and appreciation of Islam. Where the CMS have been catalysts in shaping the direction of Islamic schooling in North America has been in their emphasis on cultural identity. From the outset, CMS have aimed "to instill in each student the knowledge of his/her own uniqueness and worth."[7] Grounded in a history of enslavement and miseducation, CMS strive to cultivate a sense of pride in the students' multiple identities: Muslim, African, and American. The combination of these multiple identities has been coined by Aminah McCloud (1995) as the process of *asabiyya*, or nation building. The term originates from Ibn Khaldun's *Muqaddimah* (Rozenthal 1970) to mean "group solidarity," but in the popular usage by African Americans and in particular by Aminah McCloud in her book entitled *African American Islam*, the term is appropriated to connote a process of "nation building" in contradistinction to the building of a single *ummah*, as is common in Islamic discourses. The term *asabiyya* allows for African American Muslims to maintain their unique identities within the larger discourse of *ummah*.

The vision of African American thought has largely been directed by the influence of major historical figures. Noble Drew Ali, Elijah Muhammad, Malcolm X, Warith Deen Mohammed, and Louis Farrakhan, introduced earlier in this work, have been among the essential group of African American leaders that have shaped and reshaped African American thought in relation to Islamic beliefs. Early visionaries were instrumental in articulating the historical and ancestral lineage of African Americans. Much of the founding philosophy was based on the view that African Americans were a "lost nation" that needed to reclaim and reconnect to their origin. Each also employed Islam as the religion that would trace them back to their historical origins. McCloud (1995) asserts that this emphasis on reconnecting led to a tension between African American Muslims as a separate entity from the larger global Muslim community. The tension between *asabiyya* (nation building) and the *ummah* (the world community of Muslim believers) was not resolved until the 1960s, when Malcolm X realized the distinction. It was not until Malcolm X's departure from the NOI that a balance between *asabiyya* and *ummah* was struck under African American Muslim thought. Malcolm X's realization that the idea of nation building for African Americans was being overemphasized in the NOI came during his pilgrimage to Mecca, when he realized that an Islamic brotherhood extended far beyond ethno-cultural lines. The question that inevitably arose for Malcolm X and others who began to re-envision African American Islam was whether one can "reconcile this broader Islamic understanding with the demands of an Islam focused on African American nation-building" (McCloud 1995, 37).

The question of joining global community efforts was not the concern for Malcolm X. Rather, he wanted to ensure that African American Muslims would not overlook the importance and primacy of the issues that they themselves faced specifically in the American context. Despite the acceptance of Malcolm X's re-visioning of the direction of African American Muslims under his leadership, the primary goal of changing the condition of his people through actively addressing the discrimination and injustices against them did not change (McCloud 1995, 35–8). This tension between *asabiyya* and *ummah* has, therefore, been a foundational element in defining the balance that African American Muslims have been actively trying to establish since the 1960s, especially in relation to education (McCloud 1995, 111).

The need to legitimize both their concern for education and their soundness in understanding the Islamic tradition has pushed the community of Imam Warith Deen to develop their own model. In Imam W.D. Mohammed High School in Atlanta, a document found in their archives entitled "Implementing a Qur'anic Based Curriculum" states that part of the influence for developing a unique curriculum in the CMS is the "context of our ethnicity as African Americans."

> [W]e were a living, breathing, community working to commit ourselves to an outcome that we collectively and collaboratively agreed upon. Together we were working to shape a curriculum that preserved our Muslim and African American identity. We appreciated the billions of Muslims throughout the world and their cultural way of life [but] we discussed what we wanted our curriculum to look like.[8]

The tensions and collaborations between the indigenous and immigrant communities discussed in the previous chapter explain the need for Imam Warith Deen's community to develop and maintain a distinct sense of self.

Serving the *Ummah*: Civic Education and Responsibility

Unlike most Islamic schools established by immigrant Muslims, the community of Imam Warith Deen placed an importance on community service, community building, and civic responsibility well before the backlash of 9/11. This is clearly stated among other school aims as follows, "To foster the realization that each student is a citizen of the community, the nation, and the world; thus promoting an understanding of the privileges and responsibilities of living in our society."[9] Likewise, in another school document it states, "To enhance appreciation and respect for people of all cultures and backgrounds as one human family, and to strengthen the understanding and appreciation of Islamic, African, and African American experiences as significant developments in global history and destiny." Appropriating the Islamic concept of *khalifa* (vicegerency), CMS articulated a clear aim of their schools to be development of a sense of global responsibility among Muslim children who recognize the needs of the human family and not simply of insular Muslim communities.

The vision of the CMS is the embodiment of a balance between the aforementioned tensions of *asabiyya* and *ummah*. The African American focused curriculum, teaching staff, and school ethos serve the aspect of *asabiyya*, and the integration of teaching Islamic beliefs, values, and practices serves to connect students to the larger Muslim community. The interplay between these two aspects nurtures African American Muslim students with a self-identity that is grounded in both an ethno-cultural and religious tradition.

Shifting the balance toward greater recognition of faith consciousness over ethnic and racial identity is the definitive transition made from the University of Islam schools to the Clara Muhammad schools. Dr. Daa'iyah Saleem, professor of education and member of the CMS special committee on education, said that it was a process of "moving from ethnocentricity to Godcentricity." This transition marked "a fundamental shift that simultaneously expanded, bounded, and re-centered the philosophy much that the cultural ethos and stories—the triumphs and struggles of Africans throughout the African diaspora came to be viewed through *Tawhidic* lenses" (Abdur Rashid 1999, 57). *Tawhid* is most commonly translated as believing in a single God or being God-conscious. Daa'iyah Saleem introduces the term "Godcentricity" to incorporate the concept of seeing the world through what she has called "*Tawhidic* lenses," which by virtue also defines the vision of Islamic education for CMS. The challenge and change for African American Muslim educators is to alter their perception of the post-colonial experience of subjugation and marginalization, learning to both understand it as a God-given struggle (*jihad*) and a need for social justice (*'adl*) embedded in the moral imperatives of Islam. It is the recognition of and lived practice of Islam's moral imperatives that cultivate a sense of theocentricity. Paraphrasing the wisdom of Islam's luminary of the medieval period, al-Ghazali, Saleem says "that faith without action is flawed, knowledge without purpose is dangerous and an education without service is wasted" (Abdur Rashid 1999, 57). These two epistemological considerations of theocentricity and the socio-political realities that shape the African American experience serve as the defining aspects of Islamic education for the community of Imam Warith Deen.

From Pedagogical Principles to Practice: What Qur'an Based Instruction Looks Like

Educators in the CMS have been grappling with alternative instructional strategies that embody the philosophy of their schools since the 1980s. Unlike most immigrant established Islamic schools, CMS have been conscious of the need to alter not simply the curriculum content but also the approach in instruction, classroom management, and even teacher training.

Unconvinced by the approach of teaching conventional subjects as they are taught in public schools and limiting Islamic content to separate Islamic studies classes, the CMS initially developed a model of instruction using what they called "Qur'anic motivators." The Qur'anic motivator approach ensures that every lesson/theme/cluster of outcomes of the curriculum, regardless of the subject matter, begins with an *ayah* (verse) of relevance from the Qur'an. Educators in the CMS hope that by beginning lessons and new concepts with Qur'anic motivators, it will be ingrained in children that the "Qur'an is the foundation of human life. Therefore, it should also be the cornerstone of human knowledge" (Abdus Sabur 2005, 120). Although the Qur'anic motivator approach has evolved into a more comprehensive model of pedagogy, which I will elaborate on in the following section, most of the CMS continue to simply perfect the initial approach. The assumption is that when teachers can begin lessons with verses of the Qur'an, they will be grounded in both a deep understanding of the Qur'an as well as knowledge of their own subject areas. Connecting the two, however, can be a complex endeavor. Zakiyyah Muhammad explains how she encouraged her staff to implement this approach incrementally. Using the teachings of Imam Warith Deen, she first explains to her staff the stages of child intellectual development:

> Allah has said that human beings grow in two strains: the first thing that impacts our mind is the physical creation; that is the first textbook. There is nothing that the human beings can create in this world that has not already been observed in the physical creation. The planes came about because people saw birds. Submarines came about because some people observed the fish. A helicopter came about because somebody observed either a hummingbird or a dragonfly. So, the creation is the first textbook that impacts the mind of the human being. The second way the human beings grow, however, is through revelation. That's the internal growth. So, I would tell teachers, starting from the kindergarten, instead of telling the children one plus one equals two, show them in the physical creation first what Allah has said. Give them an *ayah* from the Qur'an; read them something in the Qur'an that talks about *mizan*, measurement. Let them know that the first source of knowledge is Allah. Not Piaget, not John Dewey, not somebody else, that all knowledge comes from Allah first and foremost. It's almost like when the baby is born, you whisper into their ear. See when you lay that foundation in their physique first then they get it. That Allah is the source of all knowledge, all knowledge comes from Allah. If they don't get that early, when they evolve and go into higher learning, when they need philosophers and thinkers, they will be confused and think that these manmade concepts are greater than Allah-made concepts.

The essence of the Qur'anic motivator approach is to nurture the foundation that God is the source of all knowledge. This is, as Zakiyyah Muhammad emphasizes to her staff, part and parcel of Islamic education. The example she gives in the previous excerpt about *mizan* (measurement/scale) is a Qur'anic concept that has mathematical implications. Using verses from the Qur'an related to math, science, language, social studies, and responsibility, for example, teaches children as early as kindergarten that they can decode the essence of life through the word of

God. The approach also makes the Qur'an central in the lives of students. The Qur'an is then used regularly and consistently to explain everyday life occurrences and as a result has a relevance beyond rote memorization.

Apart from the instructional approach, CMS educators have also actively tried to alter what is most commonly referred to as the "classroom management" method. In most Islamic schools, most faith-based schools for that matter, educators are expected and encouraged to develop more intimate social bonds with their students. Teachers are sought out, for example, on the basis of their moral uprightness, personal values, and faith practice. Principals and parents want to ensure that the teachers who will be educating their children are people whose private and public lives do not contradict one another. Along the lines of personal behavior and choices, teachers are then also expected to be moral and social role models for students, as parents would be. Put simply, the role of teachers in CMS is that of "other mothers" (Abdur-Rashid 1999, 102). Daa'iyah Saleem contends that other-mothering is a distinct aspect of the CMS philosophy. The concept of other-mothering represents a teacher's role as not only one who imparts knowledge, but also as someone who engages a student and expresses sentiments the same way a mother would. An ethic of care is where teachers develop a "motherly" relationship with their students inside, and, most notably, outside of the classroom. Discussions in the hallways, schoolyard, or outside of school hours allows teachers to assess and nurture the social and spiritual needs of students. Such a philosophy is based on a holistic understanding of child development. Each child has spiritual, emotional, and social obstacles that are often impenetrable without the nurturing of a maternal relationship based on motherly intuition, care, and trust.

The teacher plays an integral part in any school, but particularly in schools where moral upbringing and spiritual perfection is sought. The responsibility of teachers in these settings is that much greater. They must embody the qualities and habits defined by faith principles and exhibit an inner motivation to continually work toward self-improvement. The task is no small feat. And for principals of faith-based schools, identifying, nurturing, and motivating school staff to inspire their students and not solely impart content requires special people. From among these special people, I was lucky enough to speak with Sister Safiyyah Shahid, who has been the glue that brought enormous success to Atlanta's Warith Deen Mohammed High School and Clara Muhammad Elementary. As the principal of both schools currently, Sister Safiyyah told me that it all begins with the hiring process. Teachers she hires must live lives congruent with the mission of the school: the integration of a rigorous academic curriculum that is centered around Islamic principles and teachings. Teachers exhibit a commitment to embodying and learning what it means to teach with Islamic principles.

An example I was given was around conflict resolution. When conflicts arise within the school, as is common in any educational setting, the approach Sister Safiyyah espouses relies on the wisdom of the Prophet Muhammad. "Listening, trying to see both sides, not raising your voice, using Prophet Muhammad (Peace Be Upon Him), using him as a model—you know—to model that [behavior] and teach that [behavior] for students and for ourselves." Even in her own role as a principal, she employs Prophetic wisdom to build leadership capacity and teamwork.

> Every Monday morning, I meet with the level leaders to look at the work that's before us and you know to really take *shura* (counsel) in terms of what it is we have to do, what are our goals for the week, how are we trying to copy this and is this the best way to proceed, are we keeping our children at the top, is this an Islamic perspective, is the Muslim interest, is it being addressed. So, you know this is how we ensure on a daily basis, that the culture of the school is Qur'anic based.

The reference Sister Safiyyah makes to *shura* (counsel) is reflective of the Qur'anic and Prophetic wisdom at work in the CM schools. Although she is the leader and final decision maker for day to day affairs of the school, it was the practice of the Prophet Muhammad to consider the opinions of others, to make joint decisions at certain times, and to develop both ownership and motivation of the team. Nor does Sister Safiyyah assume her role as the sole source and facilitator of counsel to her staff, but also the recipient of counsel. When describing the school's philosophy based on the teachings of Imam W.D. Mohammed, she said: "Our approach is really a village. It takes a village. And everyone has a role in developing and educating our children." Among that village are committed individuals who provide support and consultation to Sister Safiyyah, the consultative board, Director of Education, and the Imam.

An essential part of the village are also parents. Sister Safiyyah said, "The parents are the first teacher. And from our perspective that's what we communicate to parents that they are entrusting us with a treasure to take on to another level." Teachers within the CMS rely on the traditional understanding of the student-teacher relationship in the Islamic tradition, where a student is an *amana* (trust) that is given to the teacher. This trust is a sacred trust to nurture and educate toward goodness and God-consciousness as a mother would a child. The role of the teacher is beyond the classroom and the formal curriculum. A great emphasis is placed on ethical conduct, moral consciousness, and deep appreciation for action in relation to intention, all guided by the tenets of the Islamic creed. The approach, as Sister Safiyyah would say, is holistic—"we see ourselves as 'mother,' we really do"—to prepare children for a future of challenge, success, and uncertainty with love and yet firmness. What defines the pedagogy of the CMS, she said, is nurture, balance, and independence. She used the analogy of animals who are given milk, nurtured for a time, and encouraged to go out on their own to grow independently and to play their part in the life cycle. For children, it is about showing them the way of the Prophet Muhammad with love and respect and then giving them the freedom to find their niche that will contribute positively to society while living within the teachings of Islam.

A Framework in Progress: Moving Closer to a Qur'an Based Model of Education

The formal curriculum format, structure, and approach of the CMS have evolved through three major stages: 1) Curriculum Draft, 2) Themed Units, and most recently, the 3) Ascension Framework. In this section, I will outline how each of these developments or models has continually built on the teachings of Imam Warith Deen and on each other to move the CMS closer to an Islam-based pedagogical model.

Imam Warith Deen encouraged educators within his community to develop a standardized curriculum since the early days of his leadership. In the late 1980s, a committee was established to begin such work. The committee consisted of Imam Saadiq Saafir, Dr. Muhammad Abdullah, Ameerah Abdul Mujeeb, Imam Qasim Ahmed, Dr. Qadir Abdus Sabur, and Dr. Zakiyyah Muhammad, of which the last two provided their insights for this book. Among the committee's first tasks was to distribute a questionnaire to the 35 full-time CMS and 50 part-time schools at the time. The questionnaire was an attempt to garner feedback and suggestions on the elements of a standardized curriculum. From the responses, the committee consolidated the ideas, some of which included fully developed local curriculum, and produced a working document that could be used to guide all schools with principles and best practices. The document was entitled "Clara Muhammad School Curriculum Draft Part I" and was completed in 1990. The completion of this document was monumental in serving as the first national collaboration between the Clara Muhammad schools in streamlining practices (Abdus Sabur and Abdus Sabur 2000, 9–12). In addition to guiding school curricula, the Curriculum Draft also served as a foundational text in training educators at the Muslim Teacher's College and as a guideline for development of Qur'anic themed textbooks. The approach of the draft was to infuse an Islamic worldview into every academic discipline from state curricula. The Islamic worldview was based on nine sets of verses from the Qur'an:

1. Man (humanity) is born good and pure, reflecting the innate good of the human being (16:78);
2. There is an Absolute Moral Authority: Allah, The Most-High (4:59);
3. There is a Single, All-Powerful, Unified Creator (Chapter 112);

4. Brotherhood is based on Faith in Universal Truths (49:10);
5. Women are mothers of civilization and different from man (3:36);
6. Domination of the Earth is for humanity by the command of Allah (31:20);
7. Unity of knowledge (which emanates from Allah) brings order (55:1–9);
8. The Islamic family is the heart of our *Masajid* and social relations (25:54);
9. Islamic thought is comparative (51:49), which requires Muslims to know what Allah's standard is at the outset (7:157; 31:21; 39:18).[10]

These are the founding principles upon which curriculum for CMS has been developed. The Clara Muhammad School Curriculum Draft sought to lay out a framework that would assist a teacher to assemble a curriculum regardless of the subject or grade level. The curriculum draft developed four large areas of knowledge: Ummatology (Social Studies), Ilm (Natural Science), Bayyan Mubeen (Language Arts/Communication Studies), and Mizan (Mathematics, Measurement) (Abdus Sabur and Abdus Sabur 2000, 12). Topic areas were mapped out combining content commonly taught in public schools along with material that defined the Muslim experience. For high school Ummatology for example, students would learn about "flaws and biases in history as recorded by the West," "the spread of al-Islam," "U.S. political structure vs. the Islamic foundation of al-Islam," and the "Islamic vs. the American ideal" in addition to the U.S. Constitution, the World Wars, political theory, and women's suffrage, among many other topics. Similarly, Bayyan Mubeen would cover topics on Islamic, Qur'anic, and Hadith literature while also teaching the Western canon of literature.

The extent to which each school continues to rely on the Curriculum Draft 1990 varies. Part of the difficulty in its longevity and systematic implementation in all schools is due to finances. Given that the initial draft was developed on countless volunteer hours and a shoestring budget for printing and on-going training and development, it has been challenging to build on. However, for many of the educators that I interviewed, it continues to serve as a reference guide for continued in-house curriculum and professional development. At Imam Warith Deen Mohammed High School in Atlanta, which serves as a model school among the CM system, Principal Safiyyah Shaheed said that the Curriculum Draft 1990 is still very much a foundational document for on-going curriculum planning. It provides a step by step outline of how to ensure that the curriculum, classroom management, delivery, and assessment mechanisms are all in line with Qur'anic principles. In addition, Principal Shaheed and her staff meet annually over the summer to review and renew their practices. Over the years, she told me that her school has taken the outline of the curriculum draft and laid it out, enhanced it, and evolved it.

The Curriculum Draft 1990 also served as the foundational text for the Muslim Teacher's College in Randolph, Virginia, directed by Qadir Abdus Sabur. Using the document, the Muslim Teacher's College has been working on developing a curriculum that fully integrates Qur'anic principles across each subject area. By the mid-1990s, the model began to take tangible shape as the second major curriculum approach of developing themed units. It began with the "Qur'anic motivators" approach discussed earlier. Over the years, Dr. Qadir Abdus Sabur and his wife developed a more extensive model where the Qur'anic motivators were not isolated to a single lesson but served as themes for cross curricular teaching. Led by the Abdus Saburs and with the help of a few others, they developed curriculum books to achieve this holistic approach. Qadir Abdus Sabur explained in one of our discussions how he used verses from the Qur'an where Allah employs analogies with bees, mountains, and the rain, for example, to develop storybooks and complimenting curriculum documents for elementary grades.

During the question/answer period of the National Muslim American Society (MAS) Education Conference held in Atlanta, Georgia, from June 2–4, 2000, Imam Warith Deen addressed the need for an indigenous curriculum. Without our own curriculum based on Qur'anic principles, we are not a consortium of schools, he said. What has often been referred to as the Mohammed School System or the consortium of Clara Muhammad schools assumes that there is collaboration and streamlined practices that define the association. But the words of Imam Warith Deen that day clarified that a unified curriculum is still a work in progress. At the same time, his words served as inspiration for educators within the community, like Dr. Qadir Abdus Sabur, who, among others, used those very words of Imam Warith Deen to continue development on a unique educational model. The brief guidelines given by Imam Warith Deen for such an endeavor were:

> Qur'anic based curricula should reflect a view of the world created by Allah and that Allah created man, in his intellectual potential, above all living things. Since the quickening of the intellect of man is the most important aspect of Muslim Education, the Qur'an should be presented in a way that appeals to and does not offend the intellect of clean hearted people.
>
> (Abdus Sabur and Abdus Sabur 2000, 4)

In the spirit of Imam Warith Deen's guidance, Qadir Abdus Sabur and his wife developed a curriculum framework for Muslim schools. The Abdus Saburs developed what they called Qur'anic thematic units over the past 15 years. Through doctoral research of the two of the more established Clara Muhammad schools (Corona, NY and Atlanta, GA), they realized that much work was already informally being done by school teachers and administrators to adopt local state curriculum. What they found, however, is that the integration of a Qur'anic worldview was being done sporadically and highly depended on the level of familiarity of each teacher with the Qur'an. As a result, the Abdus Saburs decided to embark on the development of Qur'anic based thematic units that could be used nationwide. They recognized, most importantly, that this is but a single attempt at achieving the goal of teaching from an Islamic worldview, and their work does not assume to be a panacea for Islamic schools in America. Their work also built on existing models, such as the Clara Muhammad School Curriculum Draft 1990 and the *Alim* multimedia CD, as sources for building units.

The idea of a Qur'anic themed unit was to first choose an overarching theme that was grade level specific, such as hydrology and the oceans for Grades 3 and 4. The next step searched for Qur'anic verses to frame the theme, such as Q 35:12, which states:

> Nor are the two bodies of flowing water alike,
> The one palatable, sweet, and pleasant to drink, and the other salty and bitter.
> Yet from each (kind of water) do ye eat flesh fresh and tender,
> And ye extract ornaments to wear, and thou seest the ships therein that plough the waves, that ye may seek (thus) of the Bounty of Allah that ye may be grateful.
> (Qur'an 35:12, Yusuf Ali Translation)

Through this verse from the Qur'an, every subject area was addressed in the unit. Students would learn biology through fish identification, math through concepts of ocean travel, social studies through transportation, discovery and exploration by sea, language through poetry, drama, songs, and short stories about the ocean, rain, water cycle, and Arabic and Islamic studies through reflecting on the verse, its context, and vocabulary. And all this would be done with the complementing Friday *khutba* (sermons), where the Imam would reinforce the significance of water, its essential nature, and the human responsibility to maintain and care for it by not polluting and overusing it (Abdus Sabur and Abdus Sabur 2000, 68–101). This provides a glimpse of what an Islamic school curriculum uniquely based on a Qur'anic worldview would look like. The essence is that students are taught through the Qur'an, reinforcing that all knowledge stems from a single source.

In the upper grades, this task of teaching cross curricularly has been much more complicated, but that did not affect their perseverance. Currently, the Abdus Saburs, along with their education networks in Richmond and Randolph, Virginia, recently developed the Qur'anic Education Foundation and Tawheed Prep School, the first Muslim high school in Richmond, to achieve these ends. The unique part of Qadir

Abdus Sabur's work is his perseverance to unite the disparate Muslim educational initiatives in his area first. Tawheed Prep School serves the graduates of the local immigrant established school, the Clara Muhammad elementary school, and the Muslim home schoolers in Richmond, VA. Through the Qur'anic Education Foundation, Qadir Abdus Sabur was able to find common ground between Muslim communities on the basis of the Qur'an. These are people who are dedicated to understanding how the Qur'an instructs daily life and how those principles can be instructive in developing curriculum for Muslim children. At Tawheed Prep School, knowledge is taught holistically based on the principle of *tawhid* in the purpose of creation. The core difference is that students will be nurtured to see the world for its integrated purpose—the ripple effect. They will appreciate God's creation in its magnificence—human beings, animals, plant life, constellations, time, and essence as all interrelated—all purposeful in a masterful way. The hope is that through striving to understand the wisdom of the Qur'an, which in itself is unfathomable, young students will see the world and their role in it as a journey of on-going discovery. Qadir Abdus Sabur describes the value of such an approach:

> The only immediate outcome that seems clear is that these youngsters will grow up with an appreciation for their relationship with their environment. So, through the Prophet we have plenty of examples of how we should go to war for example—you don't destroy trees, you don't destroy anything for that matter, but in American society you will study science for the sake of science so if you have to strip coal or pollute the environment we do that but these youngsters understand that science should be studied for the enhancement of humanity and the glorification of Allah. So, they say how do we extract the fossil fuel from the earth and at the same time protect the environment—it's a whole paradigm shift.

Indeed, such a model does require a complete paradigm shift, as Qadir Abdus Sabur mentioned. In his model, the Qur'an no longer fits into an existing curriculum model, nor does it strive to integrate Islamic principles with secular content, but rather the Qur'anic-based model aims to teach Muslim teachers and students to see the world through a Qur'anic worldview. Through the Qur'an, students explore and assess whether modern innovations are in reality something innovative or whether the wisdom of the Qur'an is manifesting itself. Qadir Abdus Sabur gives the example of a verse from the Qur'an:

> The sun and the moon follow their ordered course.
> The plants and the trees bow down in adoration.
> And the sky He has uplifted; and He has set the balance,

That you do not upset the balance,
But observe the balance strictly, nor fall short therein.
                    (*The Majestic Qur'an*, Nawawi
                    Foundation trans.55: 5–9)

In the Qur'anic education model, Qadir Abdus Sabur would use these verses in high school algebra, geometry, and science to understand the course upon which the sun and the moon follow. In geometry, they would use the same verses and analyze the word *mizan* in relation to balancing equations. They would explore what the word *mizan* means socially and mathematically so that students can make connections between life and creation. It is an attempt to push Muslim students to acquire higher order thinking skills through an appreciation for the Qur'an.

The work that Qadir Abdus Sabur is now focused on locally is certainly a shift from his earlier focus in developing a national curriculum for the Clara Muhammad schools in the 1980s and '90s. Although his work continues to be inspired by the vision of Imam Warith Deen and works toward a model that is useful to all Islamic schools in America (CMS and other), he realized that to truly develop something unique, it requires focus and local field testing. After years of service to the National School Board under Imam Warith Deen as well as integral roles in larger national organizations such as CISNA (Council of Islamic Schools in North America), Qadir Abdus Sabur now focuses his energies entirely on the community in Richmond, Virginia, and the work of Tawheed Prep School. However, he was judicious to point out that a Qur'anic based model is not entirely unique to the Muslim Teacher's College or to the Clara Muhammad school system. Dawud Tauhidi and his Tarbiyah Project, which will be discussed in more depth later in this book, is developing a similar model of holistic Islamic education within the immigrant supported Islamic schools.

The third model for CMS is entitled the Ascension Framework. The curriculum framework is inspired by Imam Warith Deen's Ramadan lecture in 2001 entitled the "Night Visit," where he re-traced the moment that Muslims believe the Prophet Muhammad ascended to the seven heavens. On this special night journey from Mecca to Jerusalem (*isra'*) and then from the Dome of the Rock, the Prophet Muhammad ascended to the heavens to be in the Divine Presence (*mi'raj*). This night journey is said to have reaffirmed the Prophet Muhammad's position as the seal of prophets (Lings 1991, 101–4). The night journey has been interpreted and extended by Imam Warith Deen to gain a deeper appreciation for what each prophet who preceded the Prophet Muhammad contributed to the human legacy. These contributions are outlined as follows: Prophet Adam gave mankind a sense of the original soul, *fitrah*, or a sense of our innate disposition. Prophets Jesus and John gave mankind our spirit and sense of spirituality. Prophet Joseph's legacy was intuition. Prophet Idris gave mankind a thirst for academic learning. Prophet Aaron nurtured culture and an affinity for diversity. Prophet Moses taught us how to govern politically and socially. And lastly, Prophet Abraham gave us an appreciation for ethics and morality.[11] These seven stages of evolution were then taken by believers in the community of Imam Warith Deen to develop a curriculum framework for the CMS.

The idea of such a framework based on the night journey was first initiated by a group of educators in Hartford, Connecticut, in 2004. Since then, the idea has been championed by the Mosque Cares Special Committee on Education, which includes a number of participants of my study. These educators have recognized since the beginning of the CMS that they have been working "in a philosophical box of ideas not of our own design" (Mosque Cares 2005). This working framework, therefore, has allowed educators in the community of Imam Warith Deen to reframe the way education should be imparted in a way that reflects the Islamic spirit both in content delivery and teaching methodology (see Table 4.1).

The teaching methodology relies on a rationale that is founded on principles of educational psychology through stages of development while embedded within the Ascension Framework. The first of these stages emphasizes, for example, *ain ul yaqin*, nurturing a child's "original soul" (*fitrah*) through intuition, experience, and imagination. At this stage of elementary education, children would be exposed to the wonders of creation, the natural world, and urged through experiential

Table 4.1 Ascension Framework

Prophet	Level	Representation	Description
Prophet Abraham	Level 7	"Ethical Man"	Qur'anic logic and ethics to inform the spirit and rationality
Prophet Moses	Level 6	"Man as Ruler of Government and Social Life"	Communal learning, critical analysis, collective responsibility
Prophet Aaron	Level 5	"Cultural Man"	Ideological, epistemological, reason
Prophet Idris	Level 4	"Academic Man"	Cultivating conceptual knowledge, ideas, principles, logic
Prophet Joseph	Level 3	"Intuitive Man"	Intuition, Inquiring, Investigating
Prophets Jesus and John	Level 2	"Spiritual Man"	Habit, Rote Memory, Cultivating Curiosity and Inspiration
Prophet Adam	Level 1	"Original Soul"	Experiential Learning, Inquiry, Intuition, and Imagination

activities to explore the world around them. This is what Imam Warith Deen has insisted is nurturing a child's *qadr*:[12] curiosity, natural inclinations, and intuition relating back to the first three levels of the Ascension Framework.

At the middle school level, the focus would shift to academia and culture as defined by levels four and five of the framework. Here the teaching methodology reflects a consistency with conventional teaching methodology but emphasizes *'ilm al yaqin*, or one's ability to appraise evidence, reason, infer, and make judgments about how the Qur'an relates to both the social and natural world around them. This can only be achieved, it is argued, once children have developed awe and wonder of God's creation; hence, the importance of the first stage of experiential knowledge.

The final method is based on a combination of social constructionism and recognizing *haqq al yaqin*, or the absolute Truth of reality through the teachings of the Qur'an. This approach to teach reflects the teachings of Imam Warith Deen's emphasis on rational thinking and applying the Qur'an to our everyday life experiences. Students here are encouraged to "apply logic from the natural world" and Imam Warith Deen's commentary on the Qur'an to help students make sense of science and the society that shapes the world around them. These final levels comprise the teaching methods for secondary schools, where students will gain a sense of human ethics that must inform behavior and social interaction, including leadership (Mosque Cares 2005).

The basis of the Ascension Framework is to use individual rational faculty to align the world with the teachings of the Qur'an and the Prophetic way. This method remains consistent with Imam Warith Deen's belief that all knowledge is from God alone.

> G-d gives guidance to the spirit and reason of man through revelation and the life example of the model man Prophet Muhammad (saw); Man uses reason to construct the ideas and influences of social life in agreement with revelation, the spirit and thinking of the original soul (Adam) and the logical principles of the natural world.
>
> (Mosque Cares 2005, 30)

The Ascension Framework is in theory the closest educators in the CMS system have come to developing an indigenous Islamic pedagogy that infuses the teachings of Imam Warith Deen on Islamic principles with educational methodology. It is, in the words of Daa'iyah Saleem, an Islamic educational taxonomy.

These working frameworks of Islamic education that have evolved out of the community of Imam Warith Deen are a result of his distinct approach as a scholar and community leader. Some have called him a *mujaddid* (renewer of faith), and in many ways he was. His approach on connecting with the Qur'an through one's own intellectual faculty and life experience empowered a community who could have otherwise been lost in transition. Shedding the theology of his father and adopting the universal teachings of Islam could have left his community insecure in accessing a tradition that immigrants had inherited. Yet, as a *mujaddid* does, he forged a new path by encouraging independent analysis of the Qur'an in a way that spoke to the plight of the indigenous American Muslim. In relation to education, the approach employed the Qur'an to uniquely reframe not solely the curriculum but the pedagogical principles and approach.

Islamization of Knowledge Model

The approach for immigrant established Islamic schools has been very different.

There has been less emphasis placed on developing a framework per se, or even instructional strategies similar to the CMS system, and greater development in the area of Islamic studies textbooks similar to the goals of the IIIT discussed earlier. Generally, immigrant established Islamic schools have not challenged the form and structure of secular schooling. Rather they have placed an emphasis on the lack of moral values being formally taught in schools. Supporters of Islamic schools have feared the impact that not teaching religion formally could have on the epistemological and ontological development of their children. The absence of nurturing a religious worldview in school would risk children growing up with a secularist worldview (Nord 1995). The focus of early Islamic schools established in immigrant Muslim communities was to fill the void of religious education. Organizations like the IQRA Foundation have provided an urgent service by developing Islamic studies and Arabic textbooks for elementary and secondary schools since the 1970s. Since IQRA, a plethora of textbook organizations have saturated the Islamic education market, all in hopes of developing effective teaching materials about Islam.

Two important contextual characteristics differentiate the development of Islamic school curriculum in the immigrant community in relation to the community of Imam Warith Deen. Firstly, as discussed in previous chapters, the immigrant community ought really to be labeled "communities" because of the ideological, linguistic, and ethnic diversities by which they co-exist. Unlike the CMS, which are based on the guidance and direction of a single scholar, immigrant schools have been established across North America by individual community initiatives often, but not always, associated with local mosque projects and very rarely part of any concerted effort or overseeing structural body.

Secondly, the legacy of colonial education alluded to earlier sets the stage to deeply understand how and why immigrant established Islamic schools have developed school curriculum mirroring a conventional secular public school approach. Although in most cases these schools are private institutions, it is not arbitrary that immigrant Islamic schools generally accept, if not promote, the curriculum framework of conventional public education. Inspired by the spirit of revivalism yet largely educated in schools where religion was relegated to a separate subject in colonized nations, educated, immigrant Muslims who aspired to develop their own schools modeled them after their own lived experiences. In many ways, immigrant established Islamic schools also mirrored the ideological vision of Jewish Liberal Day Schools and Catholic religious schooling in the United States. Initially establishing schools where secular subjects remained intact and only supplemented with religious studies and then later moving toward an integrated schooling model is the general historical trajectory of most religious day schools in North America (Nord 1995; Levisohn 2008; Ellenson 2008). The experience of Islamic schools, immigrant established ones in particular, therefore, mirrors the more conventional trajectory in that sense.

Pedagogical Values: Mapping the Aims of Islamic Schools in North America

The overarching rationale of early immigrants who supported the idea of Islamic schooling as an alternative to public schools was quite simply preservation and protection, as discussed in previous chapters. Adopting and adapting to a new culture produced anxieties for some around cultural norms in North American society. The acceptance of dating and pre-marital sex, for example, was viewed as the most dangerous of lifestyle choices that justified the need for Islamic schooling for many. Such lifestyles, it was feared, not only countered the ethical code of Islam but would lead to the breakdown of the family through inter-religious marriages and sexual promiscuity (Sweet 1997, 75). Speaking to the urgency of protecting our children, Sheikh Abdalla Idris has commented about his early experience as the principal of Toronto's ISNA Islamic school:

> The community suffered much within the public school in many ways, our norms, our traditions, our values. Usually we have a high level of protection for our children. And then they go to the public school and are subjected to things that Muslim families actually see as quite shocking.
> Like using bad words, using drugs, obscenity. And this is why I say, 'This is an environment that is protected to allow children to learn.'

The choice between lifestyles is seen as a compromise that young children must make and one that often distracts from student learning. For many Islamic schools, it is believed that, through separate learning environments that are "Islamically" based, educators can ideally remove or at least limit the social distractions of schooling. It is not uncommon to find Islamic school philosophies also reflecting the sentiments expressed by Sheikh Abdalla. The Islamic School of Greater Kansas City established in 1989, for example, states that the school was established out of a response "to the imperative of safeguarding our children . . . [recognizing] the ever increasing violence, the drug use, and the sexual promiscuity in public schools is a threat that cannot be ignored. . . ."[13] The threat of immoral behavior and the potential for Islamic schools to redress immorality has often only been convincing to those whose children have already adopted lifestyles counter to Islamic beliefs. Dr. Mahmoud Rashdan, once member of ISNA's Department of Education, told participants at the Islamic Education Symposium in March 1989 that he too did not consider the importance of Islamic schools "until the fire came to my home, so to say—and the smoke began to become suffocating."[14] In response to the "ills of Western society," Islamic schools served as protective agents where students could be taught in an environment where the morals taught at home could be reflected and reinforced in schools. To engage students about the relevance and superiority of an Islamic way of life, however, requires that Islamic schools make Islam attractive. Sheikh Abdalla contends that "when Islam becomes the attraction to someone—nothing can shake them because nothing else can attract them. That's the purpose of an Islamic school—to make Islam attractive to our children."

The aims of an Islamic school in this sense are then to make that which is Islamically unlawful also unattractive. According to Sheikh Abdalla, however, making Islam attractive must go beyond nurturing moral behavior. The excellence of an Islamic school, he said, must be measured by the attachment and awe that one has for the Qur'an.

Through the Qur'an, students are nurtured to think Islamically and by virtue act morally. But this is an anomaly. Most Islamic schools are far from reaching this goal, he says.

Most begin by teaching the basic beliefs and practices that makes one Muslim, but have not developed to the stage where we are nurturing Muslim children to think "Islamically" and aspire for knowledge. Sheikh Abdalla then quotes a verse of the Qur'an for me to illustrate the unending search for knowledge that he tries to nurture in children:

> And if all the trees on the earth were pens, and the sea, with seven more seas to supply it, [were ink],
> the words of Allah could not be exhausted. Allah is the August, Wise.
> *Al-Qur'an*, 31:27 (Yusuf Ali translation)

The concept of God's infinite knowledge of all things that we can only attempt to uncover is the foundation of an Islamic education, he says. The aim of Islamic education is to attempt to make sense of the Qur'an in relation to our own world. As Sheikh Abdalla puts it: "When I think of Islamic education, I am looking at someone who would say 'wow!' We need to engage the sociologists, the psychologists, the scientists, astronomers, engineers, and psychoanalysts, you name it. When are we going to get students that think that way?" Using examples of scientists who have made discoveries reaffirming Qur'anic verses, Sheikh Abdalla says this is the way to make Islam attractive to people. The Islamization approach is in principle committed to proving the relevance of and finding significance between the Qur'an and science.[15] Essential to the approach is that Islamic beliefs do not contradict modern scientific breakthroughs, but in fact, foretell modern science. The belief is that if an individual is able to deeply read the *ayahs* (verses/signs) of the Qur'an, they will discover the wonders of the universe through its signs. An Islamic education, in the way that Sheikh Abdalla envisions it, is therefore to inspire young Muslim children to see the world through the Qur'an with awe and wonder.

In practice, however, much of what Sheikh Abdalla refers to serves as the ideal.

Most parents who remained concerned about preserving and protecting stayed committed to the conventional aims measured by academic achievement. By and large, these early educated middle-class Muslims who supported the idea of their own schools were unwilling to forfeit their children becoming professionals for the sake of a strong religious-cultural identity. They wanted both. As a result, even Sheikh Abdalla admits, "Apart from that [basic religious education], it's just a regular school."

The three aims of Islamic schooling discussed earlier, to protect children from the ills of Western society, to nurture Islamic thinking, and to achieve both of those while matching academic standards of secular schools, are embedded in the immigrant Muslim experience. The language needed to dichotomize between Western culture and an Islamic way of life was instituted by the rise of revivalist rhetoric of *jahiliyyah* (the pre-Islamic period of ignorance). This rhetoric served as the catalyst for Islamic schools to provide safe havens for Muslim children (Zine 2008). The Islamization of Knowledge movement built on revivalist thought with an intellectual model for revival. Through reframing knowledge and thinking *Islamically*, the "malaise of the *ummah*" could be overcome (Faruqi 1989). Yet, after the rhetoric of revival and Islamization, Islamic schools remain, by the testament of most of my participants, structurally similar to secular public schools. When I asked Dawud Tauhidi to help me understand why Islamic schools have remained simply at the stage of rhetoric, he referred back to the impact of colonial schooling on immigrant Muslims.

After seeing Islamic schooling evolve since the early 1980s and having established his own school and model in Detroit, he concurred that Islamization had served as an impetus, but the model of Islamic schooling, he says, "thrived from the secularization of Muslim education from the colonial period."

> That's what they all knew in their home countries. You have the Western subjects and then you have Islam added on to it. You have the Islamic sciences but you don't have time for that of course so you put a little bit of Qur'an, a little bit of *fiqh* [Islamic law], a little bit of *seerah* [history of the early period of Islam], and you call it Islamic studies—none of which is based on pedagogy. So, you have a secularized framework and a watered down content and you expect to do miracles—none of it based on pedagogy—none of it.

The challenge for immigrant Islamic schools especially has been to redefine form and structure in relation to pedagogical principles that have thus far been confined to theory. Bilal Ajieb told me that this has been the challenge that CISNA initially took up in its early years in an attempt to align Islamic schools with the principles of Islamic education outlined by World Council of Islamic Education.[16] The First World Conference on Islamic education and those that followed provided the terminology and theoretical frameworks that have shaped Islamic education discourse in North America since (Durkee 1987).

The essence of an Islamic education is the development of moral character based on a foundation, which, within the Islamic paradigm, is Islam, to ensure that the *fitra* (original nature) of each and every individual is allowed to grow. From the First World Conference on Islamic Education, Husain and Ashraf (1979) define Islamic education as:

> [A]n education which trains the sensibility of pupils in such a manner that in their . . . approach to all kinds of knowledge they are governed by the deeply felt ethical values of Islam. They are trained and mentally so disciplined that they want to acquire knowledge not merely to satisfy an intellectual curiosity or just for material worldly benefit but to grow up as rational, righteous beings and to bring about the spiritual, moral and physical welfare of their families, their people and mankind. Their attitude derives from a deep faith in God and a wholehearted acceptance of a God-given moral code.
>
> (cited in Halstead 2004, 519)

In principle, the vision of Islamic education since the First World Conference on Islamic Education is theoretically holistic: mind, body, spirit. Nurturing behavior and etiquette defined by moral principles along with acts of faith, practice, and intellectual training of an Islamic worldview all serve as elements of an Islamic education. However, in practice, most Islamic schools have struggled with developing an educational framework that speaks to each element in a concerted pedagogical practice.

In the Absence of a Framework: Islam as a Subject

Apart from the administrative challenges of Islamic schools with limited resources and eclectic community support, the emphasis for most immigrant established Islamic schools has been placed in Islamic studies over altering aspects of state/provincial curriculum. Many schools have historically relied on IQRA International, based in Chicago, for Islamic studies textbooks and materials.

IQRA International is the first curriculum initiative and likely the longest standing in North America. The IQRA model is an attempt to take "modern [teaching] methodology" and apply it to the areas of Islamic studies (Ghazi 1999, 302). At the time when IQRA's work first began, discussed in more detail in the previous chapter, there was a dearth of educational material for primary school children in English about Islam. IQRA sought to fill that void by creating curriculum materials for teachers: textbooks, skill books, teacher/parent guides, enrichment books, and educational aids that would organize and package foundational Islamic teachings in a way that was accessible for schools. The initial aim was to serve weekend school programs with this curriculum, but the growth of full-time Islamic schools in North America soon increased the demand for IQRA materials. IQRA materials continue to be used primarily in Islamic studies courses and do not lean toward an integration of Islamic values across core secular subjects. The focus has been on teaching Arabic, Qur'anic studies, *Seerah* (the life of the Prophet Muhammad), fundamental aspects of *'aqa'id* and *fiqh* (basic beliefs and practices), and *akhlaq* (character).

The IQRA model soon became the default route for the majority of early Islamic schools attempting to define the "Islamic" in their schools. And for many, if not most parents, this was sufficient. A push to integrate Islam—or "Islamize"—the core curriculum did not systematically take place until well into the 1980s and continues to be a major point of contention for schools as there remains no consolidated model that has achieved this yet. Numerous educators from within the community have noted that the "appendage" of Islamic studies to a secular curriculum cannot suffice to define Islamic schooling. In addressing the curriculum challenge for Islamic schools, Dr. Freda Shamma, professor of education and supporter of Islamic schools in America, argues, similar to Dawud Tauhidi, that such a model is the result of the Muslim experience in post-colonial homelands. "When Muslims regained control of their educational systems, they kept the secular system and added the subject 'Islamic education.' It was logical for the Muslim schools in America to follow the same system, using public school textbooks for the other subjects and adding courses in religion and Arabic to make an 'Islamic school'" (Shamma 1999, 277). Maintaining the separation of Islamic studies from "secular" subjects, as they are most often referred to, has been the default model. Keeping Islamic studies as a separate subject has also been the easiest to develop because the rest of curriculum content, strategies, and methods can be adopted from public institutions, and the ingenuity of Islamic schools remains in mastering a single subject area. In addition to adopting the post-colonial educational model and considering the simplicity of the endeavor, the IQRA approach also remains in line with the model of religious schools in North America. Teaching children the language, in this case Arabic, and basic beliefs of faith mirrors the conventional model of Jewish, Catholic, and Protestant private schools in North America that all preceded Islamic schooling. For Muslim immigrants from post-colonial societies then, the IQRA framework serves as a palatable approach in that a focus on core curriculum—like any other public school—remains the focus.

Since the wide dissemination and use of IQRA materials in many Islamic schools, there has been a plethora of similar attempts to develop curriculum materials for teaching Islamic studies. *Goodword Islamic Studies* materials, for example, teach Islamic morals through themes that are aligned with teachings of the Qur'an and Prophetic tradition. Exercises to evaluate student learning follow the completion of each section of the textbook. This particular series of textbooks is designed for those families and schools where Arabic is the medium of instruction. Each textbook company attempts to raise the level of professionalism and standard of Islamic studies materials. The ICO Islamic Studies series, for example, has a similar curricular structure as the others, but emphasizes that the curriculum has been designed with a deep understanding of the target group, psychological development of children, curriculum theory, and with special attention given to superficial considerations, such as illustrations and printing standards. Most new book publishers that enter the Islamic school curriculum market concern themselves with making attractive teaching materials as opposed to altering the content. *The Right Path, Hurry to Faith, Al Amal,* and the most popular of the new textbook series, *I Love Islam,* attempt to package Islamic studies' materials with supplementary audio CDs, DVDs, posters, Islamic children's songs, interactive assignments, bright colors, and illustrations. In the case of the latter, the *I Love Islam Series* is also part of a larger Islamic educational network in the southern United States through the Islamic Services Foundation, which also manages the Brighter Horizons Academy in Dallas, Texas, and publishes the *I Love Islam Series*.

The development of Islamic studies course materials for elementary and secondary school students has to an extent been a tangible result of the past 30 years of Islamic school growth. From IQRA to *I Love Islam*, textbooks and teaching aids for imparting basic beliefs and practices of Islam have evolved with more effective instructional tools for student interest. These textbook series have also filled an important and urgent void for the day to day function of Islamic schools. However, for many Muslim educators in the field, Islamic studies textbooks remain insufficient. Teaching Islam as a separate subject, they argue, does not nurture children to think from an Islamic worldview in every aspect of knowledge—the need to "Islamize curriculum." The attempt of the Islamization approach is to "rewrite the curriculum of every subject so that Islamic knowledge/thinking is integrated into every subject" (Shamma 2004). Geography, history, social studies, and most of the social sciences have been "Islamized" with curriculum content that speaks to the contributions of Muslim societies and civilizations.

Toward an Integrated Curriculum for Islamic Schools

Freda Shamma is among a select few visionaries who have called for a *tawidic* curriculum, one that is grounded in an Islamic worldview, since the 1990s. She, among others like Dawud Tauhidi, are critical of the conventional Islamic school approaches that "assume that the American curriculum is basically sound, needing only a bit of infusion of Islamic ideas here and there" (Shamma 1999, 286). Such an approach belittles the pedagogical contributions of Islamic civilizations, Shamma argues. Education in Islamic civilizations has always been grounded in and formed by the Islamic conceptions of God as Creator, which alters the study of every subject matter from mathematics to psychology. In teaching history, Shamma uses the Qur'anic injunction that says God created humankind in nations and tribes to know one another; it is incumbent that children learn of the inherent goodness of all people. Further, when teaching about war, revolution, and the rise and fall of great civilizations, she says these must be understood through the Qur'anic teachings of ethics, morality, and the nature of power and wealth. Similarly, it is not sufficient, Shamma argues, to simply acknowledge and teach about the accomplishments of Muslim scientists and mathematicians, as is often the appendage approach. Rather, a *tawidic* approach seeks to understand how al-Khwarizmi, for example, used an Islamic worldview to discover Algebra in the 9th century (Shamma 1999, 288–9). There are few Islamic school educators that would contest the validity of such a model. The questions that remain are whether such a model exists?

I came across three integrated curriculum projects that have evolved over the years but that in their own right have far exceeded the expectations of simply an Islamized curriculum. These integrated curriculum projects are more concerned about the worldview that influences and shapes curriculum design. They question the underlying assumptions and beliefs of how curriculum has been developed. These alternative curricular designs are based on the belief that educational materials developed from a secular perspective present a "reified structure of today's world as an unchanging and unchangeable reality; it presents history from its own monochromatic view, and it may even ignore or distort solid historical data to maintain its own interpretations" (Harder 2006, xiv). The glossing over of scientific findings and traditions of Eastern civilizations in high school science textbooks is one example of such a distortion. Similarly, in elementary social studies textbooks, social Darwinism is often subtly and implicitly, if not outrightly, employed (Harder 2006, xv). Initiatives such as the Tarbiyah Project and Muslim Education Foundation call for an "epistemic correction of knowledge." A correction or re-envisioning of such magnitude requires two overarching redefinitions: the essence of life and of learning (Harder 2006, xv). The development of curriculum and teaching resources based on a Qur'anic worldview would ideally present both the physical and metaphysical significance of knowledge. Elma Harder gives the example of teaching about rain to explain that in a Qur'anic approach, it does not suffice to begin with an *ayah* (verse) from the Qur'an about rain, but to explain the water cycle in relation to its physical, natural, and spiritual significances as interrelated and interdependent (Harder 2006, xvi). Learning in this approach is integrated and theme based across curriculum as opposed to the conventional individual outcomes in individual subject areas.

FADEL

Foundation for the Advancement and Development of Education (FADEL), based out of Cincinnati, Ohio, and spearheaded by Dr. Freda Shamma, has attempted to develop an integrated Islamic curriculum since 1995. The work of FADEL began under the International Islamic University and more recently downsized into a more localized operation. The project first began by outlining a list of Qur'anic concepts that are essential for student learning. Those Qur'anic concepts were then systematically applied or integrated into history, English, Arabic language, and visual arts curriculum. Although some curriculum materials, including textbooks, have been drafted, the potential of FADEL has been stifled, as are most community initiatives, by a lack of financial and human resources. Finding specialists in each subject area has been among the most daunting of their tasks (Shamma 1999).

Muslim Education Foundation

The Muslim Education Foundation (MEF) was established by Elma Harder and her husband Dr. Muzaffar Iqbal in Edmonton, Alberta. The work of MEF began out of a concerted dissatisfaction for holistic educational alternatives for their own children. Unwilling to sacrifice the precious years of their children's formative years, Elma and Muzaffar decided early in their years of child rearing to home school. Eventually their conviction and success with home schooling caught the interest of others in their community, and a network began. What initially began as a home schooling initiative with the intent of developing resource materials to support fellow home schoolers, their work has now evolved into establishing a full-time publicly funded Islamic school in the Edmonton school system that is Qur'anically based. The work put into developing *Concentric Circles* has served as the basis for a curriculum framework that now serves as an integrated Islamic education approach within the formal confines of a publicly funded school.

Similar to the Tarbiyah framework, the MEF uses a thematic approach that is grounded in a Qur'anic worldview based on three primary concepts: *tawhid* (Oneness of God), *risalah* (prophecy), and *ma'ad* (the Return). The aim of MEF is to develop an education model that allows children to understand existence and their own place through a deeper understanding of the various levels of existence from an Islamic worldview. In 2006, Elma Harder published her first curriculum resource book entitled *Concentric Circles: Nurturing Awe and Wonder in Early Learning*. *Concentric Circles* provides a framework for educators to develop thematic units that are Qur'anically based. The ingenuity of the MEF approach is that it has not developed packaged learning and teaching resources. Rather, it has developed a model that equips educators with the tools to develop their own units of study. *Concentric Circles* walks educators through a ten-step conceptual framework that they can apply to any topic when developing an Islamic school curriculum. The essence of the framework is to define the topic, rationale, and goals of knowledge content in a way that establishes intentions and clarifies the Qur'anic orientation.

Tarbiyah Project

The Tarbiyah Project (Tauhidi 2006) was initiated by the late Dawud Tauhidi in the early 1980s. Tauhidi was among the few Muslim educators with academic training specifically in Islamic philosophy and education. A White American convert to Islam, Tauhidi's background in Arabic language and Islamic philosophy of education led him to develop arguably the most radical approach to Islamic schooling within the immigrant Muslim community. In the mid-1980s Tauhidi became the principal and director of Crescent Academy in Canton, Michigan. From his leadership at Crescent, Tauhidi developed a model of Islamic schooling that challenged the conventional outcomes based curriculum approach with a theme based, holistic curriculum grounded in an Islamic pedagogy. Structured by what the framework refers to as "Powerful Ideas" (identity, morality, belonging, God-consciousness), the approach weaves together traditional Islamic sciences with academic curriculum outcomes while centering the needs of the learner.

When conducting interviews for my research, I had the opportunity not only to meet and interview Dawud Tauhidi, but also to sit in a number of classes and watch the Tarbiyah curriculum in action. What I witnessed in sporadic, unannounced classroom observations were young middle school children making connections in classroom conversations. In a Grade 6 class that I stepped into for a few minutes, I heard students engaged in conversations about characters in a novel making moral decisions and relating those decisions to the moral uprightness of companions of the Prophet Muhammad from Islamic history. I then stepped into a math class where students were learning about clouds. It seemed awkward at first, until I comprehended the connections that were being made between science, social studies, and mathematics, all through the theme of the month that spans across grades and subjects.

The approaches of the Tarbiyah Framework and of the Muslim Education Foundation in many ways represent the organic, innovative, and authentically Islamic pedagogical model that most Muslim educators have been searching for. These frameworks challenge the logical-positivist curriculum approach that is most commonly practiced in public schools and adopted unwittingly by the majority of Islamic schools, and yet at the same time surpass the concept of Islamization by reworking the curriculum from its roots. As a result, resistance toward the Tarbiyah or MEF approach is not uncommon. Resistance is often on the basis of the curriculum not being taught in a manner that is linear and quantifiable as well as the level of dedication and commitment required on behalf of the school and teaching staff to organically develop units of study. Most schools prefer pre-packaged Islamic studies textbooks that reflect how other subjects are taught.

Toward an Islamic Pedagogy

The development of distinct models of Islamic education in North America based on diverse interpretations and ideological positions within mainstream Islamic beliefs and practices is testament to the diversity of the Islamic tradition. My emphasis on the ideological underpinnings of Islamic schooling in this chapter is not to undermine one over another or judge one model's credibility or legitimacy over another. Rather, my intent has been to highlight the complexity of aims and objectives shaped by contextual, historical, and ideological factors. In the words of Professor John Voll, who traces the growth of Islamic ideologies, "The rich diversity of the modern Islamic experience bears testimony to the continuing ability of the Islamic message to inspire people in many different ways" (Voll 1983, 389).

This chapter has attempted to provide insights into the complexity with which models of Islamic schooling have evolved. It is insufficient to understand the growth of Islamic schools solely by the historical forces, events, and personalities that shaped them, as I explored in the first two chapters. Through a deeper appreciation of historical context, however, this chapter sought to explore how developments in Islamic thought equally shaped the growth of Islamic schooling.

For the immigrant Muslim from Jordan, Syria, Lebanon, India, Malaysia, or Sudan, their readiness to adapt to a new culture and be an American or Canadian Muslim took a variety of forms. Civic engagement ranged from outright resistance to uncritical assimilation. For a large majority, the choice between resistance and assimilation left them somewhere in between; a negotiated identity formation that often elevated the connection to the global *ummah* while contributing to and gaining the benefit of Western-ness. This negotiation of identity was informed largely by the intellectual thought of a handful of revivers of faith that trickled down to the masses through writings, lectures, and at a local level, on the pulpit. The impact of reformist and revivalist ideology on the development of Muslim communities and by virtue schools in North America is immense not only for the immigrant Muslim experience but equally for the indigenous African American Muslim experience.

The settlement of ethnically diverse Muslim immigrants in North America repositioned African American Muslim authority over Islam. Ideologically, African American Muslims were by and large in a state of flux during the stages of early Muslim immigration. Transitioning from the NOI to the community of Imam Warith Deen, the initial response was to align with the aspirations of the global *ummah*. Unable to challenge authority over the Islamic tradition, however, the community of Imam Warith Deen eventually revived the need for self-identity and self-empowerment. The community of Imam Warith Deen was then able to re-establish their own mastery of the American landscape—something that immigrants found foreign. The agenda for community formation, school development, and by virtue, school curriculum was determined by these ideological tensions of: 1) plight of the global *ummah*; 2) facility with the Islamic tradition; and 3) needs of the American/Canadian Muslim community.

In her own assessment of Islamic schools, Noura Durkee explains why the CMS developed an ideology outwardly superficial of traditional Islamic sources and a greater emphasis on the American context and experience. Durkee says, "Their point of view is that they don't want to get involved in the fine points of Imam Al-Ghazali or the subtle differences between the great imams. If they can hold to what they know of the Qur'an and Sunnah they can tackle and overcome, *B'idhn Allah* [by God's permission], the overwhelming social problems faced by their communities" (Durkee 1987). The curriculum of schools serves as a microcosmic representation of larger ideological emphases between communities. The social problems, challenges, and aims that define the curriculum of CMS are unique from the objectives of most suburban immigrant established Islamic schools. The educational paradigms that have shaped the curriculum of CMS emphasize rational thought and self-help through the teachings of the Qur'an, Prophetic tradition, and leadership of Imam Warith Deen to empower his community.

For immigrant established Islamic schools, pedagogical practice has been shaped more by their own experiences of colonization, decolonization, diaspora, immigration, and settlement. Although they began for many out of a fear, distrust, and anxiety of a new life in a new land, immigrant established Islamic schools eventually developed in patterns consistent with their own colonial educational experiences while employing the rhetoric of revival against the very forces that shaped them. At an individual school level, understanding the contextual, historical, and ideological forces that have shaped the schools provides insight as to why the schools seem so outwardly disconnected from the principles of Islamic education. In his recent study of Islamic schools in the United States, for example, Michael Merry found that there is a disconnect between principles and practice in Islamic schools and that "[m]uch of the language that Islamic schools adopt to convey their mission is therefore unsurprisingly Western in origin" (Merry 2007, 60). When analyzed historically and contextually, however, this outward disconnect becomes more palatable because the vision of Islamic education is far from inherently anti-Western. What began both for the indigenous and immigrant Muslim as a distrust of Western imperialism soon translated into an ideology of Islamic revivalism. Both anti-imperialism and revivalism, however, evolved into an ideology of praxis.

The concern of educating Muslims to be Muslim is now the definitive task of North American Muslim identity formation. In a post-9/11 era, the disconnect that Michael Merry and others have recognized requires urgent reconciliation. Muslim educators are now challenged more than they have ever been to ensure that the disparate conceptions of Islamic education that have thus far been theoretically formulated are put into practice. The way forward leaves us even more questions for consideration that each school would likely answer very differently.

Notes

1. The Golden Age of Islam refers to the period of the Prophet Muhammad and his immediate successors, the four caliphs, CE 610–661 (from the first revelation to the death of 'Ali).
2. For more depth on the writings and views of the Ikhwaan (Qutb) and Jamaat-i-Islami (Maududi), see: Albert Bergeson, ed., *The Sayyid Qutb Reader: Selected Writings on Politics, Religion, and Society* (New York: Routledge, 2008); Sayed Khatab, *The Political Thought of Sayyid Qutb: The Theory of Jahiliyyah* (London: Routledge, 2006); Diaa Rashwan, ed., *The Spectrum of Islamist Movements* (Berlin: Al Ahram Center for Political and Strategic Studies, 2007); Abul Ala Maudoodi, *A Short History of the Revivalist Movement in Islam* (Lahore: Lahore Islamic Publications, 1963); Seyyed Hossein Nasr, *Mawdudi and the Making of Islamic Revivalism* (New York: Oxford University Press, 1996); Seyyed Hossein Nasr, *Islam and the Plight of Modern Man* (New York: Longman, 1975).

3. In order to distinguish his community from the theological beliefs of the NOI and more importantly in relation to mainstream Sunni Muslim communities, Imam Warith Deen had initially referred to his community as followers of a fifth *madhhab* (school of thought). Sunni Islam has had four commonly agreed upon juridical schools of thought since the period of medieval Islam. Imam Warith Deen's attempt to append a fifth school in order to keep separate from yet aligned with mainstream practices and beliefs was a short lived endeavor. He soon realized that such a position would create extreme resistance from the global Muslim community and would once again deem his attempts heretical.
4. "Sister Clara Muhammad Consortium of Schools: Statement of Philosophy," September 2003. This document was mailed to me by Safiyyah Shahid from the archives of the W.D. Mohammed H.S.
5. Clara Muhammad School in Association with Muhammad Center, Hartford, Connecticut, "Imam W. Deen Mohammed (Speaker Education Meeting, Washington, DC, May 2001)" found in the archives of W.D. Mohammed High School, Atlanta, GA.
6. Ibid.
7. "W. Deen Mohammed High School, Atlanta, Georgia U.S.A. Curriculum 1996/97." This document was mailed to me by Safiyyah Shahid from the archives of the W.D. Mohammed H.S.
8. n.a. "Implementing a Qur'anic Based Curriculum" archives W.D. Mohammed H.S., Atlanta GA, n.d., n.p. 6.
9. "W. Deen Mohammed High School, Atlanta, Georgia U.S.A. Curriculum 1996/97" archives of W.D. Mohammed H.S.
10. "Introduction" in *Clara Muhammad School Curriculum Draft (1990)*. Document produced by Clara Muhammad School Curriculum Committee.
11. The Mosque Cares Office of Education Special Committee, *The Night Visit of the Prophet (saw) and the Ascension of the Soul* (Chicago: The Mosque Cares, 2005).
12. The term "*qadr*" is generally reserved as an attribute of God and is commonly translated as "power" or "Divine Will." Imam Warith Deen's usage of the term, as with many traditional Islamic concepts, is appropriated to extend the conception and make it relevant in different contexts, as in the case of relating *qadr* to a child and their innate capacity.
13. The Islamic School of Greater Kansas City, *Accrediting Material Submitted to Missouri Non-Public School Accrediting Association 2005–2006*. In the personal archives of Sheikh Abdalla Idris's office archives.
14. ISNA Department of Education, *Islamic Education Symposium*, VHS, March 14, 1989. In the personal archives of Sheikh Abdalla Idris's office archives.
15. He refers to the work of Maurice Baucille's *The Bible, the Qur'an, and Science: The Holy Scriptures Examined in Light of Modern Science* and Amir Aczel's *God's Equation: Einstein's Theory of the Expanding Universe*, where truths of the Qur'an are confirmed scientifically, he argues.
16. World Council of Islamic Education refers to the world conferences that were held in Mecca, Kuala Lumpur, South Africa, etc. See Mabud (2016) for more information.

References

Abdur Rashid, Daaiyah. "Lessons from a Teaching Life: Towards a Muslim African American Perspective on Service Learning." PhD Diss., Ohio State University, 1999.

Abdus Sabur, Qadir. *Evolution of a Curriculum Framework: A Collection of Research Articles and Essays on the Education of Muslim Children in the West.* Richmond, VA: Dar Abdul Rahman Publishing, 2005.

Abdus Sabur, Qadir and Abdus Sabur, Beverly. *Developing Muslim School Curricula.* Richmond, VA: Muslim Teachers College, 2000.

Ahmad, Khurshid. "The Nature of the Islamic Resurgence." In *Voices of Resurgent Islam,* edited by John Esposito. New York: Oxford University Press, 1983, pp. 218–228.

Ahmed, Asma. "London Islamic School: Millstone or Milestone?" In *Discipline, Devotion, and Dissent: Jewish, Catholic, and Islamic Schooling in Canada.* Waterloo, ON: Wilfrid Laurier University Press, 2012, pp. 145–168.

Al-Attas, Muhammad Naquib. *Aims and Objectives of Islamic Education.* Jeddah: King Abdul Aziz University, 1979.

Ayalon, A. and Wasserstein, D.J., eds. "Laying the Foundation: Education, Islam, and Modernity in the Early Teachings of the Young Hasan al-Banna, 1927–1930." In *Madrasa: Education, Religion and State in the Middle East.* Tel Aviv: Tel Aviv University Press, 2004.

Barzinji, J. "History of the Islamization of Knowledge and Contributions of the International Institute of Islamic Thought." In *Muslims and Islamization in North America: Problems and Prospects,* edited by Amber Haque. Beltsville, MD: Amana Publications, 1999.

Bergeson, A., ed. *The Sayyid Qutb Reader: Selected Writings on Politics, Religion, and Society.* New York: Routledge, 2008.

Cook, B.J. and Malkāwī, Fathī Hasan. *Classical Foundations of Islamic Educational Thought: A Compendium of Parallel English-Arabic Texts,* 1st ed. Provo, Utah: Brigham Young University Press, 2010.

Curtis IV, Edward. *Black Muslim Religion in the Nation of Islam, 1960–1975.* Chapel Hill, NC: University of North Carolina Press, 2006.

Dei, George and Kempf, Arlo, eds. *Anti-Colonialism and Education: The Politics of Resistance.* Rotterdam, The Netherlands: Sense Publishers, 2006.

Durkee, Noura. "Primary Education of Muslim Children in North America." *Muslim Education Quarterly* 5, no. 1 (1987).

Ellenson, D. "An Ideology for the Liberal Jewish Day School: A Philosophical-Sociological Investigation." *Journal of Jewish Education,* 74 (2008): 245–263.

Esposito, John. "Ismail R. al-Faruqi: Muslim Scholar-Activist." In *The Muslims of America,* edited by Yvonne Yazbek Haddad. New York: Oxford University Press, 1991, pp. 65–79.

Faruqi, Ismail. "Islamic Ideals in North America." In *Muslim Community in North America,* edited by Earle Waugh, Baha Abu Laban, and Regula Qureshi. Edmonton: University of Alberta Press, 1983, pp. 259–270.

Faruqui, Ismail. *Islamization of Knowledge: General Principles and Work Plan.* Herdon, VA: International Institute of Islamic Thought, 1989.

Ghazi, Abidullah. "Toward an Integrated Program of Islamic Studies: A Systematic Approach." In *Muslims and Islamization in North America: Problems and Prospects,* ed. Amber Haque. Kuala Lumpur: Amana Publications, 1999.

Giladi, Anver. "Islamic Educational Theories in the Middle Ages: Some Methodological Notes with Special Reference to al-Ghazali." *Bulletin* (British Society for Middle Eastern Studies) 14, no. 1 (1987): 3–4.

Gunther, Sebastian. "Be Masters of That You Teach and Continue to Learn: Medieval Muslim Thinkers on Educational Theory." *Comparative Education Review* 50, no. 3 (2006).
Haddad, Yvonne. "Sayyid Qutb: Ideologue of Islamic Revival." In *Voices of Resurgent Islam*, edited by John Esposito. New York: Oxford University Press, 1983.
Hallaq, Wael. *Authority, Continuity, and Change in Islamic Law*. Cambridge, United Kingdom: Cambridge University Press, 2001.
Halstead, Mark. "An Islamic Concept of Education." *Comparative Education* 40, no. 4 (2004): 517–529.
Harder, Elma. *Concentric Circles: Nurturing Awe and Wonder in Early Learning*. Sherwood Park, Alberta: Al-Qalam Publishing, 2006.
Husain, S.S. and Ashraf, S.A. *Crisis in Muslim Education*. London: Hodder & Stoughton, 1979.
Jackson, Sherman. *Islam and the Blackamerican: Looking Toward the Third Resurrection*. New York: Oxford University Press, 2005.
Johnson, S. "Political Activity of Muslims in America." In *The Muslims of America*, edited by Yvonne Yazbeck Haddad. Oxford: Oxford University Press, 1991.
Kaloti, Sami Abdullah. "The Reformation of Islam and the Impact of Jamal al-Din al-Afghani and Muhammad Abduh on Islamic Education." PhD Diss., Marquette University, 1974.
Khan, Shujaat. "A Critical Review of Islamization of Knowledge in the American Perspective." In *Muslims and Islamization in North America: Problems and Prospects*, edited by Amber Haque. Beltsville, MD: Amana Publications, 1999.
Khatab, Sayed. *The Political Thought of Sayyid Qutb: The Theory of Jahiliyyah*. London: Routledge, 2006.
Langohr, V. "Colonial Education Systems and the Spread of Local Religious Movements: The Cases of British Egypt and Punjab." Department of Political Science, College of the Holy Cross, n.d. Retrieved from http://faculty.virginia.edu/mesp/Langohr-paper.pdf.
Lemu, Aisha. "What Makes an Islamic School Islamic?" National Conference of NAMIS Nigerian Association of Model Islamic Schools, 2003. Retrieved from www.iberr.org.
Levisohn, J. "From Integration of Curricula to a Pedagogy of Integrity." *Journal of Jewish Education*, 74 (2008): 264–294.
Lings, Martin. *Muhammad: His Life Based on the Earliest Sources*. New Delhi: Millat Book Center, 1991.
Mabud, Shaikh Abdul. "World Conferences on Muslim Education: Shaping the Agenda of Muslim Education in the Future." In *Philosophies of Islamic Education: Historical Perspectives and Emerging Discourses*. New York: Taylor and Francis Inc., 2016, pp. 129–144.
Maudoodi, A.A. *A Short History of the Revivalist Movement in Islam*. Lahore: Lahore Islamic Publications, 1963.
McCloud, Aminah Beverly. *African American Islam*. New York: Routledge, 1995.
Merry, Michael. *Culture, Identity and Islamic Schooling: A Philosophical Approach*. New York: Palgrave Macmillan, 2007.

Nasr, Seyyed Hossein. *Islam and the Plight of Modern Man.* New York: Longman, 1975.
Nasr, Seyyed Hossein. *Traditional Islam in the Modern World.* London: Kegan Paul International, 1987.
Nasr, Seyyed Hossein. *Mawdudi and the Making of Islamic Revivalism.* New York: Oxford University Press, 1996.
Nord, Warren. *Religion in American Education: Rethinking a National Dilemma.* Chapel Hill, NC: University of North Carolina Press, 1995.
Panjwani, Farid. "The 'Islamic' in Islamic Education: Assessing the Discourse." *Current Issues in Comparative Education* 7, no. 1 (2004).
Rahnema, Ali, ed. *Pioneers of Islamic Revival.* London: Zed Books, 2005.
Rosenthal, Franz. *Knowledge Triumphant; The Concept of Knowledge in Medieval Islam.* Leiden: Brill, 1970.
Sahin, A. "Critical Issues in Islamic Education Studies: Rethinking Islamic and Western Liberal Secular Values of Education." *Religions* 9, no. 11 (2018).
Saqeb, Ghulam Nabi. "Some Reflections on Islamization of Education Since 1977 Makkah Conference: Accomplishments, Failures and Tasks Ahead." *Intellectual Discourse* 8, no. 1 (2000): 45–68.
Shafiq, M. *Growth of Islamic Thought in North America: Focus on Isma'il al-Faruqi.* Brentwood, MD: Amana Publications, 1994.
Shamma, Freda. "The Curriculum Challenge for Islamic Schools in America." In *Muslims and Islamization in North America: Problems and Prospects*, edited by Amber Haque. Kuala Lumpur: Amana Publications, 1999.
Shamma, Freda. "An Overview of Current Islamic Curricula," June 9, 2004. Retrieved from www.4islamicschools.org/admin_curr.htm.
Soroush, A. "Reason, Freedom, and Democracy in Islam." In *The New Voices of Islam: Reforming Politics and Modernity—A Reader*, edited by Mehran Kamrava. New York: I.B. Tauris, 2006, pp. 243–261.
Sweet, Lois. *God in the Classroom: The Controversial Issue of Religion in Canada's Schools.* Toronto: McClelland and Stewart, 1997.
Tauhidi, Dawud. *The Tarbiyah Project: A Renewed Vision of Islamic Education.* Canton, MI: Tarbiyah Institute, 2006.
The Mosque Cares Office of Education Special Committee, *The Night Visit of the Prophet (Saw) and the Ascension of the Soul.* Chicago, IL: The Mosque Cares, 2005 (In archives of WD Mohammed High School, Atlanta, GA).
Voll, J. "Renewal and Reform in Islamic History: *Tajdid* and *Islah.*" In *Voices of Resurgent Islam*, edited by John Esposito. New York: Oxford University Press, 1983.
Zine, Jasmin. *Canadian Islamic Schools: Unraveling the Politics of Faith, Gender, Knowledge, and Identity.* Toronto: University of Toronto Press, 2008.

5 Praxis
Reviving the Tradition of Learning and Teaching in Islam

The aftermath of the horrific events of 9/11 raised the urgency for Muslims in North America to *live* Islam. For Muslim communities, the effect of 9/11 was not felt on that day, but as Zine says, on September 12th (Zine 2008). The day after 9/11 defined and redefined for many Muslims their level of civic engagement with public and private institutions. Random, calculated, and systemic acts of Islamophobia shook the faith of some and strengthened the faith of others. For some Muslims living and working amongst culturally diverse communities, the immediate response was to disassociate themselves from the global Muslim community as a primary marker of their identity. For others, the response strengthened bonds of communal obligation to correct the image of Islam through active public outreach. Jackson (2005) argues that for immigrant Muslims especially, 9/11 "tempered the isolationist impulse" (133). Muslim communities concerned about the public image of Islam in the West have been catapulted into an era of damage control. No longer could the national Muslim organizations like ISNA or the community of Imam Warith Deen worry about internal organizational building. The discourse had now shifted to speak and act publicly about the essence of Islam, whether they were ready for it or not.

In the midst of undoing a negative popular image of Islam and Muslims, the general public, including Muslims, continue to search for answers. Trying to understand what could possibly motivate a handful of disenfranchised young Muslim men to attempt to take the fate of millions into their own hands drew a myriad of voices. Many of those voices, however, felt it necessary to scrutinize more closely all private institutions considered Islamic, including Islamic schools. Parker-Jenkins et al. (2005) argue that it was inevitable that Islamic schools would come under public scrutiny. Separate school aspirations by an ethnic and religious minority community combined with the international media spotlight in light of 9/11 have drawn outright public concern and skepticism in relation to faith-based schooling.

The response of Muslim educators to the events of 9/11, however, heralded a new stage in the development of Islamic schools. Through the voices and experiences of my research participants and Zine's (2004) critical faith-centered epistemological framework, I have traced a significant shift from the previous emphasis on pedagogical practice to one of educational praxis in the post-9/11 era. Although pedagogy, as does protest and preservation of identity, all serve as on-going and overlapping visions of Islamic schooling, the particular context of 9/12 demanded a fresh vision that was defined by civic engagement. The term "praxis" is often simply held to mean the interplay between theory and practice or the move from theory to practice. However, critical pedagogues, like Paulo Freire (1985, 1998) in particular, have expanded the notion of praxis to include the ways in which dialogue and human curiosity lead one to ask the hard questions of "why" as well as "what." The process of praxis must recognize the role that power plays in shaping the aims of education. Praxis is also shaped by its dialectic between the lived experience and the experience aspired for. It is, therefore, the dialectic between teaching and learning, between transference of knowledge and knowledge that transforms, and it is the space between freedom and authority. Essential to praxis is the recognition of the complexities that arise when power is central in understanding the politics of process, in this case, education. My purpose of employing the term praxis in the way that Freire conceptualizes it is to recognize the ways in which power, most notably through anti-Islamic sentiments post-9/11, shaped a new discourse of civic engagement among North American Muslim communities and, as a result, re-shaped the aims of education as well in Islamic schools.

Islamic schools, similar to Islamic organizations, can no longer be insular or even be presumed to be insular in this new era. The urgency to move beyond religious teachings and character development must now manifest itself outwardly. In the words of Dawud Tauhidi, Islamic schools must "stop teaching about Islam and start teaching what it means to *be* Muslim." This urgency of putting Islamic school teachings into lived practice is why I have titled this current stage of development "praxis."

Beyond the conventional inter-faith dialogue and community service approaches to outreach, many Islamic schools have set out to redefine the essence of Islamic education itself. Among the findings of this chapter are that the era of praxis has brought about a deeper sense of introspection and, as a result, a dissatisfaction with the state of Islamic schooling. Largely led by second generation North American Muslims and Muslim converts, a new cadre of Muslim American intellectuals has encapsulated young Muslims to begin to think differently about their civic responsibilities. A discourse of critical social consciousness couched in the language of the Islamic tradition has equally affected the internal critique of Islamic schooling.

A push toward critical social consciousness encourages Muslims concerned about the hijacking of their North American-ness to take account of themselves first. It encourages young Muslims to question whether they are indeed living and practicing the teachings of Islam before criticizing others of ignorance and discrimination in a post-9/11 context. Riding global trends of social consciousness around issues of the environment, health, and education, Muslim intellectuals have sought to revive the Islamic tradition and by virtue respond to the backlash of 9/11 through expressing common human aspirations of global citizenship and responsibility.

The second finding that shapes the direction of this chapter is that such an explicit push toward a civics-based educational framework has stimulated new visions for Islamic schooling. The immediate response for many established Islamic schools has been to place a greater emphasis on community service, outreach, and dialogue with schools and communities of other faiths. However, for others, the response has been a more sweeping re-envisioning of Islamic schooling. Some schools, for example, have attempted to make civic engagement a central part of the school philosophy, defining Islamic education through a social justice framework. Others have taken a more spiritual/holistic approach to weave curriculum and Islamic ethics in a way that would nurture students to see the commonalities and continuities of knowledge. Still others have grown dissatisfied with both the public and Islamic schooling models and employ their critical social consciousness to develop organic alternative and home schooling communities. The diversity of educational models now gaining support in mainstream Muslim communities portrays the search for praxis. Although such ideas as home schooling existed in the Muslim community well before 9/11, participants for this stage insist that the popularity that alternative Islamic schooling models have gained over the past decade is largely a result of a new-found consciousness.

New Voices, New Visions: Reshaping Islamic Schooling

The voices and visions that shape the findings of this stage of Islamic school growth extend beyond the two umbrella communities that I have relied on thus far. Emerging during the growth and establishment of immigrant Muslims who established ISNA and the African American Muslims who formed the community of Imam Warith Deen is a third social force amongst the two: their children. The progeny of Muslim immigrants who came to Canada and the United States in the 1960s and 1970s in particular comprise a major segment of the Muslim demographic (Karim 2009). These second and third generation Muslim Americans, many of whom would consider themselves "American Muslims," have reaped the fruits of their parents' American dream (Karim 2009, 5). They are largely products of public and private elite schooling, university educated, and financially stable (Nimer 2007, 35-7). For some of them, their Islamic education came directly through Islamic schools, but the vast majority found it through Sunday schools, if not at home. But for many of the young Muslims I spoke to, gaining a consciousness of Islamic practices—often referred to as the dos and don'ts—was insufficient. As

Muslims born and raised in North America, they needed to know how to *be* Muslim. The shaping of identity for many second-generation Muslims was a journey of self-discovery. Through Muslim Students' Associations (MSA) and major national youth organizations like Muslim Youth of North America (MYNA), both under the ISNA umbrella, many young Muslims came to terms with what it meant to be an American Muslim.

Growing up in North America drew second-generation Muslims toward a leadership they could relate to. Although influenced by the organizations their parents initiated (MSA, MYNA, ISNA), the voices that could speak to the hearts and minds of young Muslims looking for an American Muslim identity were most often Americans themselves. The role of American Muslim converts who came to Islam during or soon after the Civil Rights era became crucial in shaping the discourse of identity for second-generation Muslims (Abdo 2006; Mohammed-Arif 2002; Schmidt 2004). Although the voice of Muslim converts continues to be a revitalizing force, those who came to Islam in the '60s and '70s, in particular, popularized the impact of Malcolm X and gave many young Muslims an icon that exemplified the American Muslim experience. The plight and struggle of Malcolm X was harnessed by a growing number of Muslim intellectual converts to speak about social justice as an integral part of Muslim identity. For second-generation Muslims, this was transformative. The life and teachings of Malcolm X challenged the concept of racial hierarchy that hindered collaborations of their parent's generation. It also moved them toward a social consciousness and activism that strengthened personal conviction in Islam. Interestingly enough, this new cadre of Muslim intellectuals, who redefined the American Muslim discourse, are given a platform for mass appeal at the annual ISNA conventions. It was at these conventions in the 1990s in particular where tens of thousands would pack into lecture halls to be inspired by the likes of Imam Siraj Wahhaj, former member of the NOI, Imam Jamil Al Amin, former member of the Black Panther Party, or White American converts such as Shaykh Hamza Yusuf and Jeffrey Lang. Today, many of these voices can also be heard north of the border in places like Toronto, where thousands of Muslims continue to draw together at the annual Reviving the Islamic Spirit conference to gain a sense of inspiration.

To gain a deeper insight into the shift toward a critical social consciousness that began well before 9/11 but became increasingly relevant after, I chose to interview Shaykh Hamza Yusuf Hanson. Although there are many Muslim intellectuals who have inspired young Muslims, there are few who have actively addressed education and schooling. Hamza Yusuf, a White American convert who accepted Islam in 1977, is most notably known for the many years he spent studying traditional Islam in the deserts of Mauritania. Since his return to California in the early 1990s, he has become among the foremost voices that represent American Muslims. At the height of his career, Leonard (2002) referred to him as a "rock star" because his talks were so avidly attended, recorded, and widely distributed. Currently, he serves as the president and co-founder of Zaytuna College in the United States.

In relation to education and schooling, two of his conferences in particular shook the discourse of Islamic schooling from its foundation. The first of the two was held at the University of Toronto in 2001, and the second was held at University of California Berkley in 2004. Advocating for educational alternatives, the two keynote speakers, John Taylor Gatto (notably known as the author of *The Underground History of American Education*, 2000) and Hamza Yusuf spoke to audiences of parents and educators, encouraging a critique of mass public schooling. Disenfranchised and motivated at the same time, many participants left these conferences questioning their own schooling experiences and were inspired to read more about critical educational thought. The immediate response of some was to pull their children out of public and Islamic schools and begin home schooling. To support Muslim home schoolers, Hamza Yusuf, along with the support of John Taylor Gatto, established a support network and curriculum house called Kinza Academy. For others, home schooling was deemed limiting and insular, so they sought more holistic educational models such as Montessori and Waldorf schools. And yet others have sought to transform Islamic schools from within through the discourse of critical social consciousness. The credit cannot all be awarded to Shaykh Hamza, but for the sake of depth over breadth, I chose to analyze his particular impact in relation to shifting the discourse on Islamic schooling. This section is comprised of the voices and thoughts of Shaykh Hamza Yusuf, his sister, Nabila Hanson, who was the Director of Kinza Academy, and a handful of both second-generation and converted Muslims aspiring for a different kind of Islamic education for their children. Some of my participants have been influenced by the educational thought of Hamza Yusuf, and others were not. The objective of selecting these participants was to gain insight into the alternative visions of Islamic schooling that complicate the indigenous-immigrant dichotomy established thus far.

This part will begin by establishing context with the impact of 9/11 on North American Muslims and as a result the response of a critical social consciousness. The second part will examine how such a consciousness has revived and redefined the educational aims of Islamic education from within the Islamic tradition. And lastly, this chapter will close by providing an overview of alternative Islamically based models of schooling that have developed since the early 2000s.

Impact of 9/11 on Islamic Schools: Toward a Critical Social Consciousness

In the introduction to *Muslims' Place in the American Public Sphere*, the editors outline five distinct stages that define the Muslim presence in the United States. These stages range from before Columbus "discovered" the new world to the atrocities of 9/11 that transformed the lives of American Muslims forever. The post-9/11 context, they say, "distinctively separated this phase from all other times in the history of America's relations with the Muslim world" (Bukhari et al. 2004). Nimer's (2007) edited collection traces the combining forces of Islamophobia externally and anti-Americanism from within that have shaped Muslim discourses both in North America and abroad. Post-9/11, Nimer (2007) cites studies that show "between one-fourth and one-third of Americans hold negative views of Islam and Muslims," for example (1). In a 2005 global survey, Nimer (2007) argues that the sentiments are mutual and that 51–79% of respondents from Muslim majority countries hold "unfavorable" views of America. Similarly, Ba-Yunus and Kone (2006) acknowledge that anti-Islamic sentiments or Islamophobia existed in North America well before 9/11. Both implicit and explicit forms of discrimination existed and often peaked with international conflicts in the Muslim world, but all such forms have been pale in comparison to the brunt of the aftermath experienced by American Muslims in recent years. Post-9/11, over 27,000 incidents of interrogations and raids of homes, businesses, and Islamic organizations were systematically conducted by federal authorities in the United States, for example (Ba-Yunus and Kone 2006, 112).

Among the acts of vandalism and threats were those leveled against Islamic schools. Many schools across Canada and the United States were vandalized. Safaa Zarzour, principal of Universal School in Bridgeview, Illinois, received a letter two days after 9/11 threatening him, his family, and the Islamic school (Cateura 2005). I recall visiting a local mosque and its attached Islamic school days after the arrest of the Toronto 17 and watched news reporters question young Islamic school students about the curriculum of their school, even though the arrests were made at suburban Toronto public high schools. The combination of misunderstanding and heightened Islamophobia became quite evident very quickly. Internally, 9/11 made Muslim communities in Canada and the United States question their own isolationist impulses; it made existing organizations more open to public scrutiny, and the need for public outreach reshaped internal priorities. In the case of Islamic schools, the internal critique reformed the practices of some and served as the fodder for new models for others.

A New Discourse of Civic Engagement Amongst American Muslims

In addition to outward acts of hate and discrimination that peaked post-9/11, the public perception of Islam and Muslims was also maligned in North America. Imam Zaid Shakir, co-founder of Zaytuna College, said at the time, "The apocalyptic nature of the attacks of September 11. . . led many observers to question the humanness of a religion that could encourage such senseless, barbaric slaughter" (Shakir 2003, 529). Islam became the center of public scrutiny as a religion that could motivate such abhorrence that stigmatized the faith as "anti-intellectual, nihilistic, violent, chauvinistic atavism" (Shakir 2003, 529). For many Muslims who had now made North America their home, such loss of trust was traumatic and required some form of redemption. In many ways the responsibility of reframing American Islam fell on the shoulders of the new generation of American Muslim intellectuals who could respond as both Americans and Muslims.

Among them were the voices of Muslim intellectuals, both religious leaders and academics, like Shaykh Hamza Yusuf or Muqtader Khan, respectively, who became increasingly vocal in condemning acts and even thoughts of violence (Ukeles 2003). After reading through the speeches of Muslim intellectuals post-9/11, Ukeles found an apologetic tone, regretting almost a complicity to the extent that they did not emphasize Islam's civic tradition earlier. Muqtader Khan, a professor of political science and scholar of Islam in America, said it was a time for "soul searching" post-9/11. In response to those who argue that 9/11 was a radical reaction to American foreign policy, Khan insisted that Muslims must look within and question their own policies of discrimination in the Muslim world first (Ukeles 2003, 30). Khan's call for soul searching represented but one voice of an American Muslim trying to reclaim their Islam in America. The need to right the wrongs of Islamophobia that followed 9/11 was a project taken up by many young Muslims who felt the strategies of national Muslim organizations were no longer effective (Karim 2009, 130). From elementary and secondary schools to college and university campuses both in Canada and the United States, many young Muslims became active in addressing the misrepresentation and misunderstanding of Islam. "Many young Muslims felt that the 9/11 crisis necessitated new strategies and a clearer message against religious violence" (Ukeles 2003, 33). As an immediate response to 9/11, local and national organizations were set up to address community needs. Youth groups, leadership training, and mentoring programs served internal community needs, while community outreach through new organizations for addressing, lobbying, and defending civil liberties became commonplace. Such new found social activism "created the space for young American Muslims to step into public roles to shape the future of their community" (Ukeles 2003, 36).

This new concerted voice of American Muslims is characterized by an explicit discourse of human rights, democracy, civic engagement, and global responsibility. It has sought to do what Imam Warith Deen envisioned and advocated two decades earlier, to universalize the message of Islam in America. Ukeles argued a distinct American Islam was born:

> When Muslim organizations vacillated in their condemnations of Islamic terrorism, alternate voices stepped forward with a clear mandate of rejecting religious violence and advocating peace and

diplomacy to solve conflicts. Second-generation Muslim professionals and young Muslim academics are promoting a progressive and distinctly American kind of Islam, founded on principles of democracy and religious pluralism.

(Ukeles 2003, 8)

Imam Zaid Shakir contests that such an American kind of Islam must speak of the universality of Islam that exemplifies global responsibility and connection to all, including those who are not God-centered (atheists, secularists, communists). Such a discourse must highlight the parallels and consistencies between Islamic conceptions of human rights and those globally agreed upon in policies such as the Universal Declaration of Human Rights. The new discourse of American Muslims must exhibit the universal nature of Islam to reposition ourselves as American Muslims. Sulayman Nyang, scholar of Islam in America, noted the need for such a discursive shift well before 9/11 when he said,

> It should be recognized that no serious dialogue between Muslims and the members of the larger American society can prove successful unless and until the Muslims replicate publicly and faithfully what they articulate theologically as Islam's contribution to American civilization.
>
> (Schumann 2007, 24)

This need for dialogue and to now convince Americans of the American Muslim commitment to civic contribution has also been reinforced by Tariq Ramadan's reframing of Islam's commitment to pluralism. Ramadan, Professor of Islamic studies at the University of Oxford, encouraged believers at the time living in the post-9/11 era to recognize their civic responsibility not as Muslims but as human beings.

> [W]e should work toward reform not as 'Muslims' but as citizens, inspired of course by a message and a morality, but above all aware of our responsibilities and determined by the right of every person to be treated justly and fairly (as the common law guarantees) should prevail.
>
> (Ramadan 2004, 147)

Scholars like Ramadan insist that the Islamic essence of the Qur'an and moral principles of the Prophet Muhammad can be used to direct active global citizenship without having to be oppositional: "Social commitment is a moral commandment, and reform is an obligation of conscience that, in the mind of the Muslim citizen, determines a 'moral responsibility'" (Ramadan 2004, 153). The concerted voice of Muslim intellectuals, such as Ramadan, Nyang, Yusuf, Shakir, Khan and many others, shifted the discourse of Islam in America toward a universal identity where Islam informs American civic responsibility rather than distinguishes itself from it. This discourse has sought to find parallels and connections that were empowering for second-generation Muslims who were caught between being American and Muslim. The impact of 9/11 pulled many American Muslims to identify closer with their American civil values and be more comfortable balancing their Muslim and American identities.

Second-Generation Muslims Coming of Age

On the coming of age of an immigrant's children, Albert Memmi, postcolonial theorist, argues that the distance that a second-generation child has from their parent's place of origin alters their aspirations and identity:

> There is a divide between the immigrant and his children. They don't share the same memories or the same idea of the future, they practically live in different worlds. The immigrant is, after all, a man of the past; his son and daughter are looking toward the future, even if they grow impatient, even if they despair of ever getting there, or refuse to do so. The immigrant's past, even when increasingly clouded by the fog of memory. . . . For his children there is no possible return since they never left.
>
> (Memmi 2004, 111–2)

In light of Memmi's articulation of distance, the push for a new discourse of American Islam has filled the cultural and ethnic void with a deeper sense of religious identity (Leonard 2003, 169). Second-generation American Muslims find the discourse of universality empowering because it speaks to their life experiences of being both American and Muslim by birth.

The coming of age (adulthood, marriage, progeny) of the second generation of Muslims whose parents migrated to the United States and Canada largely in the 1970s is one major factor. This second generation of Muslims were born and raised in North America, attended public schools through their elementary and secondary years, and now have begun families and professional careers. Having attended public schools and after negotiating a distinct American/Canadian Muslim identity for themselves, this particular segment of the Muslim population are more economically stable and socio-politically contributive to know that they have the right and means to challenge the status quo with regards to educating their children.

The second factor is a revival of a religious consciousness for many of these second-generation Muslims. Young, second-generation, religiously observant Muslims are looking more attentively for prolific speakers who can articulate the faith for them in a language that is defined by their generation. Malcolm X, Mohammed Ali (formerly Cassius Clay), and Yusuf Islam (formerly Cat Stevens) define the era second-generation Muslims grew up in. It was an era where Muslim converts brought their individual experiences of civil rights, sports, and music to form a distinct countercultural identity that meshed Islamic beliefs with mainstream participation. Today young Muslim participation in socio-political and artistic forms shows no bounds. From comedy to hip-hop, puppetry to poetry, and basketball to environmental awareness, young Muslims have begun to integrate in very creative ways. But the motivation for such creative engagement comes largely from the words of great orators or Muslim personalities. Initially it was the legacy of Malcolm X that served as the inspiration to generations of Muslims, young and old.

Today, his inspiration has blossomed into an array of prolific speakers who encourage Muslim millennials to negotiate a distinct identity for themselves of what it means to be a Muslim American/Canadian. Major annual conferences and retreats now draw thousands of young Muslims to listen to religious lectures by key Muslim scholars. The previously mentioned Reviving the Islamic Spirit conference held annually in Toronto since 2002 draws over 15,000 Muslims. The annual ISNA Convention in Chicago draws over 50,000 Muslims to a weekend of motivational speeches. These annual events, along with spiritual retreats that are organized by a plethora of youth based organizations, are beginning to offer young Muslims the language and knowledge that defines their unique North American Muslim identities.

The two factors stated earlier describing the position of second-generation American Muslims, achieving the American dream and being inspired by a distinct American Muslim identity, explains why a new discourse of American Islam post-9/11 has been so transformative. Through a message of universality and civic responsibility entrenched in core American values but infused with an Islamic spirit, second-generation Muslims have been equipped toward a new critical social consciousness. In search for commonality and consistencies between traditions, this new consciousness seeks to interrogate lived practices and popular trends that redefine American Islam. For many American Muslims, this discursive shift has meant jumping on the bandwagon with popular American trends that speak to an Islamic lifestyle, such as healthy eating, spiritual balance, and environmental activism. Through the Islamic tradition, many young American Muslims have become vanguards of alternative, holistic lifestyles because they are able to see its relevance to Islam. Similar to the example of the revival of a human rights discourse immediately post-9/11, American Muslims are now more consciously interrogating everyday praxis.

Arguably, a critical social consciousness aligns and extends the anti-colonial response of Muslims in 1960s and 1970s America. The initial response of early Muslims in America described in the chapters on

"Protest" and "Preservation" were guided by political inequities and procuring equal opportunities, whereas current anti-colonial responses aspire to unite disparate differences. Dei argues that anti-colonialism is deeply anchored by a spiritual synergy that characterizes the current stage of praxis (Dei 1996, 5) Muslim intellectuals like Shaykh Hamza Yusuf popularized the interrogation of everyday choices that Muslims make on the basis of basic human spirituality and wellness. In many ways, he has called for, in the spirit of critical pedagogue bell hooks, an engaged pedagogy (Namulundah 1998). A critical social consciousness within Islamic education has inherently shifted toward an engaged re-conceptualization of knowledge that questions the history, purpose, and values that inform conventional educational practices that most Islamic schools have adopted subconsciously. In pursuit of an education that is aligned with the traditional principles of Islamic education, Muslim scholars, educators, and parents are beginning to question more explicitly whether the practices of conventional schooling are consistent with Islamic principles. And lastly, some Muslim educators seek to develop an engaged pedagogy that centralizes student empowerment through social justice and activism. Although bell hooks' conception of engaged pedagogy outlines other elements as well, these three serve as new directions that have manifested within the discourse of Islamic schooling and will be discussed in the following sections.

Beyond Schooling

The beginning of a critical social consciousness specifically in relation to education and schooling sprang from Shaykh Hamza Yusuf's educational critique, my participants argued. A White American convert, Shaykh Hamza's pursuit of knowledge and traditional Islam inspired many young American Muslims. Returning to his hometown in California after ten years of travelling and studying across the Arab world, he began to articulate Islam in a way that resonated for many. By the mid-1990s, Shaykh Hamza was captivating full lecture halls of young American Muslims with a fresh critique of American foreign policy, lifestyles, and the ills of consumerism and individualism. Equally scathing were his critiques of the modern Muslim world and its pursuit of the American dream. The alternative he proposed was a deep engagement with the Islamic tradition. Within alternative American discourses, he made linkages between lifestyle choices that are consistent with a believer's *fitra* (natural inclination). One of my participants, Shaheen Rasheed, described Shaykh Hamza's influence by saying:

> He [Shaykh Hamza Yusuf] talked about the *deen* (an Islamic way of life) as inclusive of all aspects in relation to alternative lifestyles. So, a lot of people began to eat organic or considering homeopathy instead

of just popping pills all the time. He taught us that there are other options and you learn about them and then you make your choice. He influenced our lives very much in the sense of our diet, our choice of doctors, our schooling options, and even in terms of turning off our television. And because the Bay Area is largely comprised of an immigrant Muslim population that are educated, they make sense of what he spoke about but were never really introduced to such alternative thinking.

Unlike more resistant Islamic ideologies, Shaykh Hamza's critique did not call for resistance through disengagement but rather resistance through active engagement. As mentioned in the quotation, Shaykh Hamza's push for a critical social consciousness was encouragement, if not outright insistence, of the responsibility of Muslims to be critical of the world around them as part of their civic responsibility.

In my quest to first meet and interview Shaykh Hamza for this book, I traveled to meet him at New York University, where he was speaking on "God and Country" in April 2008. At that lecture he spoke about the importance of civil disobedience in the spirit of what Henry David Thoreau wrote about in 1849 as a distinctive part of our civic responsibility. He told an audience largely of young Muslim university students from across the eastern United States that we need to be "conscientious objectors" of the world around us. Speaking about the immigrant experience, the façade of "going back home," and the trap of positioning ourselves as the "other" who has no moral obligation to a country in which we live, Shaykh Hamza decried for the audience to think differently. Citing the opinions of the four Sunni founding Imams (Abu Hanifa, Shafi'i, Malik, and Hanbal), he spoke about the concept of *hijra* (migration), which many Muslims consider to be a call for establishing Muslim countries, pointing out that it may not necessarily be a physical migration but a migration of the heart toward goodness. Employing the Islamic tradition in ways that speak to fundamental American values, such as Thoreau's Civil Disobedience, Shaykh Hamza sought to show the consistency between the theoretical principles of outwardly disparate traditions. For the millennial Muslim, Shaykh Hamza's call for an interrogation of values and lived practices in North America has been empowering. These Muslims in particular needed a voice of balance and activism that would bridge the ritualistic teachings of 1980s Islam with American-speak. Shaykh Hamza became the epitome.

Among the areas of critique that Shaykh Hamza leveled at modern American values and lifestyles has been the way children are educated. It began most explicitly in April 2001 when Shaykh Hamza paired up with New York City Public School Educator of the Year,[1] John Taylor Gatto, for a conference entitled Beyond Schooling: Building Communities that Matter. The conference was held at the Ontario Institute for

Studies in Education at the University of Toronto. It garnered the international interest of 140 educators from around the world to partake in three days' worth of lectures and workshops, culminating with a closing public lecture attended by close to 1,500. For many of my participants, who are now critical of both public schooling and conventional Islamic schools, this conference was either directly or indirectly the catalyst for rethinking schooling.

Among my participants who have been aspiring for an alternative model of Islamic schools is Inayet Sahin. Inayet is a Turkish American Muslim from the D.C. metropolitan area, a teacher, and has completed her master's in education. Growing up in D.C. in the 1980s, her parents put her in an Islamic school to "preserve her Islamic identity." Unsatisfied with her elementary school experience and in search of a sense of living Islamic praxis, Inayet joined many Muslim organizations, including MYNA, MSA, and the Muslim Women of Maryland (MWM). "But there was still a spiritual void from both the Islamic school and MYNA. All they did was social work but no personal, spiritual development." Thinking back to her Islamic school experience and community activism, however, Inayet said it makes her "angry" because the "ISNA education model doesn't ask the right questions. There are no critical books, no critical questions about the system they are using." Committed to Islamic work, however, Inayet chose to do a master's in education to help raise the bar of Islamic schools. It was during her master's that she learned about and attended the Beyond Schooling conference in Toronto. She recalls,

> And then I found out about the Zarnuji conference[2] and I got a grant from the University to attend it. And at that conference I was completely blown away. Everything I was learning at that conference supported what I was learning in my master's. That was my first exposure. John Taylor Gatto was there, Shaykh Hamza was there, and it was exactly what I was looking for, it put everything in perspective. . . . And then I went back to the Islamic schools in my area and tried to explain the history and purpose of public education and tried to convince people that we (in Islamic schools) have no limitations so do something different.

For many Beyond Schooling participants, John Taylor Gatto's unraveling of the history and purpose of American mass public schooling was disconcerting. Speaking to an audience of largely young Canadian and American Muslims who had attended public schools themselves, learning about how public schools have been modeled after Prussian military training camps meant to regiment and control masses of people was disturbing. Eight years later, Uzma Husaini, another participant of my study who attended the conference from the Bay Area in California, still recalls the images of public schools that John Taylor Gatto showed in a slideshow. Images of children bored, dumbed down, apathetic, and disciplined into neat rows, lines, and rituals, she said, "it was so profound; the images of what schools are like, I could really make sense of them from my own experiences."

As disconcerting as Gatto's *Underground History of American Education* was, it resonated with schooling experiences of many of the attendees and my participants.

Shaheen Rasheed, also from the Bay Area, recalls Shaykh Hamza and John Taylor Gatto's subsequent conference held at the University of California Berkley in 2004 entitled Educating our Children in Modern Times. Gatto's views on education made sense to people like Shaheen Rasheed because she was among those who mastered the education system through academic achievement but still felt incomplete. "I was an honors student because I mastered how to follow the path. But I never questioned the education I was getting. I felt I really got the short end of the stick." She remembers Gatto's and Shaykh Hamza's distinction between training and teaching most vividly. "That was a major opening for me. I was trained in my schooling experiences. I was never really taught to think for myself, to think differently." It was a harsh realization for many American Muslims like Shaheen Rasheed, who grew convinced of Gatto's *Dumbing Us Down* argument. Like Shaheen, for many, it became increasingly clear that mass public schooling was training for mediocrity.

As eye-opening as the conferences were, the impact did not stop there. Most participants left dazed and disturbed yet committed to change. It was difficult for attendees, many of whom taught in public schools, if not Islamic schools, to not alter their practice. Some left the teaching practice altogether, others looked for an educational alternative, but most began to deeply engage if not continue to question the process of schooling. The buzz of discomfort that Beyond Schooling began among young North American Muslims, many of whom were just starting new families, began to spread largely through literature. The conferences popularized Gatto and his accessible and fluid writing in *Dumbing Us Down* and *The Underground History of American Education*. Muslim parents and educators alike began reading it along with other authors on the Beyond Schooling recommended reading list: Jerry Mander's *Four Arguments for the Elimination of Television*, Neil Postman's *The End of Education*, and John Holt's *How Children Fail*.

When Umm Umar and her husband, Shaykh Faraz Rabbani, left Toronto to study the traditional Islamic sciences in Syria and Jordan, they had the mindset that Islamic schools would be a better educational choice than public institutions. While abroad, they listened to the recorded lectures of Shaykh Hamza about education. Umm Umar recalls, "He started us off by helping us think differently. It started with critiquing television and then schooling. The stuff he teaches is very in line with what I was learning overseas and about the Islamic tradition." So she began reading John Taylor Gatto's *Dumbing us Down* and Susan Bauer's *The Well Trained Mind* because Shaykh Hamza recommended them.

> And it made sense to me. He was talking about class size and rushing through material and not really focusing on individual students and I see that in both public and Islamic systems. And you know how people study for exams and don't remember anything. There's no transformation.

What soon became clear is that many Muslim parents and educators were not directly influenced by the conferences and may not have physically attended them; few had heard or considered Gatto or classical education prior to 2001. Those in the Muslim community, for example, who home schooled prior to 2001 did so out of principle over popular critique and often did it primarily alone.

The impact of Beyond Schooling and subsequent conferences on education by Shaykh Hamza was a concerted effort to think critically through a lens second-generation Muslims could relate to. During the public lecture held at the closure of Beyond Schooling, for example, Shaykh Hamza said, "schooling is something we are all experts at because we've all been through it." Being a non-educator no longer mattered. His insistence on the reliance on personal experience now meant that parents, teachers, students, and anyone that has ever been a student has the ability to reflect critically about their schooling experiences. For many, such a lease was empowering. Arguably, no other topic that Shaykh Hamza has spoken about has allowed for such tremendous buy-in from lay audiences. Although his lectures prior to Beyond Schooling were equally critical of particular aspects of modern Western lifestyles, schooling became the mantra that ignited a widespread network of critical social consciousness. Where young Muslim parents were going to send their children to school suddenly took over dinner conversations at social gatherings. This form of active intellectual engagement was the first essential result of Beyond Schooling. The ideas presented at the conference were dismissed by some and empowering for others but served as fodder for critical discussion for all.

The second result of Shaykh Hamza's education conferences is that they inspired a new-found energy of sacrifice and commitment on the part of young parents wanting to protect their children. In Chapter 3, "Preservation," a number of my African American participants who helped establish the early University of Islam schools said that the commitment of parents to education was waning after the death of Elijah Muhammad. The era of protest had ended and parents were less willing to sacrifice lifestyle comforts for the sake of education. Although circumstantially polar, Shaykh Hamza arguably revived a level of sacrifice amongst a new second generation of Muslims in North America. Small communities of parents began establishing and considering alternative forms of schooling that include often times a hybrid form of home schooling. These are children of parents a generation ago who came to America in the 1970s and largely required two income homes in order to reach the "American dream." Inspired by a critique of public schooling, a growing handful of this generation is now willing to sacrifice the second income and its financial comforts for the sake of self-nurturing their children.

The third essential impact of the Beyond Schooling conference is that it has developed by virtue of public schooling a new-found critique of Islamic schooling. Some second-generation Muslim families have grown increasingly wary of Islamic schools not solely on the basis of isolation anymore, but now simply because Islamic schools adopt conventional practices from public schools without a critique of their pedagogical principles. Although this critique has not necessarily shifted personal commitments away from Islamic schooling, it has in many ways served as the catalyst for an impassioned search for deeply understanding what defines Islamic schooling. In many ways, this critique is based on the premise that Islamic schools are not "Islamic" enough.

Critique of Mass Public Education

The basis of the critique that Shaykh Hamza Yusuf articulated can be demarcated under two overarching areas of contention: spiritual wellness and the purpose of schooling, both of which are rooted in an anti-imperialist, anti-hegemonic response. As was described in the early Muslim immigrant experience, the concept of mass public schooling was not questioned for its purpose as it was for its content. Considering the post-colonial perception that Western forms of schooling, whether Catholic or secular, represented the height of educational development, most immigrants who came to North America were relatively satisfied, if not elated, that their children would attend American public schools.

To second-generation American Muslims who succeeded through a public school education and attained university degrees, learning about what Gatto calls the "underground history of American education" was intriguing at the very least. Speaking to sold out lecture halls largely attending to listen to Shaykh Hamza Yusuf, John Taylor Gatto gave a popular history lesson about American schooling. He connected the rise of mass compulsory public schooling to the industrial revolution and the need for order and conformity among working class citizens. The process, he argues, required a comprehensive shift from autonomous rural schooling that was largely voluntary and locally controlled to highly structured and efficiently managed compulsory schooling that would ensure particular values were imparted. Most commonly referred to as a process of social engineering, Gatto argues that schooling "was looked upon from the first decade of the twentieth century as a branch of industry and a tool for governance" (Gatto 2001, 38). In an age when waves of immigrants continued to pour into the United States and an industrial workforce was urgent, schooling served as the conduit to ensure the maintenance of a class differential through variance in the education offered.

Among his scathing historical emphases is the role that major economic stakeholders, such as the Rockefeller, Carnegie, and Ford foundations, played in the shaping of compulsory schooling. He cites examples like the announcement of Max Mason, president of the Rockefeller Foundation, on April 11, 1933, "to insiders that a comprehensive national program was underway to allow, in Mason's words, 'the control of human behavior' " (Gatto 2001, xvi). Citing examples from public lectures and private letters, Gatto attempts to piece together a history that has not necessarily been a conspiracy but a piece of history often untold. The control of human behavior was seen as an inevitability for industrializing nations at the time. Schooling had to be stratified and "dumbed down," as he calls it, in order to ensure everyone received some rudimentary form of knowledge and skills necessary for a well-functioning society. It required a "new psychology of instruction which came to us from abroad," referring to "practices of dumbed-down schooling common to England, Germany, and France, the three major world coal-powers (other than the U.S.), each of which had already converted its common population into an industrial proletariat long before" (Gatto 2001, 38–9). The American public education system, he argues, was a borrowed endeavor from 19th century Prussia. Through travelers' reports and articles in American education journals, testimony of Prussia's effective school system influenced leading American figures. Essays on Prussian schools "applauded Prussia for discovering ways to contain the danger of a frightening new social phenomenon, the industrial proletariat" (ibid., 139). It aimed at "frictionless efficiency" that was highly coveted by industrializing nations.

To illustrate the similarity to our current school system, Gatto describes the Prussian school system and its three levels of schooling: *Akadamiensschulen*, *Realsschulen*, and *Volksschule*. The first served the select one half of 1% to educate "future policy makers . . . [to] think strategically, contextually, in wholes; they learned complex processes, useful knowledge, studied history, wrote copiously, argued often, read deeply, and mastered tasks of command." The second group were "real schools," where 5–7% of the population were trained as the professional proletariat: doctors, lawyers, engineers, and civil servants. The rest of the 92–94% of the population attended people's schools, "where they learned obedience, cooperation, and correct attitudes along with the rudiments of literacy and official state myths and history" (ibid., 137).

For scholars like Shaykh Hamza, the stark similarity between the Prussian model of schooling and our current educational methods was disconcerting. Revelations of corporate interests in shaping schools begs one to question what the purpose of schooling really is. In my interview with him, Shaykh Hamza emphasized his convictions:

> I think the fourth purpose,[3] which is what John Taylor Gatto has been writing about . . . is it's more about social control, and our system, even though it's not some kind of mega conspiracy, the system itself emerged for a number of reasons that a lot of people don't understand anymore because they don't know the history of schools. They don't know why we adopted Prussian models that were used to create regimented societies.

Recognizing that compulsory schooling has not hoodwinked generations of laymen necessarily and that many extraordinary people have been nurtured through public schools with a sense of social consciousness and concern, the purpose of engaging with our history, he says, is to become better acquainted with the forces that shape our lives. Referring to Noam Chomsky's concept of the "power of culture," Shaykh Hamza told me that through history of compulsory schooling, we need to become aware of "how controlling our hegemonic culture is." As a response to elements of schooling that reinforce social control and impose a culture of conformity, there are particular aspects of mass public schooling that have shaped Shaykh Hamza's critique and by virtue those whom he has influenced.

New Educational Critique That Came Out of Beyond Schooling

To begin his essay entitled "Lambs to the Slaughter," published amongst two other critical essays for the Beyond Schooling conference, Shaykh Hamza discusses the Islamic concept of *fitrah*: "According to the Islamic tradition, children are born into a natural state, and there is sound prophetic tradition (*hadith*) that indicates this: 'Every child is born into an original state of innocence (*fitra*)'" (Yusuf 2001, 14). This original state is then "transformed by a child's society embodied in their parents. . . . [And] [i]ncreasingly, in modern society, we witness that natural state being torn away from children" (ibid.). The title of his essay which, arguably, draws an overly sensationalist analogy to illustrate the state of public schooling, characterizes the severity of immoral societal influences he believes schools have on a child's *fitra*.

The concept of *fitra* is a foundational Islamic belief that shapes much of the Islamic religious tradition (*'aqida*). It is not uncommon to find Muslim scholars elaborating on the finer points of tradition through a deeper understanding of *fitra*. Even in the canon of medieval Islamic scholarship, the concept of a child's innocence is embedded.[4] Yet in contemporary discourse on early Islamic schools, few visionaries have framed the purpose of schooling using this idea. When participants in my study who established many of the early immigrant established Islamic schools rationalized their intent, they did so through the concept of *fitrah* as well, but primarily in relation to religious practice (prayer, dress, diet, and behavior). Although practice is arguably part and parcel of a spiritual state, Shaykh Hamza has revived the traditional concept of *fitra* to critique public schools not for their inequitable teaching of religion or explicit forms of discrimination, but on a deeper societal level of being incongruent with nurturing spirituality.

Framing his critique as someone not solely as a Muslim but as someone spiritually grounded, he asked the rhetorical question in my interview: when

> you're Christian, Hindu, Buddhist, practicing Jewish or Muslim, it's very troubling to have kids growing up in a type of culture that is so materialistic and so hedonistic and so how do you then address that? How do you keep your children spiritually intact for a period of time when the most important thing is a type of isolation?

To explain the need for a period of innocence and isolation, he used an analogy of the Garden of Eden. He said:

> We have the metaphor the Garden of Eden . . . it's a period of time before the expulsion, and that's essentially what childhood is. It's a period where it's very important to maintain the type of innocent environment so the children are not exposed to the horrors of the world because they do not have the emotional, intellectual, and spiritual tools to grapple with the real core of the world.

His critique, however, should not be misunderstood as an isolationist response to the realities of modern society. Rather, his response is based on the Islamic concept of education that seeks to nurture a child's innocence for the first seven years.[5] Keeping children away from television and from mature content matter allows for their natural inclinations and imaginations to develop unimpeded by the bombardment of adult themes of war, conflict, sexuality, and death:

> When you have an environment with an immense amount of media, when you have an environment where young people, before they're ready, are exposed to the great horrors of the world. Not through fairy tales, which was one of the traditional Western means of . . . doing through telling fairy tales. The evil step-mother or the evil witch that was out to do harm to the children, that was a way of helping them generalize the horrors of the world in a non-threatening way. It created a type of fear that it wasn't non-threatening because

it was still something that was imagination. Whereas now we're dealing with young kids being exposed to the horrors of the world, but the earliest age is through television. Because of that, if you put your children into these types of schools at seven or eight or nine, then they're going to be finding out about the worst aspects of the world.

Among the books Shaykh Hamza has recommended parents and educators to read is Neil Postman's *The Disappearance of Childhood*. Interrogating the effects of media on childhood innocence has been a major theme in Shaykh Hamza's critique. Schooling not only introduces children to mature themes through formal curriculum, but more evidently, through the informal curriculum of student interaction. Many parents who have been influenced by Shaykh Hamza's educational thought will speak of the importance of *suhba* (spiritual/righteous companionship) from the Islamic tradition. Part of the purpose of protecting children from schools is to protect them from other children—Muslim or not. The first few years of childhood are important for forming habits and internalizing a spiritual worldview. On this point, Umm Umar shared an example of a time her son's moral radar manifested itself in a social interaction.

> I remember there was a time we had some friends over and my eldest son (Grade 1) was with another young child at the dinner table. And the other child started drawing bad pictures of my son on a doodle board. So my son, on his own, took his own doodle board and wrote back to that child, "Allah is watching you." [Laughs.] I was so proud of my son that he didn't come down to the level of the other child and draw something bad as well because that's often the default reaction.

For many parents, keeping their children out of school allows them to be selective in who their children interact with until children show signs of confidence in their moral identities. It is to protect children not from other children per se, but from what Shaykh Hamza calls the "powerful cultural hegemony" that influences children subconsciously out of an age of innocence. Beyond the conceptual critique of mass schooling, Shaykh Hamza also relies heavily on the structural criticisms of schooling illuminated by Gatto.

Segregating children in schools on the basis of age through grades is a foundational aspect he finds problematic. Separating students on the basis of age removes the naturalness of care, compassion, and cooperative learning between students of differing intellectual abilities. As a result, a hierarchy based on age is developed and peer pressure overrides collaboration. Shaykh Hamza argues that "when you segregate children from other age groups, a lot of things happen, but the herd-group mentality becomes exacerbated." Uzma Husaini, one of my participants who relates to Shaykh Hamza's critique, recalls her very traumatic elementary school years, as is common among many unheard voices of children. Travelling for the first few years of her childhood and then eventually settling in the United States in fourth grade, Uzma recalls her schooling experiences as being: "very traumatic for me because of the teasing from other kids . . . by seventh grade I hated school, I hated my life because of the peer pressure and the way my peers would treat me." The trauma inflicted by the "herd-group," as Shaykh Hamza calls it, places artificial markers of difference that reinforce cultural markers of hegemony based on privilege.

Based on the impact of Gatto's work on both Shaykh Hamza and those who have been influenced by the two, other areas of critique include themes of class size, learning environment, discipline, and testing. In my interviews, I found my participants in search of a method of schooling that is more natural to the needs of children. They cited angst, for example, toward the concept of large class sizes, which is a common critique of most concerned parents and educators. Participants like Uzma, who endured traumatic amounts of peer pressure, felt it could have been avoided had teachers not had 30 students in a class to worry about. She said,

> There is no way you can have 30 kids in the class and know what going on with all of them. Teachers end up spending so much more time on disciplining and you lose some people. Everyone is at a different emotional state and learning abilities and you can't do it with 30 students.

Recognizing difference and particular needs of students are important aspects, but stifling the growth and potential of students is equally problematic. In the cases of Muzaffar Iqbal and Elma Harder, two of my home schooling participants from Edmonton, Alberta, the realization was not only that curriculum is "dumbed down," as Gatto would call it, but it was their discovery that they could cover the entire Alberta curriculum in three months. Dr. Iqbal recalls teaching his children university level chemistry by the time they were conventionally in Grade 6. As a result of the time awarded to them by choosing to home school, their children, he remembers, developed a real passion for reading and read a tremendous amount of books. The potential of children if given the opportunity to excel at their own strengths is a major contention for those who find class size problematic.

In line with the curriculum being spread out to meet the needs of diverse learners, some of my participants complained about the learning environment. Similar to Dr. Iqbal and his wife Elma, Shaheen Rasheed is critical of the school day:

> I don't think children should have to sit through eight hours of class when they can learn it in four. Or the regimentation of the schools

with rules for behavior that determines when students must learn, when they can socialize, and it mandates discipline with punishment.

Referring to a prevalent theme in Gatto's *Dumbing Us Down*, Shaheen also takes issue with the rush with which students work through complex topics. "Students have to move on from topic to topic when they are told to. They never get the time to actually complete something." Based on the personal lived experiences of parents educated in the public school system like Shaheen Rasheed, reflecting on their educational experiences in relation to the concept of social control has spawned very specific contentions with the way children are schooled.

In many ways Shaykh Hamza's educational vision exhibits a more fierce commitment to protection and preservation than early Islamic school pioneers discussed in previous chapters. The difference in his approach, however, lies in his critique based on broad principles that influence practices over simply inequitable recognition within curriculum. Attacking the powerful cultural hegemony of our mass global culture, he challenges lifestyles changes that include the way we educate but are not limited to schooling. His critique is anti-colonial but not anti-Western. Nor is his approach revivalist, similar to the ideology that shaped the earlier thrust of Islamic schooling. Rather, his approach is grounded in a traditionalist approach that seeks to find commonalities and universals within modern Western discourses. Shaykh Hamza's critique relied heavily on non-dominant discourses of dissent within education to revive a particular interpretation of Islamic education.

This flurry of critique that both Shaykh Hamza and John Taylor Gatto inspired among second-generation American Muslims is rooted in a critical social consciousness that does not settle for critique but demands alternatives. For Shaykh Hamza, the need for an alternative is unambiguous: "for me the public educational system is not really an option. I know a lot of Muslims would disagree with that." Nor is the Islamic schooling system an option simply because, in his own words,

> I don't see any educational vision within the Muslim schools. The Islamization of knowledge to me is very superficial. I don't really see them really challenging the paradigms that need to be challenged. Usually they are these pale imitations of either private or public schools. At least Montessori has a real critique. The Steiner system has a real critique. There has yet to be a serious educational critique from within the Islamic community, either abroad or here.

Similar to the Montessori or Waldorf school models, Shaykh Hamza aspires to see a sense of critical engagement on the part of Muslim educators and parents to consider what an Islamic education really is. Admittedly not a scholar of education, what Shaykh Hamza has achieved is a revival of traditional Islam and a search for congruence in all aspects of Western institutions. The task ahead is not to revive teaching models from Islam's medieval past but to find a "fertile synthesis" between pedagogical principles in Islam and modern methods of schooling (Murad 2002). The new direction of Islamic education is seemingly shifting toward what Amir al-Islam, formerly professor of education at CUNY, coined a new critical American Muslim pedagogy.

> This new pedagogy, centered in Islamic epistemology and ontology, should selectively appropriate the best of traditional Muslim educational paradigms and modalities used over time. However, the traditional Muslim model must not be reified, but rather be subjected to a sharp critique which maintains the richness of its spiritual and intellectual legacy but rejects teaching and interpretations used to create false dichotomies resulting in binary constructs, particularly those which pit Muslims against the west. Finally, the new critical American Muslim pedagogy must embrace all of the best discursive practices . . . that engage us in a critical analysis of the way in which power and privilege, even in religious communities, operate to marginalize and suppress women, minorities, and people of color.
>
> (al-Islam 2006, 73)

Although in theory a new critical American Muslim pedagogy seems ideal, it remains a set of lofty aspirations still in the stage of the theoretical. Thus far any attempt to synthesize an Islamic tradition of teaching and learning either is espoused by academics disconnected from schooling at a grassroots level or is practiced by teachers on the ground but has not been articulated in a systematic way. The next section will attempt to address this gap. In an attempt to bridge theory and practice, I will outline what a critical American Muslim pedagogy looks like based on the pedagogical practice of my participants that is embedded within the Islamic tradition.

Beyond Teaching Religion: Reviving the Islamic Tradition of Education

In a period of introspection and critical social consciousness, it is not uncommon to find Muslim educators and parents committed to finding a faith-centered educational alternative to ask "why?" Dawud Tauhidi, Director of Crescent Academy in Canton, Michigan, says that he poses the question to his board members all the time:

> Why did we spend $10 million on this building? Why are we here? When they come and ask me what our standardized test scores are,

how many of our kids are going to Harvard? I say wait a minute, you know, why are we here? Are we here just to replicate another Prep school? I don't think so. If we are not here to offer an alternative vision of the human being, of life, then replicating what already exists is shameful.

Afeefa Syeed, co-founder of Al-Fatih Academy in Virginia, shared similar frustration and the need to ask the difficult question of a school's overarching purpose. She says, "I think that's why every school has to periodically if not regularly, ask the question, 'Why are we here? Why is this Islamic school here . . . What's the point? What are we doing?'" As directors of schools, both Dawud and Afeefa recognize these are scary conversations because you might not have the answer. Or you might actually have to change the way you do things in a school.

For many early immigrant established schools, these are also difficult conversations because those administering the schools are either non-educators, or the schools were established through parent-initiative with little understanding of pedagogy. Replicating curriculum from public and other faith-based institutions is not an alternative vision. And for many second-generation Muslims and converts, nor is simply "protecting" children a vision. With conviction in his tone, Dawud Tauhidi told me, "we have to be clear why we started this. And if we say that we started this school to protect our children that's a fallback position. I didn't start this school to protect them." After enduring a much-needed interrogation in light of 9/11, many Muslim educators, indigenous, immigrant, and the next generation, have moved beyond critique and quick-fix solutions to considering how to revive theoretical principles and synthesize those principles with contemporary pedagogical practice.

In search of an alternative, my participants have alluded to two overarching themes that help define a new critical American Muslim pedagogy. These are: *tarbiyah* (nurturing wholeness) and *khalifa* (global responsibility, literally "vicegerency"). Although there are many other sub-themes that could be mentioned, most concepts from the Islamic tradition that were mentioned in my interviews, I found, are dependent on or a result of *tarbiyah* or *khalifa*. I also realized that although *tarbiyah* is a concept commonly alluded to in classical Islamic educational theory, the popularization of the concept of *khalifa* in relation to education is distinctly an outgrowth of the post-9/11 era. Arguably, only Imam Warith Deen had the foresight to allude to schools as nurturers of global citizens since the inception of the Clara Muhammad schools because he was a man who understood the plight of the American Muslim. It took the second generation of Muslim immigrants and a popular American Muslim discourse expressed largely by converts to adopt the concept of *khalifa* within educational philosophy.

Tarbiyah: Nurturing Wholeness

As was described in the previous chapter, the word *tarbiyah* comes from the Arabic root *raba'* (to grow, increase). Within education, the word is often employed to mean nurturing children toward wholeness, completeness, or a God-centered consciousness. Dawud Tauhidi, who has named his educational philosophy the Tarbiyah Framework, says that *tarbiyah* is something that comes from the environment—the milieu. Explaining the lexical root meanings of the word, he mentions two other words that come from the same root: *turba* and *turab* help explain how *tarbiyah* is from the soil, it is in the air. In his words, "You just got it [*tarbiyah*] as a process of osmosis." *Tarbiyah* is a process of learning that comes from interactions, mentorship, and personal reflection. It is not something that is formally taught; rather, *tarbiyah* is a lived experience. Quoting her teacher, Shaykh Nuh Ha Mim Keller, a White American Muslim convert and renowned spiritual guide, Inayet Sahin told me that "Shaykh Nuh always tells us that you change people with your state, not with yourselves. So, it's not *what* I teach but *how* I teach. I want students to *experience* learning." Adopting the concept of *tarbiyah* puts to question the core pedagogical practices of Islamic schooling. How would a school impart *tarbiyah* systematically? Can it be systematic or must *tarbiyah* be a process of becoming that is left to chance? One possible method can be to create particular learning opportunities and moments for mentoring interactions. Afeefa Syeed, for example, cited the decision to start her school in the home of an 85-year-old Christian woman as the best decision she could have made for her students. Interacting and sharing a space with an elderly woman has been most transformative for her students, she said, because they learn life lessons about kindness, difference, and needs of people. It softens the heart, she said, and "it is the place that we're in that is feeding into their [the students] understanding. . . . By allowing the children to have those connections is a very holistic transformation." Facilitating particular interactions along with time to reflect on those interactions can be effective for students to experience learning and nurture *tarbiyah* from their environment and the people around them.

The second, more structured method of nurturing *tarbiyah* is what Shaykh Hamza emphasizes as training the *nafs* (inner desires/inclinations/ego). The essence of *tarbiyah* is to nurture a spiritual consciousness, which in this case requires training the mind to think critically. He links the idea of *tarbiyah* and education not to a form of indoctrination but the very opposite—freeing the mind of constraints through interrogating social pressures and influences. In this respect, Shaykh Hamza is convinced of the value of a liberal arts education and views the "tools" of liberation pedagogy as the most consistent aspects with the essence of an

Islamic education. Referring to grammar, logic, and rhetoric as the tools for a liberal arts education, he says:

> If you're not trained in logic, you're going to fall into certain errors of thinking, by the very nature of being a creature that has emotion, that has appetite and has rationality. And emotions and appetite can override the rationality, so if you're not careful, you could be arguing from emotion as opposed to really making a rational argument or argument from appetite. Unless you're trained in logical fallacies, unless you're trained in the ability to see the inherent flaws in much of human reasoning, then you're going to make real mistakes in thinking.

The essence of *tarbiyah* from this respect is to deeply engage with the purpose of life. Teaching children about religious belief and practice is insufficient if they are not nurtured to respond to divergent ways of thinking and living. The mind, Shaykh Hamza argues, can be swayed and influenced if the spiritual being is dormant. When the material/physical world confuses the mind to think of other than God, "the horse becomes the rider." Expressing his affinity for horses, Shaykh Hamza says that, "The Islamic ideal is to train that spiritual part, to be in control of the *nafs*, to be in control of the horse itself, because the horse becomes a vehicle that can safely take you from the beginning of the journey to the end of the journey without falling off, without losing control, without going off the trail or path."

Part of the process of *tarbiyah* is to train and control human base desires related to sexuality, personal behavior, and interactions. Without a training of the *nafs* and the intellect, an individual can fall prey to inclinations that are seemingly illogical and harmful. From this perspective, *tarbiyah* is an on-going process of life learning that is not limited to years of formal schooling. It is also something that to an extent can be formally taught in the sense of the rational tools required but must be accompanied by an informal nurturing of *suhba* (company/influence). The conception of *tarbiyah* complicates the process of Islamic schooling because it necessitates teaching beyond the conventional curriculum, and it also alters the way in which religion is taught. From this perspective, religion or faith practice cannot be limited to content of historical figures and events along with beliefs and practices, but it must be nurtured through action and lived experience. Faith belief and practice must be taught through spiritually based faith principles from which all knowledge stems. In the final part of this chapter, I will elaborate on how *tarbiyah* and *khalifa* have been integrated to reshape models of Islamic schooling.

Khalifa and Social Responsibility

The term *khalifa* traditionally holds two distinct meanings with multiple derivations, all of which are not related to education but responsibility.

Its most prevalent meaning in the Qur'an is successor, substitute, replacement, or deputy, all referring to religious and/or political authority (Singh and Agwan 2000, 277). The concept of *khalifa*, whether as *khalifat Allah* (vicegerent of God) or *khalifat rasul Allah* (successor of the messenger of God), represents a requirement of upholding social, political, and moral justice on behalf of God. The latter conception is what has most commonly been employed to serve as justification for political authority, and the former is the concept that is now beginning to find its way into American Muslim pedagogical discourse. Muslim exegetes interpret the instance in the Qur'an when God tells the angels, "I am making/creating on earth a *khalifa*." to refer "not only to Adam but also to all humanity, i.e. the children of Adam" (ibid.). Muslim scholars have employed the concept of *khalifa* and its embedded responsibility to uphold social justice as an essential aspect of Islamic education. When speaking of the essential aspects of an Islamic pedagogy, Shaykh Hamza said the ideal purpose of Islamic education is to nurture an individual "to be a *Khalifah*, to be a caretaker, a steward, to be somebody that is acting on God's behalf in their life, in their behavior, how they are treating others, and changing the world for the better." Shaykh Hamza's conception elaborates on the conventional definition of the term to presuppose an individual responsibility toward establishing goodness that extends beyond fellow Muslims. A *khalifat-al-ard* and a *khalifat Allah* makes one responsible for God's earth and all that it encompasses. This responsibility is then extended to interactions with people, taking care of the natural world, and that which God has granted one privilege over: wealth, health, livelihood, family, and community.

In Afeefa Syeed's school, the concept of *khalifat-al-ard* is the defining aspect of their school philosophy. In her own words, when she co-founded the school, she recalls that they wanted to do something different, something innovative and what they truly felt would be most definitive of an Islamic way of life: "We wanted a sense of connection not just to each other, but to the world, literally to the town we're in." The emphasis in her school is to facilitate on-going and consistent community service that connects to the curriculum. She describes how students at her school learn about the scientific aspects of environmental issues while taking care of the earth as *khalifat Allah*:

> So, if you look, you come in and have a conversation with one of our children about environmentalism, for example, or something like that, they are not going to give you what they learned in a textbook, that environmentalism means blah blah blah. They are going to talk to you about what it means to be a *Khilafah* of *Allah* [God] in that context, and what it means to create a project for the community and what that did for them, and so on and so forth. But at the same time, they will be able to tell you what's happening to the ozone layer,

what's happening to the level of pollution in such and such and so on; and that's academic to some extent. They'll also be able to break it down and tell you the chemical makeup of bad air. That's scientific. It's relevant knowledge for them.

In schools, the concept of *khalifa* is most often now employed in relation to service learning and most commonly with environmental activism. But in the case of Afeefa's example, the philosophy of the school is to connect community service to curriculum content not as appendage but as an integral part of the teaching methodology. At Al-Fatih Academy, students are regularly engaged in service learning in order for children to recognize the importance in relation to *tarbiyah*. Such an emphasis also connects children to larger issues of community that are beyond insular concerns of an ethnic, cultural, or religious community. Nabila Hanson, founder of Kinza Academy in California, agrees that service oriented learning is something that we have not emphasized enough in Islamic schools. The need for Muslim children, particularly those in Islamic schools, to integrate and interact with children of other cultures and faiths has become increasingly critical post-9/11 and an area of contention by dissenters of private schooling. The new-found emphasis on *khalifat Allah* within educational discourse has been one way of responding to and addressing insularity and stereotypes of ghettoization. The other benefit of framing an American Muslim pedagogy within a conception of *khalifat Allah* has been its potential for empowerment.

The most notable example I found in my interviews was listening to Afeefa Syeed speak about taking her class to visit the President of the United States, George W. Bush, at the time. She and one of her classes were invited for what initially was supposed to be a photo opportunity with the President, but she prepared her class by teaching about his role, democracy, elections, and the like. Initially, she recalls that parents of her students were quite resistant to the idea. Some said, "he's an evil man and I don't want my child near him." Others simply did not see the relevance of the trip. After convincing parents of the school that she wants children to understand that the President does not have "horns" on his head, they went. During the visit, the President made small talk with the kids about his dog while they questioned him about peace. But the most memorable moment for Afeefa came after the visit, when the class reflected on the experience. She recalls, "some of them said, 'well he's really old and wrinkled'. And I said, 'yeah, he's human.' And one boy, Usman said, and I'll never forget this, 'what I really feel Miss Afeefa is that I can be president,' and to me, that is our philosophy and our approach and our reason for existence, in that one sentence." For Afeefa, this moment was so definitive of an American Muslim pedagogy because it showed that students recognize that they are American Muslims and that they have a responsibility to both of those identity markers. She said she was not impressed simply because he wanted to be President but because he had the cognizance that altruism is a responsibility *"especially* as Muslims." What Afeefa Syeed has achieved with this one particular student is an inherent confidence in his dual identity that allows for his Islamic identity to enhance his American identity. No longer is there a duality laced with contradictions and incompatibilities, but rather this student is able to employ his Islamic worldview to relate to the world in a way that is inclusive.

In light of *tarbiyah* and *khalifa*, what an American Muslim pedagogy seeks to achieve is a revival of traditional Islamic concepts to redefine the practice of Islamic schooling. Although not unfamiliar with such conceptions, the context in which early Islamic schools were established did not necessitate a unique philosophy and rationale for their existence. During the 1970s and '80s, what was most urgent was ensuring the particular standards of education set by state and ministry requirements could be met. In an era of public scrutiny and a new critical social consciousness, however, defining a philosophy of Islamic schooling has grown more urgent. What has been presented are two overarching principles that my participants alluded to as distinct aspects of a contemporary Islamic pedagogy. In the following section, I explore the unique educational alternatives to the conventional Islamic school model that have evolved out of a critical social consciousness and that adopt principles of *tarbiyah* and *khalifa*.

Contemporary Alternative Models of Islamic Schooling

Early Islamic schools established by immigrant communities and the NOI/AMM were largely modeled after conventional practices in public and private secular and religious schools. They adopted conventional principles of curriculum design, instructional methodology, administrative procedures, and methods of assessment and evaluation. The essence of Islamic schooling mirrored that of other faith-based schools (Catholic and Jewish in particular), where religious studies and sacred languages (Arabic, Hebrew) were taught as individual courses of instruction in addition to conventional subject areas. A faith consciousness was also imparted through an "Islamic environment," where students would feel comfortable to practice the tenets of faith (dress, diet, prayer). For Islamic schools at least, it was not until the 1980s and into the 1990s that conversations about "integrating" Islamic content across the curriculum had begun. Following the trajectory of faith-based schooling growth, Muslim educators began to recognize the need for curriculum enhancement in the form of an integrated curriculum. Although the project for integration remains on-going, by the late 1990s and early 2000s, a new, in many ways unexpected, discourse around the aims of Islamic schooling began to brew.

What has been described in this chapter as a critical social consciousness and revived principles (*tarbiyah* and *khalifa*) has resulted in new forms of Islamic education. Some of these forms of Islamic schools have built themselves on the backs of well established schools, altering principles and practices. Other schools have relied more heavily on alternative educational discourses (home schooling, classical education, anti-racist education, holistic education, and critical pedagogy) to develop new forms of Islamic schools from the bottom up. And there are some schools, like Crescent Academy directed by Dawud Tauhidi and his Tarbiyah Framework discussed in the previous chapter, that sought an alternative vision well before the shift in discourse within American Muslim communities. The new models of Islamic schooling that I will present now will focus on those schools that have emerged through the discourse of a critical social consciousness and have been largely established by second-generation American Muslims. It should be noted that the schools, networks, and initiatives that I discuss are far from an exhaustive account of the models that exist.

Challenging the Conventional Islamic School Model: Social Conscious, Social Activist, Experiential Alternatives

If there were any of my participants that were adamant about making the distinction between the types of Islamic schools that exist, it was Afeefa Syeed, co-founder of Al-Fatih Academy. "You can't just call them African American Islamic schools and immigrant established Islamic schools," she told me. There is a distinct difference between the Islamic schools established by those who came to North America in the 1970s and those established by their children. Afeefa represents Memmi's conceptualization of the immigrant's children that I mentioned earlier best. For second-generation American Muslims like Afeefa, "the fog of memory" does not inform their decisions because this is their memory (Memmi 2004, 111).

When establishing Al Fatih Academy in 1998 in Herndon, Virginia, Afeefa says she and her co-founder did not follow the conventional route of most Islamic schools. They established a school without any particular Islamic orientation, Masjid/Islamic center support, or external affiliations. All they had was a commitment to activism. It was simply an idea developed between two friends, one a Turkish American Muslim and Afeefa, whose parents are from Kashmir. What shaped their school philosophy as distinct from all other Islamic schools, she says, is that both co-founders attended public schools, American colleges, and defined their Islamic identity through a personal journey that inspired conviction. Through MSAs and community involvement, Afeefa says that they both, as well as their hand-picked board members, see the work of this school as part of their activism. Describing the activism of people who found, work, and administer Al-Fatih Academy, Afeefa says,

These are the people we used to write plays and productions with when we were in college and high school. These are the people who went out and did homeless food drives together, and all those kinds of things. And now we're all parents. So, it's kind of an extension of all of that. I think what happened really is that we wanted to maintain that for ourselves and our children.

For these second-generation American Muslims, faith inspired activism serves as their binding ties. Cultural, ethnic, and ideological ties that bound their parents' generation are no longer relevant amongst second-generation Muslims, who "are so hybridized in many ways, creolized in some ways because our interests are connected and are so varied. And even, some of us have married interculturally so we bring so many layers of identification and of awareness." What binds these young Muslims is not simply their activism within Muslim related concerns, but around issues of social justice broadly. Afeefa, for example, cites Marian Wright Edelman, head of the Children's Defense Fund, as her personal inspiration

> not because she's religious or spiritual but because she speaks to me as a woman and as an activist and so on and so forth. . . . So that's another part of it, is that our roots are so embedded in the American experience.

Bound by the American Muslim experience, Al Fatih (The Opener) began with a commitment to "open" or forge a new American Muslim identity defined by stewardship, *khalifa*. Committed to nurturing future leaders, the school is built on principles of civic engagement and activism. In their own words, Al Fatih's mission "is to cultivate and nurture a thriving American Muslim identity that balances religious, academic, and cultural knowledge and imparts the importance of civic involvement and charitable work." Although most schools nurture civic involvement, few schools such as Al Fatih make it an integral part of the formal and informal curriculum. Definitive school programs, such as Kids Giving Salam and Peace Leaders, are two ways that the school ingrains a sense of global citizenship. The instructional method is equally transformative in that it relies more heavily on engaging with the earth and pushing the boundaries of the classroom. In our interview, Afeefa gave me one example of one teachable moment when she was digging for worms with some of the students. She recalls, "we were dirty, we were messed up and everything."

> But what was interesting for me was, before we started digging, a girl was saying, 'ew, worms are gross, disgusting, I don't want to touch it.' But in the process of digging for worms she got a worm in

her hand and stood there for 15 minutes with the worm in her hand and just realized what it was—that connection. Yes, it is a teachable moment, whatever you want to call it. The mother came in to pick her up and started screaming 'why is she so dirty,' because she was dirty, holy crow. And I said to the mother, 'Just see what's in her hand.' And she showed her the worm and the mom was scared of the worm [laughs]. But anyways, what happened was that interaction, the teacher, the parent, me, and the student, it's that moment of when the girl made that discovery, it was not recorded, it's not empirical evidence of her learning something, but that moment happened.

The approach of Al Fatih transforms the conventional marker of success for Islamic schooling. The example with the worm illustrates that, in many ways, nurturing leadership is not defined by skills but by engagement. Nurturing a sense of global responsibility, Afeefa told me, begins with local, everyday moments of connection. The connection that that young girl made in that moment connected her spiritually to the earth in ways that formal teachings of religion cannot. The approach is, as it says on the Al-Fatih website, to: "Create a culture that ensures life-long lessons for students, including a commitment to community involvement, a sense of heightened social responsibility, respect for cultural diversity, and understanding of what it means to be an American citizen and a global citizen."

For Afeefa, what such a new philosophy represents is bringing two worlds that were, for many second-generation Muslims growing up through the American public school system, separate: being American and being Muslim. Al Fatih teaches that the Islamic tradition is consistent with the core values of American society: civic engagement, dissent, respect, and responsibility, all of which are integrated in teaching so that "there is just no sense of disconnect." Al Fatih is among one of the new models of Islamic schooling that has evolved outside of the influence of Shaykh Hamza. In many ways, the critical social consciousness of Afeefa Syeed preceded the impact of the Beyond Schooling conference that popularized alternative schooling. Many other alternative models, like the Andalus Institute in Washington, D.C., and River Garden Montessori School in Chicago, illustrate alternative outgrowths of Beyond Schooling's influence.

In the case of the Andalus Institute, Hispanic American convert Jose Acevedo developed an alternative high school program that emphasizes contemporary critical issues through experiential, project-based learning. The essence of the school is to have small classes, individualized instruction, and, most importantly, developing a sense of critical engagement by looking at issues from a historical, social-political, and Islamic perspective. Taught through well-structured field experiences, students travel to places such as Colonial Williamsburg in Virginia to experience the role that religion played in the founding of America, or the Audubon Naturalist Society to study the oysters in Chesapeake Bay. The philosophy of Andalus reflects that of Al Fatih, seeking to understand the world around them through innovative, outside of the classroom teaching experiences that connect them to the Creator without formally teaching Islam.

Equally inspired by Shaykh Hamza's push for an alternative education for Muslim children that is based in the Islamic tradition, Uzma Sattar co-founded the River Garden Montessori School in Chicago, Illinois. Uzma Sattar and Kiran Younus both graduated from Northwestern University in the late 1990s, worked in professional fields, law and IT respectively, then pursued degrees in education and established educational alternatives for their children. The name River Garden is derived from a verse of the Qur'an that says, "For [the truthful] are Gardens under which rivers flow—they shall abide therein forever. Allah is pleased with them and they with Him. That is the great success" (Qur'an 5:119). The founders of the school state on their website that they were drawn to the name by the two metaphors it encompasses.

> The river represents our journey through this life, at cadences ambling at times and rushing at others, yet always with God's ever-present love and mercy as the bedrock that guides and reassures us as we strive for successes both great and small. The garden represents that most fertile of places to plant the seeds of knowledge and to develop a base for early learning and development. The garden also provides an opportunity to grow the foundation of the children's relationship with their Creator. If the flowers in a garden are properly nurtured and exposed to carefully selected elements, they will flourish. The program exposes our children to the best elements and provides a nurturing environment in which their hearts and minds may flourish, preparing them to develop as spiritual beings in their life-long pursuit of knowledge.

Unique from the social justice oriented approaches of Al Fatih and Andalus, River Garden connects more closely with the need for children's emotional growth. Rooted in the traditional and classical education principles of allowing the first years of schooling to be informal and relatively unstructured play, Montessori in many ways bridged between the home schooling that Beyond Schooling advocated and the relative institutionalization that most parents require. Integrating Islamic character and identity with the Montessori method serves as a spiritually based, student centered, alternative approach that challenges conventional practices and speaks to particular conceptions of nurturing a child's *fitrah*.

Aside from alternative model schools that are now challenging the conventional Islamic school model, the most notable shift in the context of a critical social consciousness has been a push for home schooling.

A New Wave of Parent Initiatives: Home/Community Based Models of Islamic Schooling

Home schooling is a phenomenon that boasts an extensive history. In North America, particularly among religious conservative families, home schooling has served as a form of resistance to the values of mass public schooling (Gaither 2003, 2017). For Muslims in America, home schooling equally has a long history, yet one that is largely untold because the process of home schooling is so individualistic and there are so few Muslims who have home schooled. Those who have home schooled in the Muslim community have generally been from Christian backgrounds, where the concept is relatively more widespread. Indeed, before Beyond Schooling and Shaykh Hamza's advocacy of home schooling, pockets of African and European American Muslim converts home schooled across the continent. Two notable Muslim home schooling networks that preceded the Beyond Schooling conference are the Muslim Home School Network Resource (MHSNR) in the United States and the Muslim Education Foundation (MEF) in Canada, alluded to earlier.

The Muslim Home School Network Resource (MHSNR) began in 1994. MHSNR began organically as the founder, Cynthia Sulaiman, home schooled her own children first in the eastern United States. Sulaiman later connected with and eventually amalgamated the work of MHSNR and the Islamic Home School Association of North America (IHSANA). The purpose of MHSNR has always been to serve as a network for Muslim parents who home school as well as a resource sharing mechanism. The organization's home schooling magazine, which began in 1995 and ended in 1998, called *Al-Madrasah Al-Ula (The First School)*, as well as their web presence (www.muslimhomeschool.com and www.mhsnr.com), serve these functions. MHSNR, along with Muslims Unite for Education at Home (MUFEAH), also held three successful Muslim home schooling conventions. By providing resource links, art and craft projects, and educational materials, MHSNR continues to be one of the leaders in the field of Muslim education in the U.S.

As introduced earlier, in Edmonton, Alberta, the Muslim Education Foundation similarly serves as a network for home schoolers but also for Muslim public and private school teachers. While home schooling their two children, Muzaffar and Elma established the Muslim Education Foundation to network and provide support services and resources for other home schoolers. Part of their motivation for home schooling was simple: there were few (if any) Islamic schools at the time that fulfilled the definition of an Islamic school. In the words of Muzaffar Iqbal, co-founder of MEF,

> What makes a school truly Islamic is integrated, holistic educational resources, trained teachers who are themselves rooted in Islam's

formidable intellectual and spiritual traditions, and of course an atmosphere permeated by the remembrance of Allah. One would be hard pressed to find an Islamic school with these basic ingredients.

With a dearth of Islamic schools in Edmonton, the MEF has now grown to serve as an essential educational liaison between concerned Muslim families and educational outlets. In 2007, for example, MEF formally teamed up with the Argyll Centre, a home and community based education support organization, to develop an Islamic education program for Muslim home schoolers. Validating MEF's ability to develop such a program is one of their publications entitled *Concentric Circles: Nurturing Awe and Wonder in Early Childhood Education*. Written by Elma Harder but inspired and edited both by her husband Muzaffar and her home schooled children, Basit and Nur, *Concentric Circles* serves as a handbook for Muslim educators on teaching from the Qur'anic worldview. The book is significant not simply because of its filling the need in grappling with defining an Islamic pedagogy but more importantly because of its relevance contextually to Canadians of faith. The work of Elma Harder and Muzaffar Iqbal represent both tradition and modernity in an attempt to develop a curriculum that will nurture faith conscious children with a deep sense of civic responsibility in Canada. Many Muslim home schoolers, like Elma and Muzaffar, are grappling with issues of faith, citizenship, and schooling in new ways. As converts and/or second-generation Muslims in Canada, both of whom have lived through the public schooling system in Canada and have a renewed sense of faith-identity, they aspire for a change in the way they educate their children.

Aside from the few organic home schooling communities that have existed prior to Beyond Schooling, I have found that in light of Shaykh Hamza's advocacy of alternative schooling and in particular his personal conviction of home schooling, there has been a distinct growth among second-generation Muslim home schoolers. Knowles et al. (1992) argue that the rise of home education in America coincided with the revival of the educational critique leveled by influential educational writings of the de-schooling and free-schooling movements of the 1960s and 1970s. Coincidentally, the recommended reading list provided to all participants of the Beyond Schooling conference included the works of A.S. Neill, Ivan Illich, and Neil Postman (Yusuf et al. 2001). As discussed earlier, the impact of recommended readings from this conference, which included John Taylor Gatto's *Dumbing Us Down* and Susan Bauer's *The Well Trained Mind*, served as critical literature that had a keen subset of North American Muslims seriously reconsidering the process of schooling. It may not have fully convinced Muslim parents to consider home schooling, but it created networks of parents looking for an alternative. Such networks and supports are numerous but less formally recognized. By and large they tend to be informal, local community networks of parents who home school within a particular city. Organizations like this exist in many different forms and serve various functions. Some organizations serve as small community based schools that are not exactly home schools but demand a large commitment by parents in the shaping of curriculum. In Toronto, for example, there are a number of such organizations: Lote Tree Foundation, Kitab Academy, Dar al- Ma'rifa, and Toronto Home Schooling Network. According to Shaheen Rasheed, in the D.C. area, each of its four geographical areas developed a Muslim home schooling network of home schooling families. And in the Bay Area, California, there are over a hundred families on a home schooling network that are served by a local co-op school as well as Kinza Academy.

Developed out of a growing need to support Muslim home schoolers after the Beyond Schooling conference in Toronto, Kinza Academy was established by Nabila Hanson in the Bay Area, California. Kinza had been supported by both Shaykh Hamza Yusuf and John Taylor Gatto as members of the Board of Directors since its inception. In the words of Nabila Hanson, Kinza's role

> at this point is really making it easy for the family, to really empower them, to take on responsibility of home schooling and to teach their kids at home and to keep them out of the system. And with the system I really, personally I would include Islamic schools because I think they're basically following the same model.

The critique of Muslim home schoolers is that Islamic schools do not offer a drastically different alternative from public schooling.

Individual families across North America (including Toronto, Halifax, Washington, D.C., and New York) purchase curriculum packages developed by Kinza Academy. The curriculum packages were developed using a classical education model (trivium/quadrivium) and an inherent focus on the liberal arts. *The Well Trained Mind* is an essential resource for them, and then they look for literature based readings that are age appropriate to develop a reading list for children. Shaheen Rasheed, who uses Kinza Academy's curriculum for her children, says, "Kinza's curriculum is about engaging a child's imagination and a love of reading. So, the curriculum is based on literature, liberal arts, and it is balanced between cultures and traditions. The stories are from all over the world, not just Western literature."

Kinza has been developed in the spirit of Mainard Hutchins and the classical education movement. At the core of liberal education is recognition of God, the perfection of the soul, morality and immorality in relation to the self, community, and government. Espoused most notably by the likes of Mortimer Adler, who has been revered by few and criticized by many, the liberal education he espoused was based on a return to the liberal arts though what he termed the Great Books and Great

Ideas. Insisting that every child should be exposed to a general education that includes the literature and thought of the greatest thinkers of our age (a very exclusive list of thinkers), Adler's movement has been adopted wholeheartedly by some home schoolers. The method of education revives a classical educational model of teaching through the trivium (grammar, logic, and rhetoric) and then for higher studies the quadrivium (arithmetic, geometry, music, cosmology). The model is based on a rigorous and systematic curriculum that develops virtue and mastery through gaining access to the "Great Conversation"—wisdom and thought of great minds of the past (Bauer and Wise 2004, 17).

For many Kinza supporters, they found that a classical education model was most consistent with a classical Islamic education that continues to be taught in parts of the Muslim world. The emphasis on core tools of learning (grammar, rhetoric, and logic) as foundations to further study is equally a characteristic of traditional Islamic education as it has been in the Western educational tradition (Dodge 1961, 1962; Berkey 1992; Makdisi 1981; Shalaby 1954). The Kinza Academy philosophy followed a traditional Islamic approach that considered the first seven years of a child's life to be focused on informal emotional development. Formal teaching does not begin until a child is intellectually ready. The traditional approach, Nabila said was based on four major factors:

> 1) you don't teach them until they are seven; 2) you teach at their own individual pace; and 3) you don't test them, so either they know the material in which case you move them on or they don't in which case you keep teaching them; 4) you don't segregate them by age, which really hinders their development intellectually.

Home schooling was not sustainable for many and too drastic for others who were influenced by the Beyond Schooling conference, but they were convinced enough for the need for alternatives. In the search for alternatives blossomed the hybrid home schooling approach of small community schools and networks such as those discussed here.

The case of Muslim home schoolers is particularly interesting because it illustrates the continued search for wholeness and renewal. From the handful of community based home school networks discussed earlier, it becomes clear that the push for home schooling specifically is a transitory stage until a more sustainable model is found. Yet the advocacy and rhetoric calling for alternative educational initiatives to better nurture an Islamic education mirrors voices of dissent that began this work. It is as though the community has come full circle; once again dissatisfied with existing options and committed to finding alternatives. Similar concerns over protecting and preserving through alternative pedagogies and praxis, all of these attempts exhibit an inherent element of protest against the forms of schooling that exist.

The search for new alternatives that challenge the existing conventional model of Islamic schooling has been a result of three overlapping events. Firstly, the coming of age of second-generation Muslims raised the level of experience with public educational institutions. Their reactions to the gaps in public schooling do not come out of fear of the unknown, as was common for their parents, but from attending public schools and experiencing a sense of spiritual emptiness. Secondly, a new cadre of Muslim leadership characterized by charismatic and Western-educated converts to Islam was able to speak to the experiences of the second-generation immigrant. Growing up in and able to navigate through what was once all foreign territory, second-generation Muslim immigrants and converts were able to carve out a distinct American/Canadian Muslim identity. In the wake of 9/11, the third factor, neither of these groups was willing to allow for their indebtedness to the North American fabric to be misunderstood. In search to reclaim their media-maligned Islamic identities, a discourse of a new critical social consciousness evolved that revived the pluralistic and civic aspects of the Islamic tradition. For Islamic schools, the combination of these factors has meant renewal and a push for praxis. In the current phase of Islamic school growth, a discourse of praxis has not only diversified the models of Islamic schooling but has also enhanced the practice within existing Islamic schools toward nurturing a broader sense of citizenship and responsibility.

Notes

1. John Taylor Gatto was New York City Teacher of the Year in 1989, 1990, and 1991 and then named New York State Teacher of the Year in 1991, which was also the year that he retired and sent in an opinion editorial to the *Wall Street Journal* stating that he no longer wanted to hurt kids to make a living.
2. The Beyond Schooling Conference was also known as the Zarnuji Conference, named after Imam Zarnuji, a 12th century Muslim pedagogue whose text entitled *Instruction of the Student: The Method of Learning* served as the core teaching for the conference.
3. Gatto asserts that after the first three purposes of compulsory schooling (to create good people, good citizens, and good lives) is a fourth purpose: to manage the lives of people. This fourth purpose is a scathing criticism of the ideological, political, and industrial interests that have shaped the aims of schooling historically.
4. See for example Imam Abu Hamid al Ghazali's classical treatise translated in English by T.J. Winter entitled *Disciplining the Soul: Breaking the Two Desires*, part of the classical *Ihya Ulum al Din (Revival of the Religious Sciences)*. Book One has a chapter on educating children. Many classical texts, like the *Ihya*, have sections within them on the purpose and method of education. This text was originally written in the 11th century A.D.
5. There is the Prophetic tradition that says the first seven years of life are for play and imagination, the second seven for nurturing *adab* (etiquette/proper comportment), and the third seven to nurture life-long learning. This tradition is narrated often in education circles as an ideal model of educational stages that needs to be revived. Advocates of a classical education, such as Shaykh

Hamza Yusuf, employ this tradition to support home schooling during the early years of a child's life in order to allow a child's cognition to develop without the influence of television and popular cultural forces.

References

Abdo, Geneive. *Mecca and Main Street: Muslim Life in America After 9/11*. New York: Oxford University Press, 2006.

Al-Islam, Amir. "Educating American Muslim Leadership (Men and Women) for the Twenty- First Century." *Teaching Theology and Religion* 9, no. 2 (2006): 73–78.

Bauer, Susan Wise and Wise, Jessie. *The Well-Trained Mind: A Guide to Classical Education at Home*. New York: W.W. Norton and Company, 2004.

Ba-Yunus, Ilyas and Kone, Kassim. *Muslims in the United States*. Westport, CT: Greenwood Press, 2006.

Berkey, J. *The Transmission of Knowledge in Medieval Cairo: A Social History of Islamic Education*. Princeton, NJ: Princeton University Press, 1992.

Bukhari, Zahid, Nyang, Sulayman, Ahmad, Mumtaz, and Esposito, John, eds. *Muslims' Place in the American Public Sphere*. Walnut Creek, CA: Altamira Press, 2004.

Cateura, Linda. *Voices of American Muslims*. New York: Hippocrene Books, 2005.

Dei, George. *Anti-Racism Education: Theory and Practice*. Halifax, NS: Fernwood Pub., 1996.

Dodge, Bayard. *Al-Azhar: A Millennium of Muslim Learning*. Washington, DC: Middle East Institute, 1961.

Dodge, Bayard. *Muslim Education in Medieval Times*. Washington, DC: Middle East Institute, 1962.

Singh, N.K. and Agwan, A.R., eds. *Encyclopedia of the Qur'an*, Vol. 1. Delhi: Global Vision Publishing House, 2000.

Freire, Paulo. *The Politics of Education: Culture, Power, and Liberation*. South Hadley, MA: Bergin & Garvey Publishers, 1985.

Freire, Paulo. *Pedagogy of Freedom: Ethics, Democracy, and Civic Courage*. New York: Rowman & Littlefield Publishers, 1998.

Gaither, Milton. *American Educational History Revisited: A Critique of Progress*. New York: Teachers College Press, 2003.

Gaither, Milton. *Homeschool an American History*, 2nd ed. Palgrave Macmillan US: Imprint. New York: Palgrave Macmillan, 2017.

Gatto, John Taylor. *Underground History of American Education*. New York: Odysseus Group, 2001.

Jackson, Sherman. *Islam and the Blackamerican: Looking Toward the Third Resurrection*. New York: Oxford University Press, 2005.

Karim, Jamillah. *American Muslim Women: Negotiating Race, Class, and Gender within the Ummah*. New York: New York University Press, 2009.

Knowles, G., Marlow, S.E., and Muchmore, J.A. "From Pedagogy to Ideology: Origins and Phases of Home Education in the United States: 1970–1990." *American Journal of Education* 2 (1992).

Leonard, Karen. "South Asian Leadership of American Muslims." In *Muslims in the West: From Sojourners to Citizens*, edited by Yvonne Yazbeck Haddad. New York: Oxford University Press, 2002.

Leonard, Karen. "American Muslim Politics: Discourses and Practices." *Ethnicities* 3, no. 2 (2003): 147–181.

Makdisi, George. *The Rise of Colleges: Institutions of Learning in Islam and the West*. Edinburgh: Edinburgh University Press, 1981.

Memmi, Albert. *Decolonization and the Decolonized*. Minneapolis: University of Minnesota Press, 2004.

Mohammed-Arif, A. *Salaam America: South Asian Muslims in New York*. London: Anthem Press, 2002;

Murad, Abdal Hakim. *The Essence of Islamic Education*, CD. Toronto: IHYA Productions, 2002.

Namulundah, F. *bell hooks' Engaged Pedagogy: A Transgressive Education for Critical Consciousness*. Westport, CT: Bergin & Garvey, 1998.

Nimer, Mohamed. "Introduction." In *Islamophobia and Anti-Americanism: Causes and Remedies*, edited by Mohamed Nimer. Beltsville, MD: Amana Publications, 2007.

Parker-Jenkins, M., Hartas, D., and Irving, B.A. *In Good Faith: Schools, Religion, and Public Funding*. Aldershot, England: Ashgate, 2005.

Ramadan, Tariq. *Western Muslims and the Future of Islam*. London: Oxford University Press, 2004.

Schmidt, G. *Islam in Urban America: Sunni Muslims in Chicago*. Philadelphia: Temple University Press, 2004.

Schumann, Christopher. "A Muslim Diaspora' in the United States?" *The Muslim World* 97, no. 1 (January 2007): 11–32.

Shakir, Zaid. "American Muslims and a Meaningful Human Rights Discourse in the Aftermath of September 11, 2001." *Cross Currents* 52, no. 4 (Winter 2003): 521–535.

Shalaby, Ahmad. *History of Muslim Education*. Beirut: Dar al-Kashshaf, 1954.

Ukeles, R. *The Evolving Muslim Community in America: The Impact of 9/11*. Mosaica Research Center for Religion, State and Society, 2003–04.

Yusuf Hanson, Hamza. "Lambs to the Slaughter." In *Beyond Schooling: Building Communities Where Learning Really Matters*. Toronto: IHYA Papers No. 1, 2001.

Yusuf, H., Gatto, J.T., and Sayers, D. *Beyond Schooling: Building Communities That Matter*. Toronto: IHYA Papers No. 1, 2001.

Zine, Jasmin. "Creating Faith-Centered Space for Anti-Racist Feminism: Reflections from a Muslim Scholar Activist." *Journal of Feminist Studies in Religion* 20, no. 2 (Fall 2004).

Zine, Jasmin. *Canadian Islamic Schools: Unraveling the Politics of Faith, Gender, Knowledge, and Identity*. Toronto: University of Toronto Press, 2008.

6 Conclusion
Potential and Possibilities of Islamic Schooling in North America

Among the few studies on Islamic schooling, whether in book chapters or community magazines, few recognize the complexity across races, ethnicities, and ideologies. Muslim communities within the Sunni tradition are diverse, and within such diversity there exist discourses of collaboration and tension that are necessary to adequately understand its history. What I have researched, written, and presented in this study is an attempt to unravel this complexity. Although I recognize that even my work falls short of giving due recognition to many other Islamic school initiatives, such as the *madrassa* schools, weekend school programs, the many African American schools established outside the community of Imam Warith Deen, and the many immigrant established Islamic schools that do not consider themselves under the umbrella of ISNA, I have hopefully at least extended the narrative while recognizing the need for future historical research.

Recognizing the racial, ethnic, and ideological complexity that exists within Muslim communities, this work has also sought to show continental influences. Most notably through the development of the MSA and ISNA, I attempted to show how the ideas of Islamic schooling were initiated north of the border. The work of MSA and ISNA is important because it illustrates how one particular Islamic educational visionary, Sheikh Abdalla Idris, established the first school in Canada and then became a major catalyst for schools in the United States through his work with CISNA and CIENA. More recently, Shaykh Hamza Yusuf's Beyond Schooling conference once again illustrates the importance of the Canadian-American narrative. Arguably, it was this conference in 2001 at the University of Toronto that popularized alternative Islamic school initiatives and a critical social consciousness in relation to Islamic education. The third and most notable contribution of this study is its mapping of the history of Islamic schooling in four distinct phases. The phases of Protest, Preservation, Pedagogy, and Praxis arose directly from the voices of my participants. It was not until well into my data collection and listening to the themes of our conversations that I began to see four distinct phases emerge. Although these phases overlap and even co-exist, they have assisted in giving structure to an otherwise very complex narrative. The importance of the narrative is not only in relation to time periods. My goal from the outset of this project was to deeply understand the visions, aims, and objectives that differentiate Islamic schools from one another. These stages, therefore, also speak to the evolution of the vision(s) of Islamic schools and the trajectories of discursive growth.

The earliest schools, both under the NOI/AMM and later under ISNA, began with urgency, forthrightness, and a sense of dire need. Some considered it a retreat, as though Muslims were "running from" something. And indeed some were running. It was not uncommon among immigrant voices who supported Islamic schools to talk about protecting their children until they went back home. Living in America was temporary, they thought. For African American Muslims, it was different; schools were established to take control of their children's potential in response to segregated schools and unequal educational opportunities. For the NOI, separate schools were a mechanism to liberation. In the words of Loomba (1989), schools are a form of anti-colonial resistance where "Liberation . . . hinged upon the discovery or rehabilitation of their cultural identity which European colonization had disparaged and wrecked" (181). Hall (1994) refers to this search as a search for the "one true self" that a group of people share in common (394). But one cannot be naïve about turning back to some romantic past and must forge a new identity from what has been experienced in relation to one's past and present (ibid.). In this search for authenticity, then, I feel that Imam Warith Deen was more apt than his father and the pioneers of immigrant established Islamic schools in forging a new path for his community and for an American Muslim identity that found a balance between each of the three.

Searching for an American Muslim identity, what began as protest to protect soon became a vision to preserve religious identities and values. Establishing separate schools soon became part and parcel of the American experience—establishing indigenous private institutions just like the Jewish, Catholic, and Quaker communities. Islamic schools served, similar to other forms of religious schooling, as responses to the increasing secularity of public schools. The growth of Islamic schools under the vision of by and large South Asian, Arab, and African Muslim immigrants in the 1970s and 1980s was largely a reaction to the lack of religious accommodations made by the public education system. Once mosque projects had been put underway and weekend religious schools were established, many parents began turning their attention toward what they saw as the potential loss of religious and cultural identity of their children at the hands of public schools. If public schools continued to recite the Lord's Prayer, sing Christmas carols, and not encourage religious expressions of other faiths both in the formal and informal curriculum, a growing number of parents began to fret over their child's over-assimilation. What some Muslims needed was a separate system to fill the gaps, as a founding member of CISNA adamantly put it in a 1989 conference video archive:

> Our reason for developing our own system is not to save ourselves from a burning house. No. It is to develop our own system, an alternative system that is universal, human, which fits and learns from these experiences and identifies the missing parts and submits it as a valid alternative system.

Settling on exactly what those "missing parts" are and how an alternative system of schooling should look has brought us to the present era. It began with the third stage of pedagogy and evolved into one of praxis. Raising funds, finding spaces, and establishing a school itself was one aspect of the struggle. The more important educational question was not "what are we running from?" but "what are we walking toward?" (Ombu 1983). During the era of pedagogy, Islamic schools began to define themselves and began to develop models that exemplified their uniqueness. The Islamization model and Qur'an based model served as two distinct representations of differing ideologies. These were the first attempts at recognizing that schools are philosophically based and have particular aims. It recognized that teaching Islam is different from teaching from an Islamic worldview. Although the purpose of appending and integrating Islam within a conventional educational framework remained consistent, the ideological stances that each community held shaped school curriculum differently. These two attempts were in many ways the two most widespread initial attempts at defining the unique approaches of Islamic schooling while also illustrating the role that ideological leanings played in the realm of schooling. Although there were other approaches to Islamic school design, it was not until second-generation immigrant Muslims came into adulthood that new directions began to emerge.

The coming of age of second-generation Muslims coincided with the events of 9/11, which demanded change. The final and most recent stage of praxis has been heralded by American Muslims living Islam outwardly and explicitly in ways that have revived new discourses of critical social consciousness, human rights, and social justice. Born and raised in North America, second-generation Muslims along with converts have become the new voice of Islam seeking to reclaim their faith.

In terms of schools, the discourse of what defines the "Islamic" is now articulated through more nuanced frames. Many Islamic schools are redefining the success of the school based on community involvement and civic engagement more explicitly. Students are taught about ethics not as a religious phenomenon but as a moral imperative. The *da'wa* (calling to Islam) has inherently become less with words post-9/11 and more with actions. It has revived the concept of *khalifa* to mean social responsibility. As Salahuddeen Abdul Karim put it, "If the Muslim is not going to be a voice of justice then what good are we? I don't care if you make a million prayers, if you're not the voice of saying that's wrong then something needs to be changed." The current phase of what I have called praxis has, as a result, also seen the emergence of new models of Islamic schools—home schools, Montessori Islamic schools, and community based initiatives each trying to live the vision of Islamic education in their own way. In the short 85-year history that dates back to the first Islamic school established by the Nation of Islam in the home of the Hon. Elijah Muhammad, Muslim communities in North America have come a long way in defining a distinct American Muslim pedagogy, and it will likely continue to evolve.

New Directions

Two substantial currents of change are taking place that are informing the future of Islamic schooling in North America. The first is that Imam Warith Deen Mohammed passed away on September 9, 2008. The Imam's death ushers in what Sherman Jackson coined the Third Resurrection well before his passing. The third resurrection implies a new era in the history of the African American Muslim leadership that will require less reliance on charismatic leadership, such as the Hon. Elijah Muhammad and Imam Warith Deen, and more focus on individual African American Muslims to become masters of the Islamic tradition. For African American Muslims to gain a stronger command of the sources of Islam (Qur'an, Prophetic Tradition, and Arabic) will challenge the inferiority complex that immigrants have unethically imposed.

The Imam's passing, however, not only affected the African American Muslim population but also left a mark on second-generation American Muslims. The legacy of his life and what he accomplished with transitioning an entire community of believers all while enduring the ignorance of the Muslim American immigrant is a burden that will be carried by the children of those early immigrants. After the passing of Imam Warith Deen, Azhar Usman, a second-generation American Muslim immigrant and most notably known as the lawyer made comedian, wrote a letter of apology that circulated worldwide. His apology served as a reflection of the indebtedness and appreciation that all American Muslims must have for the work of Imam Warith Deen in bringing Islam to America. But more importantly it served as an admission of guilt on behalf of Muslim immigrants who succumbed to cultural perceptions and allowed for the American Muslim *ummah* to be divided on the basis of race. He said,

> I would like to unburden myself of something that has been sitting like a ton of bricks on my heart for my entire life. I want to apologize

to my Blackamerican brothers and sisters in Islam. I know that this apology may not mean very much; and I know that our American Muslim communities have a LONG way to go before we can have truly healthy political conciliation and de-racialized religious cooperation; and I know that I am not the one who is responsible for so much of the historical wrongdoing of so-called 'immigrant Muslims'—wrongdoings that have been so hurtful, and insulting, and degrading, and disrespectful, and dismissive, and marginalizing, and often downright dehumanizing.

(Usman 2009)

Listing the numerous ways that immigrant Muslims of all ideologies enforced their own cultural Islam, unwilling to accommodate practices that were not "Islamic" enough, Azhar Usman spoke on behalf of many second-generation Muslims. He cites examples of wealthy immigrant professionals who raise funds for the superfluous beautification of their own mosques over assisting African American mosques where heating bills are going unpaid. Or the outward niceties immigrant mosque leadership show toward prolific African American speakers who are invited to speak at fundraising events, but would never consider marrying their daughters off to an African American. And then the ideological discrimination where faith practices of African Americans in their recitation of the Qur'an or prayer, or command over the Islamic tradition, is never truly "Islamic." For these perceptions that have intrinsically divided the American Muslim community, particularly by the generation of Azhar Usman's parents, he represented the voices of all those second-generation American (and Canadian) Muslims, myself included, who found conviction in Islam through the plight of Malcolm X and African American Muslims and are unwilling to adopt our parents' ingrained sentiments of racial hierarchy. To close, he said,

> I'm sorry. I'm very, very sorry. From the bottom of my heart, I want every African-American Muslim brother and sister to know that I am ashamed of this treatment that you have received and, in many cases, continue to receive, over the decades. I want you to know that I am aware of it. I am conscious of the problem. (Indeed, I am even conscious that I myself am *part* of the problem since curing hypocrisy begins by looking in the mirror.) I am not alone in this apology. There are literally thousands, if not tens of thousands of young American Muslims just like me, born to immigrant parents who originate from all over the Muslim world. We get it, and we too are sick of the putrid stench of racism within our own Muslim communities. Let us pledge to work on this problem together, honestly validating our own and one another's insecurities, emotions, and feelings regarding

these realities. Forgiveness is needed to right past wrongs, yet forgiveness is predicated on acknowledging wrongdoing and sincerely apologizing. Let us make a blood oath of sorts.

(Usman 2009)

The passing of Imam Warith Deen and the reverence with which his accomplishments are held in the hearts of second-generation Muslims will usher in a new era in American Islam. By recognizing that the ideology of Elijah Muhammad was a necessary transitory stage, the struggle of Imam Warith Deen in realigning his community with the universal principles of Islam can be appreciated. Sulayman Nyang, professor of African studies, says that Imam Warith Deen was able to achieve two remarkable feats, "One [was] the re-Islamization of the movement; the second, the re-Americanization of the movement. Here's a man who inherited an organization that most scholars of Islam would describe as heretical before [Mohammed took over]. . . . That mythology has been replaced by sound theology rooted in Islamic orthodoxy. The people had to make a 180-degree turn" (Nyang 1995, 24). The legacy of Imam Warith Deen is in his realignment of principles and practices. The appreciation of his legacy, outside of the African American community, will, however, be the catalyst toward greater collaboration between Muslim communities.

For the Clara Muhammad schools, this will also likely usher in new directions. Given the financial hardship that the Clara Muhammad schools in particular have faced, with many temporarily shutting down, others disbanding for good, and some leaning toward greater collaboration with immigrant communities, I question whether the way forward is toward a dissipation of the division as we have known it for the past 30 years. If the vision of the Clara Muhammad schools and the Islamic schools established by immigrant, second-generation, and indigenous Muslims communities are one and the same, must the distinction, schisms, and culturally based curricula remain? Dr. Qadir Abdus Sabur articulated the sentiment held by all of my participants when he said: "The climate of America has changed—it's not as important to identify with our ethnic identities as it was 20 years ago. It's more important for us to identify with our Qur'anic identity and go beyond our cultural, ethnic identities." Muslim educators have recognized the tensions that separated their initiatives because of class, race, and culture and now also have come to recognize that to unite themselves, it must come through what they all hold in common: the teachings of the Qur'an. The work of Dr. Qadir Abdus Sabur in Virginia illustrates, from what I have seen throughout North America, the way forward for Islamic schools.

Dr. Abdus Sabur has administered a Clara Muhammad school in Richmond, Virginia, where both a Muslim home schooling collaborative and an immigrant established Islamic school also reside. Since 2006, Abdus Sabur established a Qur'an class and then the Qur'anic Education

Foundation, where local Muslims interested in committed study of the Qur'an could gather. The idea was to bridge the three schools' initiatives through common personal, professional, and religious development. From the study group, sprang the idea of a central high school initiative, which all three elementary schools would feed students toward. The result has been Tawheed Prep School, established in 2007. The establishment of Tawheed Prep, of which Abdus Sabur serves as the director, has been instrumental in defining the way forward for Islamic schooling in America. The model of Tawheed Prep reframes the curriculum through theme based Qur'anic teaching that corresponds to conventional curriculum outcomes, and it unites disparate Muslim communities under a common framework that sets aside racial and cultural differences. In the words of Abdus Sabur, "such a model transcends individual names and affiliations and stands for our collective effort."

When I spoke with Dr. Zakiyyah Muhammad, she agreed that post-9/11 we should expect greater collaboration between Islamic schools that have been thus far racially divided. "We're finally getting it now. 9/11 really created an enormous amount of interesting consequences and circumstances. And we are really beginning to realize that we are in the same boat and that we have to support and help each other." The new direction of support does not, however, silence the discourse of difference, she said. Optimism of increased collaboration cannot blind us from the realities that racial prejudice is real, continues to be real, and is ingrained in the immigrant-privilege psyche. Khabeer (2016) astutely challenges, "the fallacy of postracialism, which holds that racism, particularly anti-Black racism, is over and that any talk of race is actually counterproductive to the work of antiracism" (5). For authentic and sincere collaboration between immigrant and indigenous communities, Islamic schools must continue to acknowledge that histories of immigration to those of slavery and oppression cannot be conflated or ignored (Chowdhury 2018) if we are to aspire to nurture Muslim students toward social and racial justice.

The second change current, which has also been a theme of the final section on praxis, are new generational voices that are critiquing the Islamic education project from within in search for a renewed articulation of possibilities and perspectives. Referring specifically to the impact that Qutb and Mawdudi's furious anti-Western rhetoric had on segments of the Muslim community in the 1970s and '80s, including some of the pioneers of Islamic schools, Murad (2003) insists that Qutb and Mawdudi "were not writing for the 21st century Muslim minorities in the West, but for a mid-twentieth century struggle against secular repression and corruption in majority Muslim lands." The way forward must be moving beyond simplistic ideological frameworks and toward a greater recognition of our tradition and its ability to respond to new contextual challenges in diverse ways. Islamic schools are beginning to represent this diversity of response. The ideological shift from anti-Western to civic engagement is a result of deep thinking on the part of a new generation, Murad argues:

> But we need some deep rethinking among the new generation, that minority which has survived assimilation in the schools, and knows enough of the virtues and vices of Western secular society to take stock of where we stand, and decide on the best course of action for our community. It is this new generation that is called upon to demonstrate Islam's ability to extend its traditional capacities for courteous acculturation to the new context of the West, and to reject the radical Manichean agenda, supported by the extremists on both sides, which presents Muslim minorities as nothing more than resentful, scheming archipelagos of Middle Eastern difference.
> (Murad 2003)

The phase of taking stock of where we stand is still very much in its infancy. For Muslim organizations and schools, the ideology is just beginning to shift, as is the search for alternatives. The directions in which this shift takes us in terms of models of Islamic education will only become evident with time.

Over the past decade, a burgeoning academic discourse on what defines Islamic education/schooling is taking shape once again. Similar to the wave of publication and institutional development post the landmark 1977 First World Conference on Islamic Education, a renewed effort that challenges earlier notions of Islamization, deeply acknowledges the reality of varying perspectives, and aptly questions who owns and what Islamic education means, what should be emphasized, and how educators should be prepared (Berglund 2015). The field of Islamic Education studies coined by Sahin (2018) seeks to delve toward conceptual clarity through theoretical and empirical studies of Islamic/Muslim pedagogy(ies), Islamic/Muslim education, and Islamic/Muslim schooling. He argues,

> Despite a plethora of recent publications on Islamic Education, Islamic Schooling and Muslims in Education, the attempts to define the field remain unsystematic and often lack conceptual depth and clarity. This can be attributed to three fundamental methodological shortcomings: first, inadequate theoretical reflections on the meaning of education, which gravely hinders the task of 'thinking about Islam educationally and education Islamically'; second, the absence of a rigorous 'educational hermeneutics' with which to discern the central educational and pedagogic vocabulary in Muslim core sources and narratives of education embedded within the Muslim religious, spiritual and intellectual heritage; third, lack of empirical research

in exploring the pedagogic practice and developing evidence-based policies in the field. There is a large gap in the existing literature addressing these crucial issues.

(Sahin 2018, 2)

Sahin (2018) offers a much-needed scathing critique of the existing literature in the field referring to initial articulations of Islamization to be "defensive" and contemporary efforts to either "perpetuate these reactionary postcolonial perceptions" or put forward underdeveloped conceptualizations. His work has called for a more comprehensive hermeneutic understanding of education in Islam (*tarbiyah*) to gain pedagogic insights from the Islamic tradition (2014, 2018). Contributing to the conceptual debate are those who have put forth fresh re-conceptualizations of the Islamization movement and its relevance to contemporary debates on democratic citizenship (Waghid and Davids 2016), a deeper exploration of education concepts in the Qur'an (Abdul Mabud 2016), and the potential of the concept of *ta'dib* as a comprehensive articulation of education in the Islamic tradition Ahmed (2018). A handful of important edited collections have also provided much needed scholarship on the intersections between Islamic education in secular societies (Aslan and Rausch 2013), emerging philosophical questions and Islamic Education (Memon and Zaman 2016), Islamic religious education in public schools (Berglund 2018), and Islamic school renewal in the West (Abdalla et al. 2018). These and many other academic contributions attest to the growing interest in theoretically working toward robust conceptualizations of education in light of the Islamic tradition and empirically exploring challenges and opportunities of Islamic schooling globally.

Similar to the height of Islamization in the 1970s and '80s, when a spike in research served as a catalyst to establishing higher education institutions (Abdul Mabud 2016), the past decade's Islamic education scholarship has also been complemented with new institutions. A number of research centers and graduate degree programs have been established in collaboration with universities to support the credentialing of Islamic school teachers and on-going research about Islamic schooling. In 2010, the University of Toronto collaborated with Razi Education to establish an online professional certificate program for Islamic school teachers on gaining a deeper appreciation of Islamic conceptions of education and its implications. In 2011, Bayan Claremont was established in collaboration with the Claremont School of Theology in Southern California. Among their core graduate program offerings is a master's degree in Islamic education that supports Islamic school educators with a grounding in Islamic thought and practice. And recently two new programs were established in the eastern United States. The first is Shenandoah University's Center for Islamic Thought in the Contemporary World that emphasizes a focus on training for Islamic school teachers. The second is a collaboration between the International Institute of Islamic Thought (IIIT)—a pioneer in the Islamization movement—and American University to establish a master's degree on advancing education in Muslim societies. Outside of North America, a few other notable institutional developments are the Centre for Research and Evaluation in Muslim Education (CRÈME) at the University of London's Institute of Education; the Centre for Islamic Thought and Education at the University of South Australia, who offer a graduate diploma in Islamic pedagogy, and a reader in Islamic Education at the University of Warwick. All of these research centers and degree programs are primarily geared to offer Islamic school educators a theoretical and practical understanding of education rooted in the Islamic tradition. These developments have ushered in two critical realizations: firstly, conceptions of Islamic education/pedagogy are contested and becoming. Linked to what I have tried to put forward in this book, what Islamic education means and what Islamic schooling looks like is and will continue to be different based on faith inspired pedagogical aspirations and interpretations. Secondly, educators who work in Islamic schools deserve to read, reflect on, and enact educational thought that is grounded in the Islamic tradition while engaging with educational thought that is outside the tradition. The research and programs that have sprung up over the past decade are a testament to an evolving field of Islamic schooling in the years to come that will not be consumed with solely imparting faith but with the educational thought that will inform a distinct pedagogy.

Closing Remarks

When I set out on this journey of researching the vision of Islamic schools in America, I honestly began with some defeatist misconceptions of the level of excellence in these schools. As passionate as I am about the potential of Islamic education as a valid site for indigenous knowledge based on spiritual and faith-based worldviews, I began with an overemphasis on the "potential" as opposed to the growth, development, and complexity of what already exists. My mind was set on the idea that what exists is basic and rudimentary and that much work is needed for a truly unique model of Islamic education to be defined. As I began interviewing my participants, I became increasingly embarrassed at the shallowness of my own preliminary criticisms of Islamic schools. I had reduced them in my mind, as is common in the media and among educational circles within Muslim communities, to be limited in theoretical complexity and development. Interview after interview, I have developed a deep sense of appreciation now not only for the struggle, hardship, and sacrifice of Muslim educators committed to Islamic schooling but also for the complexity of insight, thought, and vision that my "visionaries" have evolved.

It is difficult to admit, but I feel that I had presumptuously fallen into the same trap of superficially assessing the growth of Islamic schools as an outsider looking in. As much as I consider myself an insider, being Muslim and an active part of social and educational initiatives across North America, I remained and to an extent still am naïve of the depth of educational development of our schools. Conducting this oral history project has certainly been most fruitful both spiritually and intellectually as I have grown to understand nuances of my faith and the cultures that comprise its adherents more deeply. But I have also gained an admiration for individual aspiration and perseverance. Through the voices of visionaries and those who worked tirelessly to establish and envision Islamic schools in North America, I have learned what it means to have *himma 'aliya* (high aspiration). The people whom I met and others who I only know by voice are people that put aside the pleasures of the everyday for a sweetness that will only be tasted in another life. They represent to me what it means to aspire for something which you likely will not see in the span of your own lifetime. They represent a conviction in not only what they do but also in knowing that its reward will not be immediate. These are people who climbed into dumpsters to salvage used textbooks when they could not afford them for their schools. These people worked for $20 a week as PhDs in education because of what they believed in. They traveled every weekend to a different part of the country to raise funds for communities they did not even know about for the sake of Islamic education. These are people of *himma 'aliya*. These are people with a vision that few others can even comprehend.

My work is just a drop in the ocean that attempts to trace their sacrifice and vision. I hope that such work has illuminated even an ounce of the complexity, overlap, collaboration, tension, success, and wisdom that participants of this study have left behind. I hope that from this initial work, future researchers and educators will build and expand on what little my work may have contributed. And I hope that future researchers will also correct and improve what I may have misrepresented.

Dr. Zakiyyah Muhammad told me something that affected me greatly in my own journey of research. She said, "The ink of the scholar is more precious than the blood of the martyr." In an age when martyrdom is misconstrued and misused, her words of inspiration define the agenda of Islamic education from within a rich tradition of scholarship. Muslim communities have prized the importance of scholarship, but in an age of extremes when optimism turns into hopelessness, students and scholars must remember the power of the word. The Clara Muhammad schools certainly taught us this. The re-education of the Blackamerican community in the Civil Rights era was indeed a political act of protest and self-empowerment. They proved to us that through education a community can be transformed. Undoubtedly, it is a process, but with a higher aspiration there is hope.

References

Abdalla, Mohamad, Chown, Dylan, and Abdullah, Muhammad. *Islamic Schooling in the West Pathways to Renewal*. Cham: Palgrave Macmillan, 2018.

Abdul Mabud, Shaikh. "World Conferences on Muslim Education: Shaping the Agenda of Muslim Education in the Future." In *Philosophies of Islamic Education: Historical Perspectives and Emerging Discourses*, edited by N.A. Memon and Mujadad Zaman. New York: Routledge, 2016.

Ahmed, Farah. "An Exploration of Naquib Al-Attas' Theory of Islamic Education as "Ta'Dib" as an 'Indigenous' Educational Philosophy." *Educational Philosophy and Theory* 50, no. 8 (2018): 786–794.

Aslan, Ednan and Rausch, Margaret, eds. *Islamic Education in Secular Societies*. Frankfurt: Peter Lang, 2013.

Berglund, Jenny. *Publicly Funded Islamic Education in Europe and the United States*. Series: The Brookings Project on U.S. Relations with the Islamic World. Analysis Paper, No. 21, 2015.

Berglund, Jenny, ed. *European Perspectives on Islamic Education and Public Schooling*. Sheffield: Equinox, 2018.

Chowdhury, Elora Halim. "Reading Hamid, Reading Coates: Juxtaposing Anti-Muslim and Anti-Black Racism in Current Times." *Feminist Formations* 30, no. 3 (2018): 63–78.

Hall, Stuart. "Cultural Identity and Diaspora." In *Colonial Discourse and Post-Colonial Theory*, edited by P. Williams and L. Chrisman. New York: Columbia University Press, 1994.

Khabeer, Su'ad. *Muslim Cool: Race, Religion, and Hip Hop in the United States*. New York: New York University Press, 2016.

Loomba, Anita, *Colonialism/Postcolonialism*. New York: Routledge, 1989.

Memon, N.A. and Zaman, Mujadad, eds. *Philosophies of Islamic Education: Historical Perspectives and Emerging Discourses*. New York: Routledge, 2016.

Murad, Abdal Hakim. "Tradition or Extradition? The Threat to Muslims-Americans," January 2003. Retrieved from www.themodernreligion.com/world/extradition.html.

Nyang, Sulayman. "Muslims and the Challenges of American Society." *AMC Report* 5, no. 5 (1995).

Ombu, Obatala. "Letter to the Editor: 'Solution to Racism in Public Schools.'" *New York Amsterdam News*, March 5, 1983. Retrieved from ProQuest Historical Newspapers New York Amsterdam News: 1922–1993.

Sahin, Abdullah. *New Directions in Islamic Education: Pedagogy and Identity Formation*. Markfield: Kube Publishing Ltd., 2014.

Sahin, Abdullah. "Critical Issues in Islamic Education Studies: Rethinking Islamic and Western Liberal Secular Values of Education." *Religions* 9, no. 11 (2018).

Usman, Azhar. "An Apology: Heartfelt Reflections on the Passing of a Legendary Blackamerican Muslim Leader," September 11, 2008. Retrieved from www.illumemagazine.org/magazine/publish/features/an_apology.php. Accessed on April 16, 2009.

Waghid, Yusef and Davids, Nuraan. "Islamization and Democratization of Knowledge in Post-Colonial Muslim Oriented Contexts: Implications for Democratic Citizenship Education." In *Philosophies of Islamic Education: Historical Perspectives and Emerging Discourses*, edited by N.A. Memon and Mujadad Zaman. New York: Routledge, 2016.

Index

Note: Page numbers in **bold** indicate a table.

9/11 1, 21, 30

Abadi, Fazil 83
Abdalla Idris Ali, Sheikh 71, 96, 103–104; Islamic school in Canada 19, 70, 80, 85–90, 122, 145, 201; pedagogical philosophy 146–147
'Abduh, Muhammad 117
Abdul Kareem, Salahuddin 71, 94–96, 118–119, 122, 204
Abdur Rashid, Daa'iyah 51 *see also* Saleem, Daaiyah
Abdus Sabur, Qadir 22, 37, 41, 47, 70, 73, 74, 79; and indigenous educators 102, 105; and local initiatives 104; and Muslim Teacher's Training College 98–99, 138; and Tawheed Prep 141, 207; and Qur'anic education/curriculum 128, 133, 136, 140, 141, 206, 207
Abu Hanifa 172
Acevedo, Jose 192
African American 10, 13, 17, 24; agenda 57; converts to Islam 23, 37, 49, 107, 194; and equal/ civil rights 14, 90; identity 119, 131; Islam 69; Islamic schools 190; migration, urban 43; plight of 36, 75, 127; and racism 39; schools 201; and segregation 40–41; as separate and unequal 48; and slavery 44; solidarity 130; spirituality 27
African American Islam (McCloud) 130
African American Muslims 3–4, 22, 25, 26, 30; abandonment of 108; and Bilal Ibn Rabah 58; de-legitimization of 124; educators 132; and Elijah Muhammad 39, 50, 53, 56, 67, 70, 175; experience 155; and immigrant Muslims 30, 38, 79, 95, 105, 118; and Islam, orthodox 71; and Islamic movements 10; leadership 204; mosques 205; and racism 81; schools 202; struggles of 102; and Warith Deen Mohammed 60, 66, 123, 125, 129, 163, 206
African diaspora 132
African Muslims 12
Afrocentrism 38, 39, 53
Afro-Descendent Upliftment Society 55
Ahmadis 14, 29
Ahmed, Gubti Mahdi 16
Ahmed, Osman 85
ain ul yaqin 142
Ajieb *see* Bilal Ajieb
akhlaq 149
Al Amal 150
Al Amin, Jamil 164
Al-Aqsa school 90, 94
al-Attas, Naquib 14, 121, 122
al-Banna, Hassan 117, 118, 119
Al-Fatih Academy 184, 188, 190, 192
algebra 141, 151
Algerian revolution 16
al Ghazali, Abu Hamid 114, 198n4
Ali, Abdalla Idris *see* Abdalla Idris Ali
Alim multimedia CD 139
al-Islam, spread of 137
al-Islam, Amir 106, 183
al-Khwarizmi 151
Allah 57, 96, 137, 180; *B'idhn* 155; glorification of 140; and Islamic schools 195; knowledge from 124, 133; as moral authority 136; prayer to 119; and the Qur'an 138, 139, 146, 193

Index

Al-Madrasah Al-Ula (*The First School*) 194
al Zeera, Zahra 28
'*amal* 30
amana 135
American Muslim Mission (AMM) 17–18, 39, 59
American-ness 91, 162
American University 210
Andalus Institute 192, 193
Anderson, Benedict 26
anti-colonialism 116–117, 182, 202: discourse 24–27; response 113, 120, 171
'aqida/'aqa'id 149, 178
Arabia 43, 57
Arabic 49, 53, 54, 78, 153, 204; at home 85; Muslim courses in 149; studies 103, 115, 139, 144; Qur'anic concepts 152; root 185; teaching of 86, 150, 189
Arabism 121
Arabs 16, 54; in Canada 13; in Dearborn 91; girls 91; immigrants 202; Muslim 81, 91
Arab world 124, 171
asabiyya 127, 130, 131
Ascension Framework 136, 141–143, 142
Asgharzadesh, Alireza 25
Asia, Black nation of 43
"Asiatics" 43, 44
Association of Muslim Social Scientists (AMSS) 83
Atlanta, Georgia 37, 59, 99, 107, 138; Warith Deen Mohammed High School 99, 131, 134, 137
Atlanta University 51
ayah 132, 133, 147, 152

Barboza, Steven 54
Barzangi, Nimat 87
Bauer, Susan 175, 195
Bayan Claremont 209
Bayyan Mubeen 137
Beyond Schooling conference 2, 172–176, 192, 194–197, 201
Bible, Holy 42, 93, 157
Bilal Ajieb 37, 70, 77, 104, 125, 127; and the Islamization movement 113, 122
Bilalian 56–58, 77
Bilalian News 59
Bilal ibn Rabah 57, 58, 124

Blackamerican 61–62n6, 205, 211; Muslim Community 106
Black American 39, 43, 44, 95
Black American Muslim 73, 76, 106; community 106; model of schooling 79
Black body 52, 53
Black Church 39
Black Muslims 24, 57, 95
Black Nationalism 17, 18, 35, 36, 43, 47, 107; history of 49; Qur'an, shift to 77
blackness 53
Black Panther party 90, 164
Black Power 45, 53
Black Puritanism 50
Black Religion 39, 53, 56; to postcolonial religion 67–69
Black to Bilalian, shift from 56–58
Bonnett, Alastair 42
Bosnian genocide 94
Bradford Riots 7
Bridgeview, Illinois 87, 90, 166
Brighter Horizons Academy 150
Brown v. Board of Education 40, 105
Bureau for Islamic and Arabic Education (BIAE) 104

Cairo 100
Calgary 89
Canada 1, 3, 6, 7, 11, 105, 201; after 9/11 166, 167; home schooling networks 24, 194, 195; immigrant Muslims 84, 86, 105, 120, 126, 163, 169; Islamic schools 19, 21, 70, 85, 87–90, 101; Muslim presence in 13, 80; Muslim Student Association 82
Catholic schools 26, 86, 87, 145, 150, 189, 202
Center for Islamic Thought in the Contemporary World 209
Centre for Research and Evaluation in Muslim Education (CREME) 210
Chicago, Illinois 16, 17, 20; African Americans 43; Elijah Muhammad in 47; IQRA International 149; Islamic schools 86, 87, 96, 105; ISNA meeting 70; Montessori School 192, 193; Mosque Cares 37–38; Muslim Community Center 85; Nation of Islam 41; public schools 92; Warith Deen in 75, 124
Chittick, William 8

Chosen People of God 43
civilization (s) 49, 127; Eastern 152; Islamic 14, 68, 114, 120–121; Muslim 52, 117, 151; women as mothers of 137; world 94
civil liberties 26, 167
Civil Rights 4, 14, 24, 39, 82; activist 40; and African Americans 90; era 36, 48, 164; and Muslims 82, 164
Clara Muhammad schools (CMS) 18–19, 35, 60, 211; aims and objectives 129–131; in Atlanta 37, 134; civic education and responsibility 131–132; education conferences 97; elementary school 140; and Elijah Muhammad 39, 45, 55; future of 206; growth of 24; in Harlem 75; and immigrant established schools 66, 105, 107, 144; network 101; system 23, 103; organizational structure 98–99; pedagogy 126–127; Qur'an based model 127–129, 132–144; and *Tawhid* 132; and Warith Deen Mohammed 40, 71, 112, 124, 128, 184; *see also* Muhammad, Clara
"Clara Muhammad Curriculum Draft 1990" 99, 135, 137, 139, 141
Claremont School of Theology 209
Common School Movement 36
Concentric Circles: Nurturing Awe and Wonder in Early Learning (Harder) 153, 195
conversion 13, 23, 43, 51, 56, 94, 119
converts 12, 23, 45, 162, 198, 203; African American 95, 107; African Muslim 124; American Muslim 164; Black Muslim 47, 108; to Nation of Islam 37, 48, 49, 50, 73, 77; second-generation 165, 195; White 70, 71, 85, 94, 129, 153, 171, 185
Council of Islamic Education in North American (CIENA) 104
Council of Islamic Schools in North America (CISNA) 67, 70, 104, 141, 201, 203; challenges 148; establishment of 97; hindrances to 104; rise and decline of 71, 98, 101–105
Creationism 93
Crescent Academy 190
Curtis IV, Edward 43, 52, 53, 124

Dallas, Texas 150
Dantley's framework on spirituality 27
Dar al-Ma'rifa 196
da'wa 203
Dearborn, Michigan 91
deen 171
Dei, George 25, 171
Deobandi movements 29
Detroit 41, 43, 45, 52, 103; Muslim immigrants in 80; Paradise Valley 46; University of Islam 50
Dhaka 100
Dome of the Rock 141
Du Bois, W.E.B. 40, 41
Drew Ali, Noble 17, 44, 130
Dumbing Us Down (Gatto) 195

Edmonton, Alberta 152, 153, 181; Muslim Education Foundation 194, 195
education system 4; bifurcated 120; Muslim 122, 149; in Pakistan 81; post-colonial 89, 113, 121; public 127, 175, 177, 182, 202
Egypt 16, 63, 117, 119, 159
Egyptian Muslim Brotherhood 117
End of Education, The (Postman) 174
epistemology: critical faith-based 24, 27–31, 39, 113; Islamic 116
Esposito, John L. 81
Eurocentrism 29, 113, 127

fajr 28
Fanon, Franz 26, 42
Fard Muhammad 17, 54, 56, 57; birthday of 55; teachings of 42–45
Farrakhan, Louis 23, 49, 60, 63, 76, 130
fiqh 148, 149
First Gulf War 94
First World Conference on Islamic Education 208
fitrah 141, 142, 178, 193
Foundation for the Advancement and Development of Education (FADEL) 152
Four Arguments for the Elimination of Television (Mander) 174
Fruit of Islam (FOI) 17, 46, 47, 51, 57

Gaddis, John 21
Garvey, Marcus 17, 43, 44
Gary, Indiana 85

216 Index

Gatto, John Taylor 165, 172–178, 180–182, 195–196
General Civilization Class (GCC) 51
Ghazi, Abidullah 71, 80
Ghazi, Tasneema 80–82, 84, 85, 90; and CISNA 103; and IQRA 71, 80, 100, 122; and *Milestones* 119
Goodword Islamic Studies 150
Great Conversation 197
Great Depression 36, 43

Haddad, Yvonne 80, 82
Hadith literature 137
hadith 129, 178
hafiz 95
halal 28, 83
Hanafi *see* Sunni
Hanbal 172
Hanbali *see* Sunni
Hanson, Nabila 188
haqq al yaqin 143
Harder, Elma 152, 153, 181, 195
Hartford, Connecticut 142
Harvard University 80, 84, 85, 90, 184
himma 'aliya 211
Hodgson, Marshall 7, 8
holism 28
Holt, John 174
home schooling 12, 23, 107, 165, 195–197; and Clara Muhammad 45, 72; and Muslim Education Foundation 152–153; and Nation of Islam 24; *see also* Beyond Schooling
homosexuality 93
How Children Fail (Hold) 174
Hurry to Faith 150
Hutchins, Mainard 196
Hutson, Jean 75

ibadah 28, 29
Iddin, Rafiq 36, 37, 52, 72, 74; corruption controversy 22; and Nation of Islam 47, 50, 54, 60
ijtihad 117, 118, 121
Ikwaan al Muslimun 16, 117
Ikhwan al-muslimun 118, 119
Illich, Ivan 195
Ilm 137
'ilm al yaqin 143
I Love Islam series 150
Imam, Seema 91, 94, 96, 115; in Chicago 85, 86, 87, 92

Imams, founding 172; *see also* Farrakhan; Shakir; Warith Dean; Zarnuji
immigrant Muslims 3, 4, 8, 11–16, 30; aspirations 16–17; early 26; and colonialism 25, 69; communities 38–40; diasporic 28; educational aspirations 84, 85; experience 79–108; identity 82, 93; mobilizing 82–84; and "pure" Islam 68; recent 81; rights 15, 26, 86; second-generation 83; schools 84–93; support structures 66; *see also* schools, immigrant-established
India 14, 94, 155
Indianapolis 101
"indigenization" 25
indigenous-immigrant dichotomy 71, 165
indigenous Muslims 3–4, 11–14, 27, 106; American 69, 102, 107, 144, 155; Black 17, 24, 39, 79, 95, 106; communities 74, 98, 99, 101, 105, 131; converts 107; experience 21, 27, 72–79; ideas 26; initiatives 104; and Islamism 113–114, 118, 126; and Nation of Islam 67; plight of 81; private education 202; and revivalism 113–114; schools 23, 70, 92, 95–97, 115
Indonesia 16
International Board of Educational Research and Resources (IBERR) 100
International Institute of Islamic Thought (IIIT) 15, 100, 112, 120–122, 124, 144, 210
International Islamic University 152
International Negro Improvement Movement 17
Iqbal, Muzaffar 152, 181, 194, 195
IQRA 71, 89, 122, 150
IQRA Foundation 144
IQRA International 149
Iran 14, 16; immigrants from 94; Iranians 119
Iranian Revolution 82
Iran-Iraq War 82
Iraq 94, 96
Islam: and African Americans 39, 40, 58; morals 150; renewal of 119; as a subject 149–151; teachings of 44, 117, 136; traditional 183; orthodox 10, 11, 39, 55; *see also* conversion; Nation of Islam (NOI)

Islam, Yusuf 100
Islamabad 100
Islamic Circle of North America 16 (ICNA)
Islamic Community School 90
Islamic Education 208; conceptualizing 114; two models of 125–127; vision of 120–125
Islamic Fellowship 118
Islamic Home School Association of North America (IHSANA) 194
Islamic Horizons magazine 83
Islamic/Muslim pedagogies 208
Islamic Schools in North America (ISNA): aims of 145–148; Department of Education 101; practice of 114–116; rise of 116; vision of 120–125; and Warith Deeth 123–125
Islamic schools and schooling 1–11, 92–93; early 93–95; in Canada 87; context and conflicts of 24–27; growth of 7–10, 18, 20; history 19, 21, 35, 54; ideology 93–95; and immigrants/indigenous Muslims 95–98; initiatives 84–86; oral history 18–19; organizing 100–101; pedagogy 11; practice 114–116; praxis 12; preservation 11; protest 10–11; Qur'an-based model of 112, 113, 114, 118, 123–144, **142**; revivalist beginnings 116–120; rise of 116; in the United States 90–92; *see also* Nation of Islam
Islamic Schools League of America (ISLA)104
Islamic Society of North America (ISNA) 15–19, 97, 102–104, 106; in America 164, 170; in Canada 87–90, 100, 122, 145; Department of Education 98, 101, 113, 146; Education Forum 71; and Islamization 123; public image of 161; and Warith Deen 123; work of 201–202
Islamic Spirit conference 164
Islamism 116, 117, 118
Islamization 28, 53, 112, 123–127; approach 147; challenges to 28; concept of 154; conception of 121; model 125, 203; movement 126, 209; re- 206; theory of 109

Islamization of Knowledge 182; model 87, 144–145; movement 113–114; project 14, 122, 127
Islamophobia 30, 161, 166, 167
Ismail, Muhammad 87
Ismail, Sha'ban Mufta 87, 101
Ismailis 14, 24, 29

Jackson, Jesse 75
Jackson, Sherman 39, 42, 55, 56, 107, 161; on Islam in America 67, 68; on legacy of Black racism 124; on neofundamentalism 117; on the Third Resurrection 204
jahili 15
jahiliyyah 119, 147
Jakarta 100
Jamaat-e-Islami 16, 118
Jame Mosque 85, 86, 88
Jewish schools 145, 150, 189
Jews 94, 179; scholars 84, 85
jilbab 91
Jim Crow laws 36, 40, 59, 60, 61

Karumanchery, Leeno 25
Kashmir 69, 190
Khabeer, Su'ad 207
Khaldun, Ibn 114, 130
Khalid, M.D. 80, 84, 88, 93
khalifa 9, 131, 184, 186–190
Khalifah 187
khalifat Allah 9, 187
Khomeini, Ayatollah 16
khutba 88, 139
Kinza Academy 165, 188, 196, 197
Kitab Academy 196

Lang, Jeffrey 164
Lebanon 155
'-l-m 30
Leonard, Karen 164
liberation theology 30
Loomba, Anita 26, 202
Lote Tree Foundation 196

ma'ad 153
madaris, madrasa 88; traditional 5, 24, 87, 96
madhhab 126, 157
Malaysia 122, 155; Malaysians 16
Malcolm X 51, 54, 55, 73, 130; impact of 164; martyrdom of 119
Malik 172
Maliki *see* Sunni

Mander, Jerry 174
marriage 93, 94, 169
masjid 74, 84, 106, 190
Masjumi Party 16
Mason, Max 177
Mattson, Ingrid 15, 16, 82
Mauritania 164
Mawdudi, Abu'l A'la 117, 118, 120, 125, 207
McCloud, Aminah 13, 63, 81, 129, 130
Mecca 54, 55, 56, 100, 113, 122; journey from 141; pilgrimage to 130
Medgar Evans College 106
Mississauga, Ontario 70, 87, 88, 89
mizan 133, 137, 141
Montessori schools 165, 182, 192, 193, 204
Montreal 89
Moore, Thomas 75
Moorish Science Temple 43, 44, 61
moral code 43, 44; principles 168; values 144
Mosque Cares 37, 142–143
mosques 6, 16, 29, 56, 66, 80, 83, 144; establishing 97; in Toronto 85–86, 88
Mohammad, Warith Deen *see* Warith Deen Mohammad
Muhammad, Clara 45–46, 55, 72
Muhammad, Elijah 62; death of 21, 23; and the Nation of Islam 10, 50–56, 63; racial inequality under 67; and University of Islam 35–36; and Warith Deen Mohammed 11, 18, 38
Muhammad (Prophet) 43, 51, 57, 79, 98, 154; ascension of 141; biographies of 129; model of the 123, 124, 126, 140; way of the 136; wisdom of 135; *see also* Seerah
Muhammad, Zakiyyah 37, 59, 70, 78, 98, 211; and racism incident 22; and school transition 77–78; and the Universal Institute 99
mujaddid 118, 143, 144
Murad, Abdal Hakim 207, 208
Murata, Sachiko 8
Muqaddimah (Khaldun) 130
Muqawwi, Faisal 83
Muslim Alliance of North America (MANA) 38, 106, 107
Muslim American Society (MAS) 138
Muslim Community Center (MCC) 85

Muslim Community Organization (MCO) 17
Muslim Education Foundation (MEF) (Canada) 152–154, 194–195
Muslim Girls Training (MGT) 46, 51–53
Muslim Home School Network Resource (MHSNR) 194
Muslim Journal 18
Muslim Students Association (MSA) 15–17, 66, 71, 82–85, 90, 97, 106, 112; and identity 164; and Islamization 122; pioneers of 87, 113; and revivalism 120, 123; and Warith Deen 124; women in 84
Muslim Teacher's Training College 98
Muslim Women of Maryland (MWM) 173
Muslim Youth of North America (MYNA) 164, 173
Muslim(s): African American 71; American 17–18, 81, 108, 164, 169, 201, 205; aspirations 16–17; Canadian 169, 201, 205; diversities and complexities 13–15; history in North America 12–13; millennials 170, 172; organizational structures 15–16; South Asian 3, 16, 80, 81, 87–90, 113, 202; *see also* African American Muslims; Black Muslims; immigrant Muslims; indigenous Muslims; Sunni Muslims
Muslims, second generation 12, 23, 83, 162–165, 204–206; American and 192; Canadian 198, 205; coming of age 169–171; home schooled 195; identity 198; progressive 168; and "protecting" children 184; reclaiming faith 203; sacrifices of 175–176; social consciousness 182, 190
Muslims Unite for Education at Home (MUFEAH) 194

nafs 185, 186
Nasr, Seyyed Hossein 14, 28, 114, 121, 122
Nation of Islam (NOI) 10–12, 16–18, 37–61, 76–79, 189, 202; and African Americans 23, 38; Black Nationalist teachings 35; context of 35–37; conversion to 37; and racial segregation 40–43; protest 127; and University of Islam schools

42–50; voices of 37–40; *see also*
  Black to Bilalian; converts; Fard
  Muhammad; Muhammad, Elijah;
  Warith Dean Mohammad
Neill, A.S. 195
New York City 38, 41, 43, 77, 198
New York University 172
Northwestern University 193
Nyang, Sulayman 13, 206

oral history 4, 18–19, 20, 37, 53;
  limitations of 21–23
Ottawa 89

Pakistan 1, 16, 81; Pakistani 3, 96,
  119
pedagogy 2, 5, 9, 10, 11, 12 73;
  alternative 197; American Muslim
  99, 183, 187–189; curriculum
  151–152; Islamic 112, 149–151,
  154–156, 185, 195, 208; practices
  92, 112–114, 209; Qur'an based
  127–129, 132–144; values 145–149
Philadelphia 22, 37, 38, 41, 76, 106
piety 91, 120
Plessy v. Ferguson 40
Postman, Neil 174, 180, 195
praxis 10, 12, 23, 161–163, 171,
  204; discourse of 198; everyday
  170; ideology of 156; Islamic 173;
  liberatory 30; phase of 5, 9, 201,
  203, 204, 207
promiscuity 54, 93, 94, 145, 146
Prophetic tradition 5, 18, 30, 58, 113,
  128, 204; guidance of 73; teachings
  of the 150, 156; way 125, 143;
  wisdom 135
prophets **142**; Aaron 141; Abraham
  142; Idris 141; Jesus 141; John
  141; Joseph 141; Moses 142;
  Muhammad 141
public school 25, 26, 46, 72, 89, 92; and
  control 174–175; curriculum 127,
  137, 154; religious education 209;
  "mis-education" by 50, 52; second-
  generation Muslims in 169; secularity
  of 202; and spiritual emptiness 198

qadr 143, 157
Quaker 202
Qur'an 51, 54, 93, 155; approach
  152; from Black Nationalism to 77;
  education in 206; essence of 168;
  on good and evil 16; and Islamic
  knowledge 5, 74, 98, 99, 204;
  knowledge of 78, 94; memorizing
  87; model of education 127,
  136–144; primacy of 72; reciting
  205; in school 93, 100; studies 149,
  207; teaching 85, 86; teachings of
  42, 150, 151, 156; verses 57, 74,
  147 193; wisdom of 8; worldview
  of 152; *see also* Islamic schools and
  schooling; Prophetic tradition
Qur'anic Education Foundation 139
Qureshi, Iffat 85
Qureshi, Marghoob 85
Qutb, Sayyid 16, 108, 117, 119, 207;
  activism of 120; influence of 123,
  207; and Muslim Brotherhood 118

race relations 43
racial segregation 10, 40–42, 44, 68;
  systemic 35
racism 10, 22, 58, 76, 205; anti- 42,
  67, 207; Black 124; harms of 119;
  ingrained 39; systemic 25
Rahnema, Ali 117
Ramadan 60, 141
Ramadan, Tariq 168
Randolph, Virginia 98, 138, 139
Rashdan, Mahmoud 87, 146
Rashid, Hakim 37
Razi Education 209
Resurrection: First 55; Second 40, 55;
  Third 204
revivalist ideology 116–118; in
  America 118–120
Rida, Rashid 117
Right Path, The 150
risalah 153

sadaqah 30
Sahih Bukhari 129
Sahih Muslim 129
Sahin, Abdullah 208, 209
Sahin, Inayet 173, 185
Sahnun, Ibn 114
Sakr, Ahmed 83
Salafi doctrine 117
Salafism 125
Salafiyyah movement 29, 117, 128
Salahuddin Abdul Kareem *see* Abdul
  Kareem
Saleem, Daaiyah 37, 79, 132, 134, 143;
  see also Abdur Rashid, Daa'iyah
Sarroub, Loukia 90–91
Sattar, Uzma 193

Saudi Arabia 56, 59, 122
Saviors Day 55, 57, 62, 107
saw 143
Schomburg Center for Research in Black Culture 38
schools: African American Islamic 190; Blacks in 40–42; Nation of Islam 36; age segregation 180, 197; gender segregation 49; racial segregation 40, 41, 61, 202; separate 77; *see also* Islamic schools and schooling; public schools
schools, faith based 2, 4, 29, 161, 189; decreasing support for 7; educators in 134; establishing 80; purpose of 29, 94; stigma of 1
schools, immigrant-established 20–23, 37, 70, 206; in Canada 87–90, 101; curriculum 149; early 179, 184, 189; growth of 67, 105–108; influences 113; initiatives 84–87; organizing 100–101; pedagogy 155, 156; in the United States 90–108; vision of 163, 165; weekend 85, 91; *see also* Clara Muhammad Schools; Warith Deen Mohammad
Seerah 129, 149
seerah 148
Shabazz, Abdul Alim 37, 48, 50, 51, 59, 73, 107
Shabazz, Tribe of 43, 54, 58, 63
Shafi' *see* Sunni
Shafi'i 172
Shahid, Safiyyah 37, 72, 74, 107, 134
Shakir, Zaid 166
Shamma, Freda 149, 151
Shuaibe, Faheem 103
shura 135
Sister Clara Muhammad schools (SCMS) 18, 24, 72, 112
Sister Safiyyah *see* Shahid, Safiyyah
slavery 26, 35, 44, 207
South Asia 14, 68, 113; South Asians 3, 16, 80, 81, 87–90, 113, 202
Spook theology 49, 56
stigma 1, 2, 92, 167
Sudan 85, 155; Sudanese 124
suffrage 137
Sulaiman, Abdul Hamid Abu 100
Sulaiman, Cynthia 194
Sultan, Talat 87
Sunnah 30

Sunni Muslim 3, 14, 21, 24, 29; African American 26; and immigration 67; two communities 126
Sunni Islam 29, 107, 172; and African Americans 56; orthodox 18, 107; schools 23; and Warith Deen 37, 125
Sweet, Lois 94
Syeed, Afeefa 20, 184–185, 187–192
Syria 12, 13, 117, 119, 155, 174

ta'dib 209
Tafsir 129
tafsir 123, 129
taqlid 118
taqwa 22, 116
tarbiyah 184, 185, 186, 188, 189, 190, 209
Tarbiyah Framework 190
Tarbiyah Project 70, 152–154, 185–186
Tauhidi, Dawud 70, 129, 141, 147, 149, 151; on Islamic schools and education 162, 183–184; and the Tarbiyah Project 129, 141, 153, 185, 190
Tawheed Prep School 139–141, 207
tawhid 28, 52, 132, 140, 153
"Tawhidic lenses" 132
Temple University 121
Third Resurrection *see* Resurrection
Thompson, Paul 18
Totonji, Ahmed 83
Torah 93
Toronto 38, 70, 80, 84, 96, 104; home schooling 196; Islamic schools in 90; Ministry of Education 88; Muslims in 164, 170; public schools 166; South Asian community 89; *see also* mosques
"Toronto 17" 166
Toronto Home Schooling network 196
Turks 16

ul Mulk, Ishaq Abdul Malik 102
Umar, Umm 174, 180
ummah 130, 204; global 97, 155; "malaise of" 147; plight of 69; revival of 121; serving the 127, 131–132
Umm al Qura University 59
Ummatology 137
Underground History of American Education (Gatto) 174

Universal Institute 99
Universal Negro Improvement Association 43
University of California Berkeley 174
University of Illinois 83
University of Islam (UofI) 10, 35, 37, 38, 40, 72; and Black identity 45; and Farrakhan 23; and Nation of Islam 66; renaming/restructuring 11, 61, 72; roots 76; schools 40, 46–50, 53–54, 58–59, 77, 78, 108
University of Oxford 168
University of Toronto 1, 85, 165, 173, 201, 209
Usman, Azhar 188, 204, 205
uswa, 'uswa 125, 126

Vancouver 80, 89
Venture of Islam (Hodgson) 7

Wahhabi movements 29, 129
Wahhaj, Siraj 164
Warith Deen Mohammed High School *see* Atlanta
Warith Deen Mohammed, Imam 3, 11; and American Muslim Mission 15, 17–18; and authenticity, search for 202; on Clara Muhammed 45; death of 204, 206; followers of 44, 125; ideology 113, 126; indigenous curriculum, need for 142; influence of 123, 124; and Islamic schooling 18, 21, 45, 69; leadership of 74, 98, 156; and Nation of Islam 38, 54–61, 66, 68; Patriotism Act 60; and Sunni Islam 37, 107; teachings of 128, 133, 136; and the Qur'an 143; vision of 22, 71–76, 78, 99, 141, 167
Warith Deen Mohammed, Imam, community of 11, 18, 20, 24, 38, 142, 144; American Muslim 3; decentralizing of 79, 98; educators 127; home schoolers in 24; indigenous 97; immigrant 124, 125; and Islamic schools 105, 112, 113; and Muslims 39, 163; outside 201; ousting from 23; overhaul of 66; re-education of 35, 73; repositioning of 61; selective engagement of 16
ways of knowing: indigenous 29; faith-based 27, 31, 113; Western 29
Washington, D.C. 94, 96, 192, 196
Well Trained Mind, The (Bauer) 196
Western-ness 68, 155
White supremacy/superiority 36, 45, 53, 107
Whiteness 26, 68
White race 36, 37, 40–44, 47; accepting 56; integrating with 60; *see also* converts
Wholeness and Holiness in Education (al Zeera) 28
World Community of Al-Islam (WCIW) 59
World Council of Islamic Education 148

Yakub 43, 44
Younus, Kiran 193
Yusuf, Hamza 24, 164, 165, 167, 168, 171; Beyond Schooling conference 194, 196, 201; critique of mass public education 176; and Kinza Academy 196

zabiha 83
Zarnuji, Imam 2, 173, 198
Zarzour, Safaa 166
Zaytuna College 165, 166
Zine, Jasmin 27, 30, 89, 91, 113, 161; critical faith-centered epistemology 27, 30; final 29; framework 27, 162; second principle 28; third principle 29

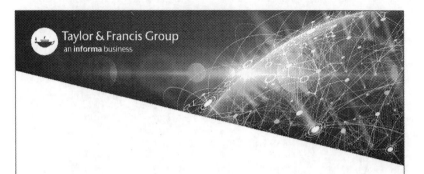